This book examines the meaning and practice of political representation in Britain. It reveals the intricate connections between theory and action and how different notions of representation coexist in a complex and potent mix. The thoughts of major theorists – from Edmund Burke, Jeremy Bentham, John Stuart Mill, through G.D.H. Cole to Paul Hirst – are used to outline the diversity of ideas and practical forms of representation in Britain. Clear accounts of microcosmic, trustee, party, interest, functional, associational and territorial modes of representation are provided as a foundation from which ideas about 'post-parliamentary governance' and the 'crisis of legitimacy' are analysed. A wide-ranging review of representation at local, subnational, national and European levels reveals the concept's fundamental significance in the practice of modern politics.

David Judge's study addresses the central paradox of representation whereby citizens are simultaneously included in, and excluded from, the processes of decision making in politics. His study provides students with extensive contemporary examples and access to the ideas of key theorists, giving an excellent insight into political representation, a key concept in the understanding of modern British politics into the twenty-first century.

David Judge is Professor of Politics, University of Strathclyde.

Theory and practice in British politics
Series editors: Desmond King, Jeremy Waldron
and Alan Ware

This series bridges the gap between political institutions and political theory as taught in introductory British politics courses. While teachers and students agree that there are important connections between theory and practice in British politics, few textbooks systematically explore these connections. Each book in this series takes a major area or institution and looks at the theoretical issues which it raises. No other textbook series offers both a lively and clear introduction to key institutions and an understanding of how theoretical issues arise in the concrete and practical context of politics in Britain. These innovative texts will be essential reading for teachers and beginning students alike.

Other titles in the series

The Law
Jeremy Waldron

Electoral Systems
Andrew Reeve and Alan Ware

The Civil Service
Keith Dowding

Political Parties and Party Systems
Moshe Maor

Representation
Theory and practice in Britain

David Judge

London and New York

First published 1999
by Routledge
11 New Fetter Lane, London EC4P 4EE

Simultaneously published in the USA and Canada
by Routledge
29 West 35th Street, New York, NY 10001

Typeset in Baskerville by Routledge
Printed and bound in Great Britain by Redwood Books,
Trowbridge, Wiltshire

British Library Cataloguing in Publication Data
A catalogue record for this book is available from the British Library

Library of Congress Cataloging in Publication Data
Judge, David.
Representation: theory and practice in Britain / David Judge.
 (Theory and practice in British politics)
 Includes bibliographical references and index.
 1. Representative government and representation – Great Britain –
 2. Great Britain – Politics and government. 3. Democracy –
 Great Britain. I. Title. II. Series.
JN956.J83 1999
321.8'043'0941 – dc 21   98–8110

ISBN 0–415–08196–3 (hbk)
ISBN 0–415–08197–1 (pbk)

Contents

Preface

As the title indicates, this is a book about the 'theory' and 'practice' of representation in Britain. Four beliefs have driven the writing of the book.

First, the concept of representation is central to an understanding of modern British politics.

Second, in examining 'theory', named 'theorists' should be identified and, wherever possible, their own words used to outline their ideas. This enables the student to understand what theorists actually said, rather than what commentators interpreted them as saying. In addition, the citation of the original works of identifiable theorists allows me to remind my own students that there is no theorist called 'some' (as in: 'some argue that' or 'some maintain that'!).

Third, in analysing political practice, the words of practitioners should be examined, contemporary examples should be provided, and evidence should be substantiated.

Fourth, there is an inextricable linkage between theory and practice. Political analysis, like political life, is complex. Students should not be shielded from complexity; but should be guided through complexity to understanding.

Acknowledgements

It has taken me far longer to produce this book than I had originally intended. For nearly a decade it has been a part of the changing tapestry of my life as I moved from: academic role to administrative duty (as Head of Department for three years, and then back to being an academic); continent to continent (from visiting Fulbright Fellow in Houston, USA, and back to Strathclyde in Scotland); office to office (six changes of room); and house to house (three changes). Fortunately, apart from the production of this book, there have been other more important and pleasurable continuities in my life: Lorraine, Ben and Hannah have been a constant reminder that there is more to life than writing books.

Many people have offered me advice, information, technical assistance and encouragement in preparing this book. Thanks are due particularly to Alice Brown, Mike Keating, Dave Marsh, Murray McVicar, James Mitchell, Michael Rush, Thomas Saalfeld, and Gerry Stoker for providing assistance at various stages and sustaining my 'just-in-time' work-style. Fiona Macintyre sorted out a succession of temperamental computers and IT problems with good humour (and a temperamental author with biscuits).

Patrick Proctor, at Routledge, will be relieved that he does not have to hear any more heart-rending explanations as to why another deadline has been missed (at least not for this book!).

1 Representation, representative democracy and representative government

There is by now a well established formula in the writing of books on representation whereby, in rapid succession, introductory sentences point to the longevity of the concept, differences in meaning of the word, and the inherent contestability of the idea of representation itself. Thereafter it is customary to pay homage to Hanna Pitkin's *The Concept of Representation* (1967) to establish one's seriousness as a writer on representation, and to engage in a debate about whether Pitkin is correct in her belief that there is a discernible single meaning that has not changed much over the past three hundred years (1967: 8). Certainly this debate indicates the centrality of the concept in political theory throughout these centuries – but, equally, the very intensity and abstruseness of the debate is likely to discourage many students.

At the risk of disappointing those readers who expect such a familiar and well-worn linguistic approach, this book focuses instead upon the *political* dimensions of representation and the interconnections of the theory and practice of political representation in Britain. However, in preface, we do need, of course, some indication of what representation means. We need some etymological certainty in the conceptual uncertainty to follow. Here, indeed, the work of Hanna Pitkin is invaluable in providing the clue that 'representation, taken generally, means the making present *in some sense* of something which is nevertheless *not* present literally or in fact' (1967: 8–9). In saying this Pitkin recognises that there is a paradox here and that 'a fundamental dualism is built into the meaning of representation' (1967: 9). This simple paradox will guide most of the discussion in this book, but it is also linked to a wider, more complex paradox, that:

> Political representation is primarily a public, institutionalized arrangement involving many people and groups, and operating in the complex ways of large-scale social arrangements. What makes it representation is not any single action by any one participant, but the

over-all structure and functioning of the system, the patterns emerging from the multiple activities of many people. It is representation if the people (or a constituency) are present in governmental action, even though they do not literally act for themselves.

(Pitkin 1967: 222)

In other words, we should examine the systemic nature of political representation – over time and as a *system* of government. In doing so, our attention is immediately drawn to the wider concepts of *representative democracy* and *representative government*. Both of which have inherent within them the initial 'present/absent' paradox noted above, where the people (however conceived and constituted) are held to be present through their representatives (however conceived and constituted) in the making of political decisions – yet are not literally present at the point of decision. They are, therefore, simultaneously included and excluded from the process of decision. Exactly where the emphasis is placed – upon inclusion/participation, or exclusion/non-participation – depends upon one's ideological predilections and one's conception of democracy.

From starting with a simple etymological statement about the meaning of representation we have immediately become immersed in the exceedingly deep and complex conceptual waters of 'democracy'. In fact we cannot avoid being embroiled in these waters, as one variant of democracy has at its very core – as one of its 'indispensable components' – the notion of representation and a representative assembly. This variant – liberal democracy – justifies representation through an elected assembly 'as the most effective device for reconciling the requirements of popular control and political equality with the exigencies of time and the conditions of the modern territorial state' (Beetham 1992a: 41). Exactly what these requirements and exigencies are we will return to shortly – but first we need to examine the democratic claims made on behalf of representation in the term 'representative democracy'.

Democracy

Democracy, as Bernard Crick observed 'is perhaps the most promiscuous word in the world of public affairs' (1964: 56). Indeed, the various usages of the word, both throughout history and in the modern world, have led some commentators to maintain that there is little in common between these variants of democracy other than the word itself (see Parry and Moran 1993: 3). Indeed, the problem starts with the word itself, for although deceptively simple in its Greek origin *demokratia* – drawn from *demos* (people) and *Kratos* (rule) – their combination, in 'people rule', raises all sorts of questions about 'who' the people are and 'how' they rule? One perfectly defensible answer to these questions is to argue that democracy is an ideal, that it does not exist in practice (see Burnheim 1985: 1). However, such a simple answer generates its own complexity and results in a new conceptual language of, for example, 'polyarchy' (Dahl 1989) or 'demarchy' (Hayek 1982: 39–40; Burnheim 1985: 9), designed to differentiate practical political systems, from the ideal. What both of these concepts have in common is the starting premise that 'democracy' – defined as rule by the people – is impractical in the modern nation-state. At its simplest there are limits, both theoretical and practical, as to how far political participation (if this is how rule by the people is to be conceived) can be effective in a diverse and large mass public. Or as Dahl puts it: 'The theoretical limit of effective political participation, even with modern electronic means of communication, rapidly diminishes with scale' (1989: 217). A fully participatory political system, where all citizens participate directly in collective decisions, is thus seen to be an ideal. What is required is some practical institutional structure which will promote the 'democratisation' of decision making in order to ensure 'the highest feasible attainment of the democratic process in the government of a country' (Dahl 1989: 222). It should be noted, however, that the claim is not that this is democracy itself, but that polyarchy is a process as close as can be achieved in a large scale polity. Similarly with 'demarchy', we do not need to understand the complexities of this system other than to understand that it is not a system of *direct* and universal participation in collective decision making. It is not, therefore, 'democratic' in the ideal sense, but is an attempt to 'democratise' the procedures of decision making in a large scale society/polity.

Direct democracy

The position we have arrived at from these negative postulates is that 'democracy' does not exist. A conception of fully participatory politics, with all of the necessary social, economic and political rights required to sustain such activity (see Parry and Moran 1993: 4–5) is thus either an ideal, and unattainable, or is an aspiration, something to be striven for. A fully participatory process of decision making would entail each and every individual in the making of each and every decision. Even if the scope of decision is limited merely to participation on each and every decision which affects the individual, or is believed by the individual to affect him or her directly, this still imposes a significant time burden upon the individual. Moreover, it also assumes that individuals are equally capable of making consensual decisions in terms of knowledge, interest and resources

– and that they are free and willing to do so in the absence of social, economic or political impediments. Direct democracy may thus conceivably require: a 'democratic citizen' who is capable of participation when given the opportunity to do so; a 'democratic society' which institutionalises the values of equality and liberty, and; a society sustained by a 'democratic culture' which actively encourages informed deliberation and the dissemination of information among the citizenry. These requirements are drawn from different models of direct democracy but they emphasise the inherent and inextricable interlinkage of social, economic and political factors in an adequate conceptualisation of democracy.

Athenian democracy

This interlinkage was apparent in Athenian democracy. In ancient Athens, between 461 BC and 322 BC, citizens (a small proportion of the total population, given that only male, non-slaves over twenty years old were eligible for citizenship) constituted 'the people'. Formally, citizens faced no obstacles to involvement in public affairs – indeed the concept of citizenship itself entailed taking a share in legislative and judicial activity. In other words, there was an expectation that 'the people' would participate directly in the affairs of the *polis*. The political culture was thus one of 'a general commitment to the principle of *civic virtue*: dedication to the republican city-state and the subordination of private life to public affairs and the common good' (Held 1987: 17). The institutional features of Athenian democracy reflected this political culture. As Aristotle noted:

> From these fundamentals [liberty and equality], and in particular from the principles of ruling and being ruled, are derived the following features of democracy: (1) Elections: all citizens eligible for all offices; (2) rule: all over each and each in turn over all; (3) offices filled by lot, either all or at any rate those not calling for experience or training; (4) no tenure of office dependent on the possession of a property qualification, or only on a very low level; (5) the same man not to hold the same office twice or only rarely...; (6) short term of office for all offices or for as many as possible; (7) jury-courts all chosen from all the citizens and adjudicating on all or most matters...; (8)...the Assembly is the sovereign authority in everything, officials having no sovereign power over anything except quite minor matters....
>
> (Aristotle [c.335–322 BC] 1962: 237)

Hence, the Assembly, as the meeting of eligible citizens, institutionalised the concept of popular sovereignty. All major issues came before the

Assembly for deliberation and decision. Unanimity was normally expected in reaching decisions, but on exceptional, intractable issues decisions could be reached by a formal majority vote. The Assembly in turn was 'assisted' by a Council of 500 members whose composition was determined by lot and whose function was to organise the agenda of the Assembly. Even in ancient Greece, therefore, the notion of direct democracy was not taken literally – with the whole people deciding unanimously on each and every issue freely and equally. Instead, there was provision for majority decision and for institutionalised leadership in the Council. As Manin notes: 'In the Athenian democracy, then, the populace itself did not wield all power; certain important powers and even a portion of the decisive power belonged to institutions that were in fact, and were perceived to be, other than the *demos*' (1997: 25). What was important was that members of these other institutions were mainly appointed by lot. The use of lots to assign political power serves to differentiate direct democracy in Athens from later representative variants of democracy. Hence, in Manin's (1997: 41) view, what makes a system representative is not the fact that a few govern in the place of the people, but that they are selected by election only. Nonetheless, 'the democracy of antiquity was undoubtedly the closest possible approximation to a literal democracy in which governors and governed stood side by side and dealt with each other face to face' (Sartori 1987: 280).

Marx: the 'end of politics' and direct democracy

Since ancient times there has been a protracted, heated and inconclusive discussion as to whether such direct self-government can be recreated. Throughout the ages alternative schemes for direct participatory democracy have been articulated – with Marx providing one particularly influential model. Starting from the belief that 'democracy' was impossible in capitalist society, in view of the fact that its political institutions systematically and exclusively served the interests of a dominant economic class (for reasons see Miliband 1977: 17–42; Femia 1993: 11–67), Marx maintained that both civil society and the state would have to be replaced by a higher unity where neither would be distinct from the other. 'Civil society as a differentiated arena of private interest would therefore vanish. In the political realm, class or rank would no longer stand between the person and the universality of the body politic' (Femia 1993: 71). In these circumstances, with what Held refers to as 'the end of politics' (1987: 123), public business would become the activity of ordinary citizens, with political deliberation and decisions being the concern of everyone. 'What makes democracy "true" is not the equal opportunity of every citizen to devote himself to public life as something special, but the "immediate participation of *all* in deliberating and deciding" on political matters. There should be no professional bureaucrats, no professional politicians' (Femia 1993: 72). 'Rule of the people' would thus entail equal opportunities for all to participate in decision making in all aspects of daily life (Parry and Moran 1993: 4). The full complexity of this argument and its intellectual challenge to liberal democracy need not detain us here (see Held 1987: 105–39; Femia 1993; Judge 1993: 55–67), all that we need to note at this stage is that Marx's argument echoes the radical tradition of direct democracy in ancient Greece (see Held 1987: 130–1; Sartori 1987: 476).

The new technologies and direct democracy

For different reasons the societal models, of direct democracy in ancient Greece and those contained within Marxist analysis, have proved inappropriate in the late-twentieth century – the conditions for direct citizen participation have long since passed, as in ancient Greece, or have not yet arrived, as in Marx's communist society. Thus, for Held, 'the classical participatory model cannot easily be adapted to stretch across space and time' (1993: 23). On the one hand, the social exclusivity and the small-scale of the city-state contrasts sharply with the size and organisational complexity of modern mass industrial societies; on the other, Marxian notions of 'true' participatory democracy remain untested without the overthrow of the capitalist state.

If direct democracy is equated solely with mass participation in public decision making bodies then it becomes a small step in logic, but a quantum leap in principle, to argue that 'direct democracy is impracticable in the modern state. And this must surely be the correct view' (Holden 1974: 28). Yet, from what we know already, the concept of democracy is inherently contestable. Not surprisingly, therefore, some modern political scientists vigorously advance the counter view that direct democracy is now *practicable* in the modern state (see McLean 1989; Budge 1996). Their basic contention is that the technology for extending popular participation in decision making has been available for a long time and that the union of computers with telephone and television, and the universal access to this technology, now allows for the institutionalisation of direct democracy in modern form (Budge 1996: 27). In which case, the argument against the practical feasibility of direct democracy is, in Budge's view, 'totally invalid' as electronic media now provide the means for direct popular participation in decision making via debate and voting, and also reduce, if not eliminate, the costs associated with such participation (Budge 1996: 28).

Indirect democracy

However, even allowing for the technical advances in recent years which facilitate direct participation, there are still those willing to argue in defence of the 'inevitability' of indirect forms of democracy in the modern state. Bealey (1988: 36), for instance, advances the commonly held view that there are compelling practical reasons for the ubiquity of indirect democracy. First, total participation in decision making is impossible, given the vast numbers of people in the modern nation-state. Second, in handing decision making over to others, this form of democracy allows the citizenry to pursue other necessary daily activities. Underpinning such statements is a conception of a political division of labour where citizens limit their political activity essentially to voting, and so leave a small number of representatives to concentrate their attention on decision making. Indeed, it is the overriding practical consideration of time that leads David Beetham to conclude that: 'any society with similar require-ments to our own in terms of production and reproduction (including the work of domestic care) could only afford to have a relatively small number devoted to full time [deliberation and legislative decision making]' (1992a: 47).

With such considerations in mind, Lijphart argues that there is thus one major amendment that needs to be made to the literal meaning of democ-racy as 'government by the people':

> that the acts of government are usually performed not directly by citi-zens but indirectly by representatives whom they elect on a free and equal basis. Although elements of direct democracy can be found even in some large democratic states, democracy is usually representa-tive democracy: government by freely elected representatives of the people.
>
> (Lijphart 1984: 1)

Representative democracy

If indirect democracy is taken essentially as a synonym for representative democracy (Holden 1974: 29), then decision making is no longer conceived in terms of direct participation by the collectivity of citizens. Instead, it becomes the preserve of a few 'decision makers' – leading some to talk of 'rule by the politician' rather than 'rule by the people' (Schumpeter [1943] 1976: 269). But on what grounds can such a system be described as democratic?

One answer, of course, is that it cannot be democratic: as only direct democracy fulfils the fundamental requirement of self-rule by the people. Despite his claim that democracy had not and could not exist, Rousseau ([1762] 1973) is frequently cited in defence of the position that citizens cannot delegate their voting rights to representatives. In his opinion, if citizens are truly to be decision makers they must be able to gather together in a sovereign assembly. Only direct participation in government, in small, homogeneous communities could provide the framework within which freedom and government could be reconciled. In Rousseau's view freedom was dependent upon people governing themselves. Representative government, in contrast, only resulted in a position where, as in England, people are 'free only during the election of members of parliament. As soon as they are elected, slavery overtakes it, and it is nothing' ([1762] 1973: 26).

A related, but diluted, answer is that representative democracy is not democratic because representation entails the practical *exclusion* of the mass of the people from decision making. This second answer is willing to admit that representation is necessary in the modern world, but then contends that there is now too little representation concentrated in too few representative institutional forms. It acknowledges that limited participation is an institutional feature of representative democracy but then proceeds to argue that such a democracy has at best a 'limited virtue' and only insofar as it upholds the possibility of periodically changing decision makers through the medium of elections (Hirst 1990: 30). What is required, therefore, is a 'democratisation' of representation, through supplementing traditional representative political institutions with a diversity of other representative associations (see Hirst 1994; Beetham 1992a: 52–3).

A third answer recognises that 'representative government includes both democratic and undemocratic features. The duality lies in its very nature, not just in the eye of the beholder' (Manin 1997: 236). If representative democracy constitutes a division of political labour between citizens and rulers, between represented and representatives, it not only distinguishes between levels of political activity but also between levels of *perceived* political competence. Representatives are seen to be different from those they represent. This is what Manin calls the 'principle of distinction' (1997: 94). This principle holds that representative democracy produces elected elites, and that representatives are perceived by the represented to hold 'distinctive qualities'. Traditionally these qualities were defined in terms of local standing and social prominence, but in an age when elections are dominated by mass parties, the qualities are defined in terms of activism and organisational skill. Some commentators now argue that in an age when elections are becoming increasingly 'personalised' the image of a political elite is built upon qualities of 'trust', 'competence' and 'style' (see Denver 1997: 41; Kellner 1997: 625). Representatives are still distinguished from the bulk of the populace – but now the basis of differentiation revolves around 'lifestyle', 'education', and 'vision'. Only a minority possess the perceived attributes for election – and hence representatives continue to constitute an elite. Indeed, Manin goes so far as to argue that 'the elective procedure impedes the democratic desire that those in government should be ordinary citizens, close to those they govern in character, way of life, and concerns' (1997: 238). Instead, 'election is…an aristocratic or oligarchical procedure in that it reserves public office for eminent individuals whom their fellow citizens deem superior to others' (1997: 238). Representative democracy culminates, therefore, in the *self-exclusion* of the bulk of the population from systematic involvement in decision making. Elections, by definition, are mechanisms for the selection of elites: but they are simultaneously mechanisms for mass participation. This duality is at the heart of the practice of representation examined throughout this book. It is particularly apparent in Chapter 2 in the consideration of microcosmic representation, in the theory and practice of 'trusteeship' examined in Chapter 3, and in the analysis of party theory in Chapter 4.

Defence of representative democracy

Its defenders maintain that, 'against the contrary claims of perfectionists, participationists and populists…representative democracy is not a sham' (Sartori 1987: 170). It is not, in essence, a polity in which people are effectively excluded from decision making, rather the reverse. Yet to make this argument requires that the nature of the debate be redirected away from etymology and from general principles of 'rule by the people'. These might constitute the starting point of debate, but, in Sartori's words, they leave discussion 'hanging in mid-air' (1987: 30). What is required, instead, in this view is 'to clear away the myths of rule by the people' and recognise that democracy is 'a set of political mechanisms' (Hirst 1990: 28), or a set of political 'techniques' and 'instruments' whereby popular power is exercised (Sartori 1987: 30).

Representative democracy subsequently comes to be conceived as a *political process*. As a process it is deceptively simple: with 'the people freely choosing representatives, those representatives debating and enacting policy and later standing for reelection, and administrators enforcing that policy' (Murphy 1993: 4). In which case, the basic claim to be 'democratic' is dependent upon the process itself.

However, the union of representation and democracy in 'representative democracy' generates its own problems. It may be argued that 'the institutions of representative democracy removed government so far from the direct reach of the *demos* that one could reasonably wonder...whether the new system was entitled to call itself by the venerable name democracy' (Dahl 1989: 30). Those who are willing to call this system 'democracy' do so primarily by stipulating a cluster of institutions and rules which define the relationship between governed and governors in the determination of how representatives are chosen and how popular control is exercised over representatives. Sartori (1987: 30) provides one of the clearest summaries of this position. In his view modern democracies hinge on limited majority rule; elective procedures, and; the representational transmission of power.

Limited majority rule

Limited majority rule is restrained rule where the majority respects minority rights. Throughout recent history the issue of majority rule has been, for different reasons, a prime concern of political philosophers (see for example Madison *et al.* [1788] 1987; Tocqueville [1862] 1968; Mill [1861] 1910). The 'tyranny of the majority' has haunted both critics and advocates of democracy alike. Recognition that society is necessarily divided by wealth, status, class, gender, religion, or ethnicity, for example, leads to a political concern over majoritarian decision making. In fact, there is a dual concern. On one side, there is the concern of the 'economic haves' that the majority of 'have nots' should not be capable of using their numerical superiority to redistribute economic resources in their favour. This was of primary concern during the course of the development of liberal capitalist states. Linked to this was a concern with 'social tyranny' whereby a minority of individuals with special ability, enterprise or wisdom needed to be safeguarded from the 'mediocrity of the masses' (see Tocqueville [1862] 1968; Mill [1861] 1910).

The second concern was that 'minorities' (traditionally religious or ethnic minorities) should not have their civil liberties violated by the majority. The problem here is how to prevent the practical exclusion of sections of the people, because of their minority position, from influencing decisions. The danger is that some minorities might become 'non-people' effectively excluded from influencing decisions which affect them directly. To offset this danger democracy has to be conceived as majority rule limited by minority rights because it 'corresponds to the people in full, that is, to the sum total of majority plus minority. It is precisely because the rule of the majority is restrained that *all* the people (all those who are entitled to vote) are *always* included in the demos' (Sartori 1987: 32–3). This theoretical justification of limited majority rule has practical consequences for the second institutional feature of representative democracy – elective processes; for, without the protection of minorities, elections could be used by a majority to determine its political dominance.

Elective procedures

Free elections are undoubtedly a central characteristic of representative democracy; but, in the sense of a universal franchise of all adult citizens participating in competitive elections, this form of democracy is a modern phenomenon. Indeed, in Britain it is essentially a late-twentieth century phenomenon – with all adults over the age of 18 securing the vote only as late as 1969.

Elections are central to representative democracy because 'they provide a means of making democracy possible in bodies much larger than those which permit direct participation in decision making' (Reeve and Ware 1992: 23). In other words, the 'participatory' claims of the system are justified in terms of the participation of citizens in elections. However, both election (participation) and representation (indirect decision making) are required to constitute representative democracy. If the democratic claims of the system are to be sustained, elections have to be free, with an equal weight assigned to each citizen's vote, and open to all adults who must be able freely to organise, speak and inform themselves of the alternatives. In essence elections decide who will make decisions rather than deciding issues themselves (see Riker 1982: 236; Sartori 1987: 108; for a qualification of this statement see Chapter 4 and the notion of electoral mandate in Britain). However, this returns us to the exclusion paradox again, for if elections are primarily concerned with the choice of leaders, then does not this limit the contribution of voters to the process of decision making to a few seconds once every four or five years – and so residualise notions of citizen participation to the discontinuous and minimal act of voting? The answer of Rousseau, Marx and participatory theorists, such as Pateman (1970), is of course: yes.

An alternative answer is: no. The basis of this negative response is to assert that elections not only choose representatives but also provide the mechanism for *controlling* them. In this view, the fact that empirical studies reveal that individual voting is not based upon rational choice – nor is it necessarily informed as to who representatives are, nor as to what they have done – does not undermine the fact that elections implant uncertainty in the minds of *representatives*. Representatives are thus aware that they may be only temporary occupants of their positions *unless* they maintain some connection with their voters. Elections become periodic and dramatic demonstrations of the fact that possession of decision making power by representatives is contingent upon the continuing support of their electorate. The ballot is thus 'the ultimate weapon' (Mayo 1960: 78) in enforcing popular control over decision makers in representative democracy. From Thomas Paine ([1792] 1984) in the eighteenth century through to William Riker (1982) in the twentieth century there has been a recognition that 'elections do not necessarily, or even usually, reveal popular will. All elections do, or have to do, is to permit people to get rid of rulers' (Riker 1982: 244). This view is shared by Manin (1997: 177) in his statement that: 'In representative government negation is more powerful than affirmation: the former constrains those in power, while the latter remains an aspiration.'

From this perspective, elections are not primarily 'democratic' as a means of expressing voters' preferences on policy alternatives, but rather as a means of controlling those who effectively choose between policy alternatives. 'In contrast to dictatorship, oligarchy, actual monarchy,…or other forms, representative democracy signifies a radical chastening of political authority.…[P]olitical authority is, at every moment, a temporary and conditional grant, regularly revocable' (Kateb 1981: 358). Popular control, exercised through the medium of elections, is thus institutionalised as one of the democratic 'rules of the game'. Elections come to exert an effect well beyond the actual day of the election itself. As Beetham (1992a: 47) points out: 'The fact of the vote casts a long shadow in front of it, as it were. It acts as a continuous discipline on the elected, requiring them to give public account of their actions and to take constant notice of public opinion.' Thus, voting exerts more continuous control than the simple act of casting a vote at first seems to allow. Indeed, free competitive elections have been identified as 'the genius of representative democracy' (Kornberg and Clarke 1992: 9), they allow for the peaceful transition of decision making power and provide the essential mechanism by which that power can be checked.

The representational transmission of power

Thus far the discussion has been 'impersonal' and abstract: neither specifying who voters or representatives 'are', how they are 'constituted' respectively, nor specifying the precise form of their relationship. The reason for this is that once specifics are introduced then the discussion becomes ever more complicated. Essentially, therefore, to make any progress the discussion has to be disaggregated into discrete but interlinked questions. The first is: how are 'the people' to be conceived – as individuals; or as collectivities organised around, for instance, geographical constituencies, workplace, functional interests, or social class? The answer to this question gives rise to various *types* of representation: territorial/geographical; functional; corporatist; associational; pluralist, and; collectivist. The second question is: how are representatives to be conceived – as individuals; or organised into collectivities of assemblies, parliaments, communes, guilds, work councils or some other organisational form? Much of the discussion on representation assumes a one-to-one relationship between individual voter and individual representative, but, as we have noted already, to make much headway in the discussion requires us to examine aggregate relationships at the level of the political system as a whole.

Nonetheless, the third question is: *what* do representatives 'represent' when they act for their electorates? Do they represent them as individuals, or as collectivities? If the former, do they represent their constituents' opinions or interests? Moreover, who decides what is to be represented, the electorate itself or the representatives? If the voters are conceived as collectivities: what is the organising focus of the collectivity – the entire nation; geographical constituencies; functional interest, or membership of some other social group? Linked to the issue of 'focus' is the question of 'style': of *how* the electorate is to be represented (see Wahlke *et al.* 1962). This raises the question of the extent to which policy discretion and independence is afforded to the representative by the represented. It specifies a power relationship. The answer reveals the extent to which the representative should be seen as a 'trustee' with significant policy independence; or as a 'delegate' bound by instructions and limited in the degree of policy discretion (see Chapters 3 and 4). The answer thus takes us to the heart of the 'representational transmission of power' and to the issues to be considered throughout this book. However, before embarking on a detailed consideration of these questions, it is important, first, to note the distinction between the terms representative *government* and representative *democracy*.

Representative government

But perhaps it is a mistake to approach political representation too directly from the various individual-representation analogies – agent and trustee and deputy. Perhaps that approach...leads us to expect or demand features in a representative relationship which are not there and need not be there. Perhaps when we conventionally speak of political representation, representative government, and the like, we do not mean or require that the representative stand in the kind of one-to-one, person-to-person relationship to his constituency or to each constituent in which a private representative stands to his principal. Perhaps when we call a governmental body or system 'representative' we are saying something broader and more general about the way in which it operates as an institutionalized arrangement. And perhaps even the representing done by an individual legislator must be seen in such a context, as embodied in a whole political system.

(Pitkin 1967: 221)

This logic leads Pitkin to maintain that political representation should be conceived, and analysed, in terms of the overall structure of the political system itself. At this macro-level the analysis of representation becomes ever more complicated – but for our purposes we simply need to note the distinction to be made between 'representative democracy' and 'representative government'. In practice, many commentators use the terms as synonyms (see Bealey 1988: 36–42; Birch 1993: 66), and manifestly there is significant overlap in their meanings. For the sake of simplicity, however, representative democracy will be used as an overarching term to describe the fundamental organising principles of a political system, whereas 'representative government' will be concerned primarily with the issue of leadership within that broader political framework.

Thus far in the discussion we have assumed that representatives are equal and undifferentiated decision makers or political leaders. However, representative *government* points to a fundamental distinction to be drawn between the institutions of representation (parliaments, or legislatures), and the institutions of decision or leadership (political executives). Only in the United States are both executive and legislature separately and directly elected, giving rise to the simultaneous claim of both executive and the legislative branches to have distinct popular authorisation for their actions. In all Western European countries, however, and in Britain in particular, the political executive is drawn from the legislature itself and has no independent source of legitimacy other than that derived from the legislature. Hence, the claims of governments to be democratic depend upon the wider claim of legislatures to be the meeting place of the people's representatives.

In fact, the claim of a government – a political executive – to be 'representative', ultimately distils into a claim of that government to be 'responsible'. As Pitkin points out, representative government 'requires that there be machinery for the expression of the wishes of the represented, and that the government respond to these wishes unless there are good reasons to the contrary. There need not be a constant activity of responding, but there must be a constant condition of responsive*ness*' (1967: 233, original emphasis). By this definition of representative government it is possible to have representative government without that government itself being democratic in the sense of being elected by a mass electorate.

Indeed, representative government in Britain has traditionally been conceived, and functioned, as a means of legitimating executive power through the condition of responsiveness. The emphasis has been upon consent and the legitimation of the change of governors by a representative body encompassing the 'political nation'. As already noted, only in the twentieth century did the 'political nation' come to approximate to 'the people'. Thus, while Britain may have been a 'representative government' for centuries, it has only been a 'representative democracy' for decades.

The tradition of representative government: relationship between theory and practice

The tradition of representative government in Britain has been concerned with the transmission of opinion between 'political nation' and governors. Government has been 'controlled' to the extent that governmental actions have required the consent of representatives of the 'political nation', and that changes of leaders has required legitimation through the representative process (see Judge 1993: 6). A brief historical survey reveals the significance of this point. Starting in the thirteenth century, the notion was already established that the English parliament should act as a corporate body of the representatives of the 'political nation', as the focus of deliberation of common business, and as the aggregation of 'informed' opinion upon public policy. The political system rested on the premise that decision making (at the time the monarch's prerogative) was conditional upon the consent of the king's most powerful subjects. Medieval English parliaments thus incorporated, in embryonic form, the elemental principles of consent and representation. In their proceedings could be 'discerned many of the elements of a system of representative government' (Birch 1971: 27). From this early stage, therefore, the principles of consent, limitation and the authorisation of decision making were enunciated. Thereafter the history of the English state up to the seventeenth century reveals the gradual restructuring of power between the monarch and an increasingly corporate body of representatives in parliament. Responsible government became institutionalised insofar as the king's ministers came increasingly to sit in the Commons and were expected to secure election to that House. As Pollard notes: 'responsible government was not established by summoning representatives to Westminster, but by embodying those representatives in the government or the government in those representatives' (1926: 296). As executive responsibility came to be institutionalised in this period, so too was the affirmation of the responsibility of representatives to support and legitimate executive actions.

In the seventeenth century representatives came also to raise popular grievances in the Commons, and no longer simply those grievances pertinent to the political elite. In a period of heightened electoral competition, MPs became conscious of an interested public beyond Westminster and beyond what had thus far constituted the 'political nation' of an aristocratic, landed class (Hill 1986: 41, 44). Indeed, MPs became trapped between the crown's rapacious demands for increased finance and a growing resentment within their own constituencies at the immiseration caused by such monarchical demands. It is significant that in the face of increasingly arbitrary government, representatives in the Commons responded by claiming their historic right to consultation in the making of decisions and in the consent to taxation.

What is particularly important for our purposes, is to note that the concepts of 'representation' and 'representative government' in England in the seventeenth century were directly linked to the actual *practice* of government. Political theory tended to reflect, and refract philosophically, the operation of political institutions and emerging constitutional relationships. This point is emphasised by Pitkin (1967: 245) who finds that in the debate preceding and surrounding the Civil War the term 'representation' underwent a widening in its meaning and became a *political* term. An important part of this debate was the contention that 'by virtue of election and representation: a few shall act for the many' (quoted in Pitkin 1967: 248). In asserting sovereignty over the crown, parliament invoked a collective right to authority and power derived from its representative status. The concept of representation thus applied to the Commons as an institution and parliament as a whole rather than to the actions of individual representatives. Indeed 'the individual member is said to 'represent' only after he has come to be thought of as acting for the whole realm, and only after the body of Parliament of which he is a member has come to be thought of as representing the whole nation' (Pitkin 1967: 251). At this time the claim to authority – to sovereignty – was made in terms of parliament being more representative of, and more responsible to, the political nation than the monarch. This claim came to be substantiated in the Constitutional Settlement of 1689 when the Bill of Rights confirmed the historic principles of consent and representation. The balance of sovereignty in 1689, in the constitutional formulation of the crown-in-parliament, tipped unquestionably in favour of parliament.

The true significance of 1689, therefore, was that it enabled historic representative principles to be attuned to the emerging principles of a liberal economy. Thereafter, the logic of parliamentary development for most of two centuries was that those with an 'interest' in the market system, primarily those with property, had the right through their representatives to influence public policy. In reverse, the inclusion–exclusion paradox manifested itself in ensuring that parliamentary representation excluded from decision making those sections of society whose interests were seen to be incompatible with prevailing liberal values. The franchise was used effectively to 'filter out' the property-less. In practice as well as theory, representation was rarely linked with notions of democracy.

By the nineteenth century, Britain had thus developed both representative government and a liberal system of government – one based upon a liberal, competitive economy and with developed social freedoms. Yet Britain was far from a democracy. At heart the system was one of responsible, not democratic, government. While the reasons prompting the transformation of representative government into representative democracy in the nineteenth century have been hotly contested (see Judge 1983b), it is clear that many leading politicians and political theorists at the time regarded the process of democratisation neither as an unmitigated blessing nor as a logical step for the liberal state to take. Rather they saw it as a 'problem', as something to be opposed and frustrated. When 'democracy' came in Britain, therefore, it came late. And it came as an appendage to an established system of representative government based upon the constitutional precept of parliamentary sovereignty. The term 'representative democracy' thus came to subsume 'representative government'. Thereafter, the central paradox in Britain was that the latter not only predated, but continued to predominate over, the former.

'Representative government' and 'representative democracy' in the modern British state

If 'democracy' has become part of the 'common coinage of political speech' in Britain (Miliband 1982: 27), 'democracy', as popular participation, has not, until very recently, greatly impinged upon the practice of British politics. If the pre-democratic institutional structure has accommodated itself numerically to 'the people' – as the 'political nation' was successively enlarged through franchise reform – the organisational principles and the governing ethos of the British state were not really enlarged and enhanced to include the democratic precepts of 'participation' and popular sovereignty. In fact, throughout the course of political transition in nineteenth century Britain, 'democracy' was largely seen as a purely political process of government, as a way of doing things, rather than an ethical ideal.

Ultimately, as Roper points out, democracy was conceived in a limited institutional context: 'It involved an appreciation that there should be a widespread right to vote for the only representative national institution, the House of Commons' (1989: 13). This institution was already legally sovereign within the state structure, so that popular elections created their own problems in reflecting the principle of 'popular sovereignty'. For some 'parliamentary sovereignty and popular sovereignty are incompatible' (Lijphart 1984: 9); for others 'popular sovereignty' is a fiction (Mitchell 1992: 103); for Dicey ([1885] 1959), however, there was no problem. Indeed, Dicey maintained that legal (parliamentary) sovereignty and political (popular) sovereignty were essentially in harmony. The established conventions of the British constitution served to ensure that 'Parliament, or the Cabinet which is indirectly appointed by Parliament, shall in the long run give effect to the will of that power which in modern England is the true sovereign of the state – the majority of electors'. In which case 'our modern code of constitutional morality secures, though in a round-about way, what is called the "sovereignty of the people"' (Dicey [1885] 1959: 431).

Dicey's critics have consistently maintained that the connection between the people and the point of decision in government is so mediated as to become almost vacuous. They point to the fact that the ephemeral act of casting a vote every four or five years cannot be seen to be 'very active citizenship' (Brazier 1991: 40). Other commentators have difficulty in deciding whether 'ultimate authority' rests with public opinion or with parliament (Camerilleri and Falk 1992: 32). Yet, in political practice, the concept of the 'legal' sovereignty of parliament has prevailed over the concept of 'popular' sovereignty. As Birch observes: 'In Britain, which has no written constitution,…the constitutional doctrine [is] that sovereignty belongs to Parliament, there being no mention of the people' (1993: 59).

It has to be recognised, therefore, that Dicey's view was always an idealised view. His simple, symmetrical conception of the representational transmission of power – of the serial flow of authority from the electorate to their representatives in parliament and then to the government – rapidly became far more complex and asymmetrical in practice. Organised parties interposed themselves between individual electors and individual representatives; parliamentary government was transformed into 'party government'; limited government becoming ever more active; and a host of organised sectional interests engendered a system of political representation which was only tangentially and intermittently linked to parliamentary representation in Westminster.

Throughout these changes representative government continued to provide for: the recruitment of decision makers as members of the political executive; an institutionalised role for opposition, and the sustenance of an alternative government in waiting, and; the symbolic responsibility of government, if not directly to the people then at least indirectly to their representatives. What the organisational principles, and the governing ethos of the British state, did not provide for was the inclusion of the democratic precepts of 'participation' and 'popular sovereignty'. In these circumstances, 'democracy' constituted 'a problem' for representative government in Britain throughout the twentieth century (Wright 1994: 13–14). A problem which confronted the new Labour government after 1997 and one the new administration sought to address, but a problem which was itself at the very heart of the difficulties entailed in 'democratising' the British state.

Representation: language of legitimation

'Representation' has traditionally formed an essential term in the language of legitimation used by decision makers to establish their credentials to act on behalf of those not actually present at the point of decision, and also to assert their responsibility and accountability for decisions taken. As such it is not exclusively a part of the lexicon of 'democracy'. Certainly in Britain, representative government pre-dated representative democracy, and, although there is a tendency to use the terms 'representative government' and 'representative democracy' as synonyms, their historical distinctiveness should be borne in mind. In other words, when we come to examine the theory and practice of representation in the 1990s we need to remember that, although the concept is now commonly associated with democratic government, it had its origins in pre-democratic times. Similarly, the institutional structure of representative government pre-dates the growth of representative democracy in Britain, and has never fully accommodated itself in practice to the idea of popular sovereignty inherent within democratic theory.

One consequence of this conceptual and institutional inheritance is that discussion of representation in Britain is replete with paradoxes. Representation both serves to include 'the people' in decision making – indirectly and infrequently through the process of elections – yet, simultaneously, to exclude them from direct and continuous participation in the decision making process. If limited participation is an institutional feature of representative democracy, then this poses a dilemma for those who seek to 'democratise' the British political system through the supplementation of representative political institutions with self-governing participatory associations (see Chapter 6). Moreover, if representative government entails 'the principle of distinction' as identified by Manin (1997) then the electoral process which incorporates the principle of mass participation culminates in the choice of elites distinguished, by definition, from the mass. This, in turn, poses a dilemma for those who seek a more proportionate or pictorial representation of social characteristics among elected politicians (see Chapter 2). Similarly, if a basic tenet of representation is not only the choice of representatives but also the popular control of representatives, then the nature of control – whether active in the form of mandates and delegation, or passive in the form of policy independence and trusteeship – reflects a further duality in the conception of representation (see Chapters 3 and 4).

But perhaps the most fundamental paradox of all is that the very concept of 'representation' often poses a challenge to the established pattern of representative government in Britain. This is most clearly seen, for example, in the tension between functional forms of representation in their modern pluralist, corporatist, and associative variants and territorial representation in the Westminster parliament (see Chapters 6 and 7). The ultimate dilemma for proponents of the enhancement of representative democracy in Britain in the 1990s is that the language of legitimation is rooted in the process of territorial representation. The constitutional 'rules of the game' – to which the electorate subscribe, and from which the legitimacy of public policy outputs derive – are defined formally in terms of geographical representation. Other forms of representation and attendant forms of legitimation – for example through 'function' or 'presence' (see Chapters 2 and 6) – have been subsumed within these broader, and fundamental, 'rules of the game'. In this sense the authorisation of public policy made by elected representatives is afforded priority over any other form of authorisation (derived, for example, from expertise or functional knowledge, or social characteristics).

What follows, therefore, is an examination of the theory and practice of representation in one country with a unique representative tradition. Whilst most theories of representation are universal, their practice is specific, and in Britain the practice is often peculiar. What we need to remember most of all throughout the following discussion, however, is that: 'representation is not any single action by any one participant, but the over-all structure and functioning of the system' (Pitkin 1967: 222).

2 Microcosmic representation

The concept of representation is inextricably linked with the concepts of legitimacy and legitimation, and, as we saw in Chapter 1, representative assemblies provide *the* characteristic political institutions of legitimation in modern liberal democracies. Indeed, they have been identified 'as the most effective device for reconciling the requirements of popular control and political equality with the exigencies of time and the conditions of the modern territorial state' (Beetham 1992a: 41). Their 'effectiveness' is linked in turn to the nature of the 'inputs' and 'outputs' of the process of representation. On the input side, direct elections are an integral part of the legitimation process providing simultaneously: the decision makers themselves; authorisation for decision making, and; information upon popular preferences. In addition, the periodic nature of elections also provides incentives for representatives to remain informed about popular preferences in between times. Equally, however, what representative assemblies 'do' is as of much importance as what they 'are' (in terms of their composition and origins). On the 'output' side, therefore, representatives, as authorised decision makers, have the capacity to bind those in whose name they act. In these circumstances, it is of some significance to individual citizens, so bound, that their representatives act responsively to them and responsibly on their behalf. Finding ways of ensuring this policy-responsiveness subsequently has been one of the prime concerns of representation both in theory and practice over the past two centuries.

If we assume that representation is essentially about political action – about how and why representatives can act for others, and so 'make present' those who are not actually present at the point of decision – then we have to start by considering 'how' the people are made present in the first instance. One answer, at the institutional level of the representative assembly, is that the composition of the institution itself 'reflects' the composition of the wider electorate – insofar as there is some correspondence between the social characteristics of the population at large and the membership of the legislature. Representation, in this sense, is less about what the legislature does than about how it is composed. Pitkin, for example, summarises this view in terms of: 'The representative [not acting] for others; he "stands for" them, by virtue of a correspondence or connection between them, a resemblance or reflection' (1967: 61). In part, Pitkin's summary is misleading in the use of the singular pronoun, for no single individual can reflect 'proportionately' the characteristics of a social group. At its simplest: no single representative can be half woman and half man, or 5 per cent black and 95 per cent white, or whatever other demographic characteristic is deemed important. Only at an institutional, or aggregate level can such reflection, or proportionality, be offered. Second, Pitkin's summary is also misleading because it places the emphasis upon what representatives are 'like' rather than what they 'do' – upon resemblance rather than action. Yet, even Pitkin eventually has to recognise that 'proportionalists…are interested in what the legislature does; they care about its composition precisely because they expect the composition to determine the activities' (1967: 63).

This dual concern with 'composition' and 'action' provides the foci of discussion in this chapter and prompts an examination of the concept of 'microcosmic' representation itself. This might seem a strange place to start if we were to accept Philip Norton's statement that 'in both British political thought and practice, the argument for a socially typical House has never taken root' (1981: 55), but, on both counts, Norton is mistaken. Whilst few have argued that the House of Commons should be an *exactly proportionate* reflection of all social groups and interests in the electorate at large, nonetheless, there have been persistent and pressing claims for a *more* proportionate representation of *some* groups in the legislature. Exactly which groups merit more proportionate representation, and why, has changed over time.

Why 'microcosmic' representation?: theory

As we have noted already, notions of representation over the centuries have become entangled with ideas about legitimate government and, eventually, democracy. If a representative democracy is to function 'democratically' it has to make present 'the people' who are not, and cannot literally be, present in decision making. If representative democracy is a mechanism, a process, then one recurring argument has been that the representational transmission of power would be 'more perfect in proportion as it accurately duplicates the working of the people as a whole' (Pitkin 1967: 86). Implicit within this idea is the assumption that representation is a second-best option: if direct participation by 'the people' is impractical then, as a second preference, representation should at least attempt as close a reflection of the constituent elements of 'the people' as possible. An implicit criticism is thus often present at the outset in the 'proportionalist' case: representation is already less than the ideal of direct democracy; in which case, the task should be to ensure the *representativeness* of the legislature of the wider electorate. While 'representation' and 'representativeness' are conceptually distinct, successive 'proportionalist' theorists have argued, however, that *they should* be linked. The representative assembly *should be* a proportionate reflection of society (even if it cannot be exactly so in practice). In this sense, microcosmic representation provides a critical standard by which the representativeness of existing institutions can be measured. Not surprisingly, such a criterion will always find existing institutions wanting (Birch 1971: 58).

Contrary to Norton's view, therefore, such notions of proportionality have had, and continue to have, 'a good deal of influence' in Britain (Birch 1971: 55). This influence was particularly pronounced in the agitation for franchise reform in the nineteenth century in the writings of Jeremy Bentham, James Mill and John Stuart Mill, and still finds reflection in the debate about 'democratisation' of representation in the writings of Anne Phillips and others in the 1990s. The unifying thread in these works is the linkage between the 'composition' and 'action' of representative assemblies, between inputs in terms of representativeness and the outputs in terms of legislation and policies.

Notions of microcosmic representation in the nineteenth century

Jeremy Bentham

One powerful advocate of franchise reform in the nineteenth century was Jeremy Bentham, the utilitarian philosopher. His conception of representation was:

> essentially microcosmic....The essential function [of members of the representative assembly] is to constitute, in themselves, a microcosm of the nation, so that if (leaving aside their temporary and peculiar interests as politicians) they pursue their personal interests, they will reach decisions which will maximize the happiness of the community.
>
> (Birch 1971: 55)

Generally, endorsement of the principle of representation in utilitarianism was secured on the grounds of ensuring that governments would pursue the principle of utility, that is the greatest happiness of the greatest number. The basic problem of a political system based upon this principle, however, was that the maximisation of individual utilities – of the calculus of individual pleasure minus pain – was the motivation of representatives as well as the represented. In which case, the actual result of government was likely to be the promotion of the happiness of *governors* at the expense of the pleasure of the governed. What was necessary, therefore, was to ensure that a correspondence existed between the happiness of governors and governed, and this could best be achieved by bringing the particular interests of rulers into accordance with that of the ruled. Fortunately we do not have to examine how congruence could be attained between the universal interest and the competitive self-interest of individuals, other than to note that Bentham believed they could be brought into harmony. What is important for our purposes is that Bentham identified *popular* representation as 'the method' for ensuring the 'junction of interest' ([1830] 1843: 6) between rulers and ruled.

On these grounds he was critical of the pre-1832 system of representation because it secured the 'sinister interest' of the propertied minority at the expense of the universal interest (Bentham [1817] 1843). Intermittently, after the French Revolution of 1789, Bentham expressed his views on the methods whereby the 'ruling few' maintained their political control over the 'subject many'. Indeed, events in France convinced him of the need for the French to adopt a system of representation based upon free elections and a near-universal franchise (Arblaster 1987: 45; Dinwiddy 1989: 11–12). But his case for the extension of the franchise and popular representation in Britain was initially advanced more hesitantly, and was conducted according to simple utilitarian logic (Eccleshall 1986: 30). Nonetheless, by 1830 and the publication of *The Constitutional Code* there were no doubts that 'the best form of government' was one in which 'the greatest happiness principle requires that, be the governors who they may...it is the will of the governed, that during each moment their existence in that situation should be the result: that is to say, that after having been placed, they should at certain intervals of no great length, be displaceable by the governed' ([1830] 1843: 95). The means of exercising this 'dislocative power' was, of course, to be through elections, which were to be (nearly) universal, secret, free, equal and annual ([1817] 1843: 452–3).

Good government could be secured through representation based upon popular elections because:

> there *does* exist [on the part of electors] the disposition to contribute towards the advancement of the universal interest, whatsoever can be

contributed by their votes: by those votes…will be determined the individuality of the several persons on whom, in the character of their representatives, will be incumbent the duty of acting their parts respectively, towards the accomplishment of the same ultimate and comprehensive end.

(Bentham [1817] 1843: 455)

This accomplishment would be guaranteed through representation of *all* the interests of the nation in parliament. 'Legislation requires a variety of local knowledge, which can only be obtained in a numerous body of deputies chosen from all parts of the empire. It is proper that all interests should be known and discussed' (Bentham [1789] 1843: 301). Moreover, 'the composition of a legislative assembly will be the better in proportion…as its interest is similar to that of the community' ([1789] 1843: 301).

The purpose of representation for Bentham was thus to provide information about, and an accurate reflection of, the interests of the electorate. This mirroring of interests would ensure that: 'A numerous body of amoveable [*sic*] legislators participate too strongly in the interest to the community to neglect it long' ([1789] 1843: 301). Hence, the composition of the representative assembly was of importance to the determination of the nature of legislative outputs. The *representativeness* of parliament mattered in a democracy. It was a claim for the institutionalisation of democratic authority. In the early nineteenth century this claim was radical, and was to prove influential in the debate about franchise reform in Britain thereafter (see Pitkin 1967: 65–6; Birch 1964: 47).

James Mill

Bentham's views were echoed at the time by his close colleague James Mill. Indeed, in 'An Essay on Government' ([1820] 1992) it was Mill who set out the clearer exposition of the case for microcosmic representation. Along with Bentham, Mill believed government was merely a means to an end, namely the happiness of individuals within the community. He also shared the utilitarian assumption that individuals are motivated by a desire to experience pleasure and avoid pain. The primary problem of government remained that of minimising the extent to which rulers could encroach upon the wider maximisation of individual and community happiness. One possibility would be direct democracy, but 'it is obviously impossible that the community in a body can be present to afford protection of its members' ([1820] 1992: 7). Moreover, direct democracy was deemed impractical and inefficient. It was impractical because 'to assemble the whole of a community as often as the business of Government requires performance would almost preclude the existence of labour; hence that of property; and hence the existence of the community itself'. It was inefficient because 'a community in mass is ill adapted for the business of Government' ([1820] 1992: 7). However, if only the community as a whole could be trusted to pursue the general good, Mill appeared to have created a dilemma for himself in summarily rejecting direct democracy. The way out of this dilemma was through the process of representation, for 'the system of representation' was 'the grand discovery of modern times' in which was to be found 'the solution to all the difficulties [of good government], both speculative and practical' ([1820] 1992: 21).

But the fundamental problem of government remained that, 'if power is granted to a body of men, called representatives, they, like any other men, will use their power, not for the advantage of the community, but for their own advantage, if they can' ([1820] 1992: 23). What had to be ensured, therefore, was that they could not. The solution, for Mill, was to ensure that 'the interests of the Representatives...be identified with those of the community' ([1820] 1992: 23).

> The general conclusion, therefore, which is evidently established is this; that the benefits of the Representative system are lost, in all cases in which the interests of the choosing body are not the same with those of the community.
>
> ([1820] 1992: 27)

If left like this then Birch's (1971: 55) assessment that 'this concept of representation is essentially microcosmic' would undoubtedly be correct. However, Mill does not leave it like this and proceeds, in the next paragraph, to claim that the interest of the whole community is 'identical with that...to be found in the aggregate males, of an age to be regarded as *sui juris* [over 40], who may be regarded as the natural representatives of the whole population' ([1820] 1992: 27). Hence, although generally in favour of universal suffrage (see Fenn 1987: 124), Mill ended up proposing a system of representation based upon the exclusion of over 80 per cent of the adult population from the franchise (see Macpherson 1977: 39).

Women, and the representation of their interests, did not appear to be a particular problem for Mill as the interest 'of almost all of whom is involved either in that of their fathers or in that of their husbands'. Certainly, as an activist in the reform movement, he was keenly aware that public opinion in the early-nineteenth century was far from ready to admit women into the franchise (Macpherson 1977: 40). In this he shared Bentham's belief that women should be excluded: 'Because the prepossession against their admission is *at present* too general, and too intense, to afford any chance in favour of a proposal for their admission' (Bentham [1830] 1843: 108, emphasis added). Yet, other than on grounds of political expediency, Bentham found little cause to exclude women from the vote: on grounds of intellect, there was no basis upon which women could be deemed inferior, and; on grounds of political skills, history pointed to the capacities of female monarchs – in England, Russia, Austria, Sweden and Portugal – to govern ([1830] 1843: 108–9). Moreover, he pointed to the 'practical good' that the incorporation of women into the franchise would probably be secure in the nature of legislative outputs ([1830] 1843: 109). Ultimately, however, Bentham baulked at admitting women representatives into parliament because of 'the reciprocal seduction that would ensue in the case of a mixture of sexes in the composition of a legislative…body….It would lead to nothing but confusion and ridicule' ([1830] 1843: 108). To avoid such contemporary 'confusion' he stopped short of recommending women for membership of the representative assembly.

John Stuart Mill

Pitkin (1967: 63) has no hesitation in including John Stuart Mill as a 'proportionalist'. She chooses to single out, and edit, Mill's statement that 'Parliament…is an arena in which not only the general opinion of the nation, but that of every section of it, and as far as possible of every eminent individual whom it contains, can produce itself in full light and challenge discussion' (Mill [1861] 1910: 239). Unless 'opinions' are directly correlated with specific social groups, however, there is no necessary linkage in this quotation with microcosmic conceptions of representation.

Where Mill appears to be more explicit in his endorsement of microcosmic representation is later in *Representative Government* when he considers the merits of Thomas Hare's proposals for a system of proportional representation. There he states that:

> Mr Hare's plan [is] among the very greatest improvements yet made in the theory and practice of government.
>
> In the first place, it secures a representation, in proportion to numbers, of every division of the electoral body:…every minority in the whole nation, consisting of a sufficiently large number to be, on principles of equal justice, entitled to a representative.
>
> (Mill [1861] 1910: 263)

The proportional nature of representation is brought out even more clearly when Mill considers how representative democracy can secure enlightened decision making. Unlike his father, he argued without qualification for female suffrage, and, he did so primarily on developmental grounds. Utility, in John Stuart Mill's opinion, 'must be utility in the largest sense, grounded in the permanent interests of man as a progressive being' ([1859] 1910: 136). He believed that higher moral culture could be encouraged through democratic participation and by promoting an interest in public affairs. Promoting the developmental capacities – of intellect and moral virtue – of all individuals was thus a distinctly different concern from that of the earlier utilitarians and their promotion of the greatest happiness of the greatest number.

Yet the concern with both individual development and the extension of the franchise was driven by an identical logic. It was, as Coole notes, a logic 'especially applicable to the question of female suffrage, since it is women who must languish in privacy and thereby threaten public integrity' (1993: 107). Without doubt the exclusion of women from the public sphere infringed the developmental principles at the centre of Mill's conception of utility. Perhaps not surprisingly, therefore, Mill's advocacy of universal suffrage was to place women's political and social emancipation firmly on the theoretical and practical political agenda of liberalism in mid-nineteenth century Britain (see Eccleshall 1986: 34; Coole 1993: 109–17).

Nonetheless, it should be remembered that Mill basically conceived of interests in terms of class or socioeconomic status rather than of gender. Parallels can of course be drawn between his concern for class and sex oppression and the need in both cases to break with paternalism and to promote responsible self-government, but, as Coole (1993: 112) argues, Mill's commitment to liberal economics severely limited his feminism. Equally his commitment to liberal economics ultimately also limited his commitment to 'microcosmism'. Mill never really explicitly acknowledged the contradiction between capitalist economic relations and the democratic ideal of equal self-development. Implicit throughout his work was the assumption that an equal and universal franchise would result in the class government of an uneducated mass. His fear was that, in curbing the 'sinister interests' of an economically dominant class, the extension of the franchise would bring in its wake 'collective mediocrity', as, 'superior intellects and characters will necessarily be outnumbered' by placing 'the principal power in the hands of classes more and more below the highest level of instruction in the community' (Mill [1861] 1910: 265–6). One way to secure and sustain the representation of a gifted elite in parliament was through a system of plural voting where votes would be heavily weighted in favour of intellectuals and professionals. Another, perhaps more effective and politically practical way, would be through the adoption of a proportional electoral system. In this manner, 'if the *elite* of these classes formed part of Parliament, by the same title as any other of its members – by representing the same number of citizens, the same numerical faction of the national will – their presence could give umbrance to nobody' ([1861] 1910: 269). Mill thus believed that the intellectually gifted minority would wield a disproportionate amount of political influence to offset their numerical proportionality. Moreover, he hoped that this would guarantee what 'a democratic people' would not normally be guaranteed: 'leaders of a higher grade of intellect and character than itself' ([1861] 1910: 269).

Clearly, Mill was exercised by the potential for representative democracy to slide into majoritarian tyranny, but equally he was concerned by the other major issue which we identified in Chapter 1: what exactly was a representative assembly supposed to do? In fact, Mill's conception of what a representative assembly 'is', in terms of its composition, was inextricably linked to what he thought it should 'do'. In his discussion of these matters he intertwined the meanings of 'representative democracy' and 'representative government'. Given the very title of Mill's work – *Representative Government* – there can be no doubt which took precedence. This is hardly surprising because he drew directly upon the historical experience of representative government in Britain (see Judge 1993: 45). Although he believed that 'practical supremacy in the state should reside in the representatives of the people' he also acknowledged that 'it is an open question what actual functions, what precise part in the machinery of government, shall be directly and personally discharged by the representative body' (Mill [1861] 1910: 229). Thus, in making his case that representative bodies should control the business of government rather than 'actually doing it' he drew directly upon British experience. His preference for a position where a political executive made decisions, and a representative parliament consented to and controlled executive actions, reflected that experience.

His view of what a parliament should do is thus conditioned by what the British parliament already did: it 'is not expected, nor even permitted, to originate directly either taxation or expenditure' (Mill [1861] 1910: 230); 'in reality the only thing which [it] decides is which of two, or at most three, parties…shall furnish the executive government' ([1861] 1910: 234); 'a popular assembly is still less fitted to administer, or to dictate to those who have charge of administration' ([1861] 1910: 231); and that 'the only task to which a representative assembly can possibly be competent is not that of doing the work, but of causing it to be done; of determining to whom or to what sort of people it shall be confided, and giving or withholding the national sanction to it when performed' ([1861] 1910: 237). The truly effective function of a representative assembly, therefore, is deliberation:

Representative assemblies are often taunted by their enemies with being places of mere talk and *bavardage*. There has seldom been more misplaced derision. I know not how a representative assembly can more usefully employ itself than in talk, when the subject of talk is the great public interests of the country, and every sentence of it represents the opinion either of some important body of persons in the nation, or of an individual in whom some such body have reposed their confidence. A place where every interest and shade of opinion can have its cause even passionately pleaded, in the face of the government and of all other interests and opinions.

(Mill [1861] 1910: 240)

Here the historic principles of parliamentary government are fused with radical notions of microcosmic representation. This mixture was to prove highly potent in successive debates about representation in Britain.

Notions of microcosmic representation in the twentieth century

Concern about the representativeness of parliament did not end with the development of a universal franchise. Simply admitting the working classes, women and young adults into the franchise was no guarantee that those groups would gain membership of parliament itself. As we will see below, many argued, and continue to argue, that there was no logical requirement for parliament to reflect the precise composition of the electorate in this way, and moreover that it would be a practical impossibility to do so. Despite these cautions, echoes of the 'proportionalist' case have continued to be heard throughout the twentieth century.

Birch (1971: 58) characterises this case as 'neo-Benthamite' in that it uses microcosmic ideas – that parliament should in some sense be a proportionate reflection of the wider electorate – to criticise the present 'unrepresentativeness' of the elected assembly. Birch then proceeds to identify the works of J.F.S. Ross as providing 'a notable example' of neo-Benthamite analysis. From a detailed study of Ross's writing, however, it is far from clear that he subscribed unambiguously to a microcosmic conception of representation.

The point of departure for Ross's (1944: 12) analysis is the application of the 'scientific method' to the study of parliamentary representation. All that this means in practice is a quantitative analysis of the socioeconomic backgrounds of MPs. Ross maintains that: 'When we have really found out the facts, when we know something definite of the hitherto neglected natural history of the genus MP, we shall be in a better position to criticize

the laws and customs that have evolved that genus and that now perpet-
uate it. When we know what *is* we can better determine what *ought to be.*'
'What is', is apparent:

> the House is not in any sense…'an average sample of ordinary men'.
> In no single respect – age, education, occupation, sex, social standing,
> party – does the composition of the House of Commons reflect that
> of the community. The differences, moreover, are not the minor devi-
> ations inseparable from any system of representation: they are radical
> divergences.
>
> (Ross 1944: 116)

Does that mean that parliament should be 'an average sample'? If it was,
Ross (1944: 180) argued, it 'would be much younger than our present
House of Commons, it would be more than half feminine, it would be
predominantly hard up and inexperienced and ill-educated'. This is not a
prospect Ross contemplates with equanimity. The thought of a House
'consisting largely of youthful ignoramuses and with men in the minority'
convinces him that 'the "average sample" theory is untenable' (1944: 180).
We are back, therefore, to the spectre raised by John Stuart Mill of an
unthinking and ignorant mass. The dilemma remains that: 'if we are
honest we must recognize the political limitations of the great majority of
ordinary men and women; but if we really believe in democratic government we ought to see that they are given every opportunity and
encouragement to take that share in which they *are* capable' (Ross 1944:
174, original emphasis). For Ross their 'share' is conceived in terms of the
choice of candidates (1944: 174–7), for he believes that in 'favourable
circumstances the electors can and will choose their members wisely'
(1944: 176). The electorate's choice should, however, be limited.

Thus, in dismissing the 'average sample' theory as an 'absurdity' (1944:
180), Ross reaches the conclusion that 'in the most general terms, some
kinds of people could do the job better than most others' (1944: 181).
Ideally, therefore, representatives should be 'enlightened men and women
who, whether or not they are in the formal sense well educated, have read
and thought widely, have a good knowledge of affairs, and possess an
understanding of fundamental facts and principles' (1944: 193).

From Ross's perspective it 'is highly improbable that [the working
classes] could normally supply more than a very few candidates capable of
fulfilling all the exacting conditions [of an MP's job]' (1944: 196). Quite
why members of the working class, or young people or most women for
that matter, would fail to match Ross's criteria of 'enlightenment' is never
explained: it is merely asserted. Such comments limit, however, his claim to

be a 'proportionalist'. He still retains *some* claim, insofar as his basic intention is 'to secure a better balance of occupational experience among members' (1944: 196); in his belief that 'the House should not be so elderly as to be out of harmony with the thoughts and feelings and outlook of the community it represents' (1944: 194), and his desire to ensure 'a broad correspondence between the political views of the community at large and the political complexion of the House of Commons' (1944: 177). In practice this would not entail 'a mathematically precise representation of every shade of opinion in exact proportion to the number of electors holding it' (1944: 177), or 'a strictly proportional representation of all occupations' (1944: 196). Instead, the objective was to secure 'a better balanced House, one more truly representative of the community it exists to serve' (1944: 199). What this last statement demonstrates is the implicit linkage made between representativeness and representation: 'true' representation requires some, though not an exact, correspondence to the broader socio-economic characteristics of the electorate.

Many subsequent quantitative studies of the composition of the House of Commons have operationalised 'microcosmic' criteria as a test of the 'representativeness' of MPs. In this regard, Bentham and Mill's preoccupations continue to have contemporary resonance. Mellors' (1978) study of the socioeconomic background of British MPs from 1945–74 was driven in part by the assumption that the composition of a representative assembly affected the 'character of its decisions' (1978: 1). His conclusion pointed to an implicit linkage between representativeness and quality of representation: 'it seems not unreasonable to contemplate how far apparently wider disaffection with parliamentary politics and government is compounded by a narrowing of the social base from which British MPs are drawn' (1978: 119). This linkage was made even more explicit in the last sentence of the book: 'All of this means a Parliament which has become increasingly...uncharacteristic of, and some would argue isolated from, the electorate whom it represents' (Mellors 1978: 126). Although Mellors was not arguing for 'proportionate' representation, nonetheless, there is a pervasive underlying theme that the House should be *more* representative in its socioeconomic composition than it had been in the post-war period.

Similarly, Rush, whilst agnostic on the claim that the electorate would be better served by 'a House of Commons which were more nearly a microcosm', goes on to note that 'it is difficult to resist the argument that a more representative House...would be able to draw on a broader and deeper range of knowledge and experience in performing the roles demanded [of it]' (1988: 33). More recently still, Adonis (1993: 49–50), in observing that British MPs are a 'select breed' raises the question: 'After all,

Parliament is supposed to represent the people as a whole. How can it do so when its composition is such a poor reflection of British society?' (see Table 2.1). Although Adonis then avoids answering the question directly, the very manner in which it is posed reveals the continuing influence of microcosmic notions of representation in Britain in the 1990s.

Anne Phillips: politics of presence

Anne Phillips answers the question posed by Adonis from a radical perspective. In examining the shift from direct democracy to representative democracy she observes that concern has shifted 'from *who* the politicians are to *what* (policies, preferences, ideas) they represent, and in doing so, has made accountability to the electorate the pre-eminent radical concern' (Phillips 1995: 4). With this concern comes a linkage of the quality of representation to the mechanisms of accountability that bind representatives more closely to the ideas and opinions of the represented. Attention has come to be focused, therefore, upon the congruity between the political beliefs and ideals of the representative and the represented – with the additional expectation that the former would possess some superior ability to articulate and register opinions (Phillips 1995: 6). By this view the 'role of the politician is to carry a message. The messages will vary but it hardly matters if the messengers are the same' (Phillips 1995: 6). For Phillips

Table 2.1 Backgrounds of MPs: May 1997

	Labour		Conservative		Liberal Democrat	
	n	*%*	*n*	*%*	*n*	*%*
Age of MPs						
20–39	65	16	22	13	17	37
40–9	178	43	61	37	9	20
50–9	140	33	61	37	15	32
60+	35	8	21	13	5	11
Education						
Public school	67	16	109	66	19	41
University	275	66	133	81	32	70
Occupation						
Professions	188	45	61	37	23	50
Business	37	9	65	39	11	24
Miscellaneous	139	33	38	23	11	24
Manual workers	54	13	1	1	1	2
Women	101	24	13	8	3	7
Black/Asian	9	2	0	0	0	0

Source: Criddle (1997).

(1995: 1) this constitutes the 'politics of ideas' which regards social difference as primarily a matter of ideas. This form of politics has been associated with representation through political parties, and entails a 'secular understanding of politics as a matter of judgement and debate, and expects political loyalties to develop around policies rather than people' (Phillips 1995: 1). Part of this understanding is that ideas and interests are detachable from experience. Hence, if social class is regarded by parties as the pre-eminent group inequality, then shared beliefs about discounting or eliminating such differences are sufficient qualifications for membership. However, class identities and personal experiences of class inequality, are not essential in themselves for the representation of 'class interests', and so for example, the 'labour interest' in Britain can be, and has been, promoted by representatives other than workers themselves. In these circumstances, 'one person may easily stand for another: there is no additional requirement for the representatives to "mirror" the characteristics of the person or people represented' (Phillips 1995: 6).

This is not the case, however, for the 'politics of presence', as, the 'politics of presence' is 'identity based' rather than 'ideas based':

> Once difference is conceived…in relation to those experiences and identities that may constitute different kinds of groups, it is far harder to meet demands for political inclusion without also including the members of such groups.…Adequate representation is increasingly interpreted as implying a more adequate representation of the different social groups that make up the citizen body, and notions of 'typical' or 'mirror' or 'descriptive' representation have then returned with renewed force.
>
> (Phillips 1995: 6)

With the rise of new social movements, and a recognition of inequalities stemming from sources other than social class in recent years, Phillips argues that the focus of the debate about representation should move from the 'politics of ideas' to the 'politics of presence'. Whereas the politics of class was grounded in the differences arising from underpinning economic and social conditions, the politics of identity is more directly grounded in political activity itself. The point is thus to enable those groups presently under-represented or excluded from the political process to engage more directly in political debate and political decision making.

The emphasis upon political exclusion stemming from 'identity' rather than 'class' allows Phillips to insert the issues of group difference directly into the normative and practical debates about representation. Her objective is to generate 'identity-based politics' around differences of gender, race or ethnicity and, in so doing, to develop a 'different understanding of representation'. More particularly, it is to build a case for changing the nature of representation based upon historically-specific analysis of the existing structures of exclusion. She seeks therefore to identify which groups have been systematically excluded from decision making and to identify the conditions for their political inclusion. This gets around the problem of calling for equal representation of all disadvantaged groups (pensioners, the physically disabled, the blind, etc.), and concentrates attention instead upon 'those particularly urgent instances of political exclusion which a "fairer" system of representation seeks to resolve' (Phillips 1995: 47). Women and ethnic minorities stand out as 'particularly urgent instances of political exclusion'.

Representation of women

Nowhere in the 1990s is the continued potency of microcosmic theory better illustrated than in the campaign for increased representation of women and women's interests in the House of Commons. Since the early 1980s there has been increasing interest in the 'problem' of female representation in the British parliament specifically, and in legislatures generally. The essence of the 'problem' is captured in two simple questions: first, why so few women in parliament – and, second, does it matter?

The answer to the second question for many feminists throughout the 1960s and 1970s was: no, it did not matter. It did not matter because elections and representative institutions themselves were seen not to matter. Indeed, the preoccupation of radical feminists in these decades was with 'self-organisation' and direct participatory forms of engagement in the broader social movement of feminism. The principles governing the wider polity were hardly a matter of urgent concern. ' "Getting women into politics", where politics meant parliament or national assembly, was very low down the list, and the real issues of democracy and participation were thought to lie elsewhere' (Phillips 1991: 61; see also Lovenduski and Randall 1993: 4–8; Phillips 1993: 93). This perspective changed in the 1980s, however, when a reconsideration of the importance of mainstream politics was undertaken by feminists (Lovenduski 1993: 1–6).

Indeed, a fundamental part of this reconsideration was to move from a focus upon women as voters to women as office-holders and representatives. For long periods after the majority of women were first enfranchised in 1918, and after the extension of female suffrage in 1928, the issue of women representatives was not really seen as a problem. Representation had been secured through the vote, women were eligible to stand as parliamentary candidates, it was up to women, thereafter, to use their vote to influence policy. Who they voted for was not a primary consideration. Yet, whilst women's participation rates in elections have consistently equalled that of men, their participation rate in Western legislatures, with the exception of the Nordic countries, has remained far below that of men. As Table 2.2 reveals, for nearly seventy years in Britain, the proportion of women MPs never exceeded 5 per cent of the total House of Commons. Only relatively recently, however, has the lack of female representation in legislatures been regarded as a puzzle or a problem (see Darcy *et al.* 1994: 25).

The 'problem'

For those who maintain that microcosmic representation is impractical, impossible or undesirable (see pp. 44–5) there is no problem in the 'under-representation' of women, or of any other social group or minority for that matter. It is only to be expected that representative democracy based upon geographical constituencies cannot produce a perfect reflection of society:

Table 2.2 Women candidates and MPs 1918–97

	Conservative		Labour		House of Commons	
	PPCs	MPs	PPCs	MPs	MPs	% HoC
1918	1	0	4	0	1	0.1
1922	5	1	10	0	2	0.3
1923	7	3	14	3	8	1.3
1924	12	3	22	1	4	0.7
1929	10	3	30	9	14	2.3
1931	16	13	36	0	15	2.4
1935	19	6	33	1	9	1.5
1945	14	1	41	21	24	3.8
1950	29	6	42	14	21	3.4
1951	25	6	41	11	17	2.7
1955	33	10	43	14	24	3.8
1959	28	12	36	13	25	4.0
1964	24	11	33	18	29	4.6
1966	21	7	30	19	26	4.1
1970	26	15	29	10	26	4.1
1974 Feb	33	9	40	13	23	3.6
1974 Oct	30	7	50	18	27	4.3
1979	31	8	52	11	19	3.0
1983	40	13	78	10	23	3.5
1987	46	17	92	21	41	6.3
1992	62	20	138	37	60	9.2
1997	66	13	155	101	120	18.0

Source: F.W.S. Craig (1989: 114–5).

hence there is no problem. But Phillips counters this by maintaining that 'arguments that rely on the impossibility of one extreme in order to justify its opposite are always suspect, and as long as those who speak for us are drawn from such an *un*representative sample, then democracy will remain profoundly flawed' (1991: 65). The fundamental problem identified in this view is one of democracy itself: of how can 'the people' be adequately reflected if one half of them are effectively excluded from formal positions of decision making? Equally, the problem is one of power as well. If this is the case then it is not accidental that women are under-represented in most major Western democracies. Indeed, such under-representation is a *systemic* feature of those political systems and reflects wider power inequalities in the economic and social realms. These disadvantages and the disproportionate representation of women are thus 'too striking for any democrat to ignore' (Phillips 1991: 77).

The first aspect of the 'problem' therefore is one of 'democratic justice' (Norderval 1985: 84), or of 'symbolic equity' (Norris and Lovenduski 1989: 107). Increased female representation is conceived as an end in itself, and the 'problem' is self-evident: for it is 'patently and grotesquely unfair for men to monopolise representation' (Phillips 1995: 63). At its strongest this case maintains that the 'unfairness' of women's representation is a reflection of the inequitable and 'unnatural' consequences of the current sexual division of labour. It reverses the standard argument by asking what makes men so 'naturally' superior in talent or experience that they claim a right to dominate representative assemblies. In shifting the burden of proof to men, feminists are not persuaded that men possess some genetic distinction as decision makers nor some socially derived advantage which enhances their political skills, but rather that their position depends upon structures of discrimination (Phillips 1995: 65). In which case 'there is no argument from justice that can defend the current state of affairs: and in this more negative sense, there *is* an argument from justice for parity between women and men' (Phillips 1995: 65, original emphasis). At its weakest the 'justice' argument simply treats women as but another 'group', and their claim for justice is located within the broader claim that only if parliament acts as a public forum for all points of view can it function democratically (Norris and Lovenduski 1989: 107).

A second aspect of the 'problem' is closely related to the prescriptions of this 'neo-Benthamite' position. Here the focus is changed to consider the legitimacy of the wider political system, and the claim is made that if representation is designed to secure legitimation for political regimes then 'political decisions made by all-male or predominantly male governmental processes can no longer serve this legitimizing function' (Darcy *et al.* 1994: 18). The exclusion of women may undermine 'the democratic legitimacy and public confidence in institutions' (Norris 1996: 89; Norris and Lovenduski 1995: 209). Basically this is a pragmatic argument on behalf of maintaining the stability of liberal democratic regimes, and in this perspective the representation of women becomes a major test of specific electoral mechanisms and the degree of legitimation afforded by, and through, them more generally to the wider political system.

But these claims for more proportionate representation logically stand independently of the actual impact of increased female representation upon policy outputs. The first and second dimensions of the 'problem' are not concerned primarily with whether or not women have any practical impact on decisions, but rest, instead, on the assertion that it is only 'fair', it is only 'right', that they should be represented more proportionately. Rarely, however, is the case for 'symbolic equity' pressed by itself and without reference to claims for the substantive impact of increased female representation upon policy outputs. A third dimension of the 'problem' covers the assumption that female under-representation 'means that women's interests are poorly represented' (Norderval 1985: 84). In other words, it is driven by a belief that more women decision makers and representatives would have an impact upon the substance of public policy.

The basis of this third case is that women have identifiable interests as women. At one level it is a claim that there is a 'universal' women's interest derived from shared biological experiences. 'Women are not [therefore] women by achievement, they are women by birth' (Darcy *et al.* 1994: 17). Hence, their 'interests' are not analogous to other groups with 'interests' conceived in terms of 'functional', 'class' or 'sectional' interest. At another level, however, women are identified as having 'a materially different position in society [with] objectively different interests from men' (Phillips 1991: 70). Women are held to have distinct interests from men no matter how 'interest' is conceived – whether derived from biological, patriarchical or economic sources. In which case 'proportionalists' argue, it is of some importance for these interests to be represented in decision making.

There is a further conception of interest, however, which posits a 'common' women's interest but avoids most of the pitfalls associated with the preceding notions of interests. The difficulty with notions of interest determined by biology is that they do not automatically translate into 'common interests'. Attitudes to abortion provide a good example: 'The experience of being a woman increases both the importance women attach to legalizing abortion *and* the reluctance they feel towards abortion itself. Each of these is a "women's" perspective' (Phillips 1991: 73). There is, therefore, no single, homogeneous and readily identifiable 'interest'. Equally with notions of 'interest' derived from shared experiences of patriarchy, sexual inequality and women's oppression, there are, in reality, manifestly profound differences (invariably associated with class position) among women. Inequality and oppression might be universal phenomena but it does not mean that women experience them equally or uniformly. For some this undermines the force of the arguments for gender parity in political representation, for others (Phillips 1995: 68) the 'argument from interest does not depend on establishing a unified interest of all women: it depends, rather, on establishing a difference between the interests of women and men'.

Conceptually, the specification of women's 'interests' or women's 'attitudes' is fraught with difficulties. Nonetheless, much of the contemporary case for enhanced female representation is posited upon the existence of 'distinctive values, attitudes and concerns which may have an impact on legislative behaviour and the content of public policy' (Norris and Lovenduski 1989: 106). The 'bottom line' argument is that gender parity matters if the inclusion of women leads to a change in what representatives do.

Do women make a difference?

The answer to the question: 'do women make a difference?' is inconclusive. In fact, there are two dimensions to the question; the first concerns attitudes towards the performance of, and styles of, political roles and the second relates to policy priorities once elected. On the former, there is some evidence, though far from systematic, that women have a different style of politics and are perceived as more compassionate, caring and collaborative than male politicians (see Witt *et al.* 1994; Norris and Lovenduski 1995: 135; Norris 1996: 91).

On the second dimension – the relationship between gender and public policy in Western democracies – the findings from comparative studies point to *some*, but not necessarily profound, differences between the policy stances of men and women. Thus, women representatives in the US have been found to be more 'liberal' in their attitudes and legislative behaviour (Welch 1985), and to have made a difference to public policy (Thomas 1991, 1994). Women tend to place a greater priority than men on certain types of legislation – on issues relating to family, children and women (Saint-Germain 1989; Thomas 1991, 1994; Thomas and Welch 1991). Similarly in Nordic countries women representatives tend to concentrate their parliamentary activity on 'reproduction issues' (social policy, education, health, family, consumer policies) (Skard and Haavio-Mannila 1985: 75–80).

When it comes to Britain, however, relatively few empirical investigations have been conducted into the relationship between gender and policy preferences, and the resulting evidence is at best inclusive (Norris and Lovenduski 1989: 107). The most exhaustive surveys to date, conducted by Norris and Lovenduski (1989, 1995), of women candidates at the 1987 and 1992 general elections found that *within political parties* there were indeed 'gender differences in priorities' and that 'women tended to give slightly stronger support for feminist and leftwing values [and] to express stronger concern about social policy issues' (Norris and Lovenduski 1995: 224; see also Norris and Lovenduski 1989: 111–14). Overall, however, party remains the dominant variable explaining the policy priorities and attitudes of representatives. This was forcefully illustrated in December 1997 on the issue of lone parent benefits and the decision of the Labour government to end the additional premium of £6 per week added to child benefit for lone parents. In the vote in the House of Commons, 47 Labour MPs voted against the reduction, only 8 of whom were women. Of the 64 newly elected women Labour MPs, only Ann Cryer cast a dissenting vote. This prompted Clare Longrigg (*Guardian*, 5 January 1998) to ask: 'So what happened to our hopes for a female-friendly policy?' Her answer was that the new female intake 'have been easier to mould to the party model than their more experienced sisters…They follow the party line, whether it is an issue that affects women or not.'

While gender differences should not be exaggerated, therefore, there is some evidence that they impact on the choices of representatives. Olive Banks (1993), for example, in a study of the legislative activities of female MPs from 1918 to 1970, concluded that although female MPs gave priority to their party there were a number of issues, such as equal pay, the marriage bar, sexual and child abuse and abortion, which led them to campaign actively as *women* rather than party politicians. Equally, other studies have revealed the historical concentration of female MPs' activities in the House upon 'women's issues' such as health, education and welfare (Vallance 1979; Pugh 1992: 194–6). Hence, despite significant party differences between women, and despite the fact that by no means all were feminists, 'very few could be described as anti-feminist' (Banks 1993: 66).

From these studies there does appear to be, therefore, *some* empirical evidence in support of the 'substantive' dimension of the 'proportionalist' case. What further strengthens this case are research findings which show that gender effects on policy become more marked the greater the proportion of female representatives in a legislature. In the US, for example, Thomas' study of twelve state legislatures revealed not only that women 'make a difference' but that 'that difference is enhanced…in situations in which they may find support – in…circumstances of increased numbers' (Thomas 1991: 974; see also Darcy *et al.* 1994: 183). The best indication of the impact of increased representation of women upon public policy is provided, however, in Norway and Sweden, with respectively 36 per cent and 38 per cent of women in their national parliaments. In Norway, Bystydzienski's research indicates that 'as more women entered Parliament and county and municipal councils, they made it possible for women's issues, concerns, and values to be discussed, debated, and legislated more openly and frequently' (1992: 20). Indeed, Bystydzienski (1992: 15) concludes that when female representation reaches at least 15 per cent then it begins to make a difference. Others set the threshold somewhat higher at 20 to 30 per cent (Norris and Lovenduski 1989), but still maintain that at this level a 'critical mass' is attained whereby women representatives are capable of transforming the legislative agenda. There is agreement, however, that below 10 per cent 'gender attitudes will fail to make a major impact upon public policy' (Norris and Lovenduski 1989: 115).

A case can thus be made that the number of women representatives and gender policy effects are closely related. If women are to have a substantive policy impact then it appears that the size of overall female representation within a representative body is of some importance. Effectively, this allows 'proportionalists' to move the argument away from symbolic equity – that there *should be* a more proportionate representation of women – to 'substantive equity' that there *needs to be* more women to have a significant policy impact. Once the argument is couched in these terms it then becomes of major importance to secure greater electoral success for women candidates and hence a more proportionate representation of women in parliament. This then entails strategic assessments of how to enhance female representation and leads to a consideration of the wider roles of political parties and their candidate selection processes (see Lovenduski and Norris 1989; Norris and Lovenduski 1993a, 1993b). We will return to these wider considerations in Chapter 8, but for the moment we need to examine the claims made on behalf of more proportionate representation of ethnic minorities.

Representation of ethnic minorities

During the [1992] general election campaign all the political parties claimed that race was no longer an issue in British political life....Yet,...the claim that race was no longer an important feature of the electoral process was premature in its optimism....Britain's ethnic minorities are questioning whether they are fully included in and represented through political institutions.

(Solomos and Back 1993: 328)

Certainly before the 1987 general election ethnic minorities had every right to raise such questions, as no 'non-white' MP sat in the House of Commons. In fact, no representatives of ethnic minorities had sat at Westminster for fifty-eight years, despite the proportion of the non-white populace increasing to 4.5 per cent by the end of that period. In the 1890s two Indian MPs, Dadabhai Naoroji and Mancherjee Bhownagree – Liberal and Conservative respectively – had been elected, and another Indian, Shapurji Saklatvala served as an MP from 1922 until 1929. Yet it was not until 1987 that more non-white Members – one Asian and three Afro-Caribbean MPs (all Labour) – were elected. All four Labour MPs – Dianne Abbott, Paul Boateng, Bernie Grant and Keith Vaz – held their seats in the 1992 general election and were joined by two Asian MPs, Piara Khabra for Labour and Nirj Deva, for the Conservatives. Even so, the six non-white representatives still constituted less than one per cent of MPs. At the general election in May 1997 there were 42 major party candidates from ethnic minority backgrounds (13 Labour, 10 Conservative and 19 Liberal Democrat), but only 9 non-white MPs were returned to Westminster. The sole Conservative Asian MP, Nirj Deva, lost his seat while four new Labour MPs (Ashok Kumar, Oona King, Mohammed Sarwar and Marsha Singh) joined their five Labour colleagues from ethnic minorities.

The arguments in favour of a more proportionate representation of ethnic minorities replicate almost exactly those advanced on behalf of women. First, there is a case to be made in terms of democratic justice. Thus Saggar notes an increase in interest in the question of black parliamentary representation which has been 'conducted against the backdrop of microcosm politics; that is, a renewed interest in the composition of Parliament to reflect the social make-up of contemporary society' (1992: 166). On grounds of equity 'at just under 5 per cent of the population the expectation has been to see something in the order of 32 black MPs' (Saggar 1992: 166). Yet, as with women and ethnic minorities, black 'proportionalists' normally link the concept of democratic justice to the substantive case in favour of greater black representation. Hence, the second argument is made that blacks have their own common interests and policy 'agendas' which need to be reflected in public policies. The evidence of shared 'black interests' in Britain is however mixed. Surveys of black public opinion have, as Layton-Henry cautions, been 'plagued by problems of inadequate sampling procedure and the possibility of environmental effects due to the geographical distribution and residential concentration of the minority ethnic communities' (1992: 108). What these surveys have indicated is that there appears to be no distinctive set of political priorities that divide black and white voters in Britain (Studlar 1986). Similarly,

Saggar notes that 'according to empirical investigations of black political attitudes [there appears] a remarkable degree of similarity between black and white outlooks...broadly speaking, race-specific issues do *not* play an important role in the political priorities of black voters' (1992: 140). Despite this similarity in outlook, ethnic minorities, nonetheless, display a markedly different pattern of party allegiance. Blacks have traditionally been much more inclined to vote for the Labour party than white voters in similar economic and social positions – whether these be class location, housing tenure, or geographical area (see Heath *et al.* 1991: 113). Not surprisingly, this focused much attention upon the organisation of blacks within the Labour party. In 1975 the Labour Party Race Action Group was established to raise the profile of the party in 'ethnic marginal' constituencies. Thereafter, black activists in the party sought the creation of 'black sections' modelled on Labour's women's section. After a protracted campaign, a compromise was reached at the party's 1990 annual conference whereby Black and Asian Socialist Societies were allowed to form at local and regional levels and to have direct representation on the party's National Executive Committee.

Significantly, Harris opinion polls in the late 1980s revealed that the majority of black respondents disapproved of separate black sections in political parties (Geddes 1995: 279). Moreover, responses to general survey questions often fail to discover specific black or Asian concerns about, for example, education, housing, unemployment or police powers. Nonetheless, some analysts (Goulbourne 1990: 10) still maintain that there is a 'black political agenda' which is driven by the experience of discrimination, racism or even racial attacks in education, housing, employment, and relations with the police. These experiences define specific black policy issues within broader policy domains. However, it is recognised that for this black agenda to impact upon public policy requires black politicians 'to articulate black interests in terms which are acceptable to, because complimentary with, the interests of sizeable proportions of the majority population' (Goulbourne 1990: 11). There is a recognition here that black politicians alone cannot achieve a significant policy impact; even a truly proportionate House would draw less than 5 per cent of its Members from ethnic minorities. What is important is that more black MPs should be capable of articulating black concerns and informing policy debates as to the interests of ethnic minorities. As Doreen Cameron, Labour candidate for Ashford in 1992, put it: 'Issues that affect blacks happen to blacks first, so we must incorporate a black perspective into British politics' (quoted in Cashmore 1991: 32).

The case against microcosmic representation

There are three main grounds upon which opposition to microcosmic representation has traditionally centred: it is impractical, it is undesirable, and, ultimately, it is impossible. First, it is maintained that it is impossible to represent every social group in proportion to the wider social structure. Even before strict proportionality could be attempted it would be necessary to decide *which* groups of people warrant representation in their own right: fat people, short people, deaf, blind, disabled, lesbians/gays, unemployed, Catholics, Jews, and so on. It is easy, therefore, to reduce the principle of proportionality *ad absurdum* in order to highlight its impossibility. Yet the answer is simple: *political movements* establish which social categories are deemed sufficiently important to warrant more proportionate representation (Phillips 1991: 66). Hence, in Britain in recent years it has been women and ethnic minorities who have pressed most vociferously and determinedly for increased group representation. More intermittently the case has been pressed by Muslims (particularly in 1992 when a separate 'Muslim parliament' was established in protest at the lack of representation afforded to Muslims within Westminster), and on behalf of greater 'working class' representation (by Joe Ashton MP, who advocated in the 1980s, partly facetiously, the creation of a 'working class' section within the Labour party to offset the demands for women's sections and black sections within the party).

Even if agreement could be reached upon which groups should have more proportionate representation, critics proceed to argue that it would be impractical to secure greater representativeness through established electoral procedures. In this manner Birch (1971: 57) argues that, 'there is no country in which competitive elections based upon manhood suffrage have produced an assembly which could fairly be described as a social microcosm of the nation'. He later maintains that: 'unless the House of Commons comes to be composed of conscripts chosen by computer, it will never be fully representative in the microcosmic sense of the term' (Birch 1975: 57). Norton (1981: 55) takes this argument a stage further in claiming that 'a computer, a list system of election, and the nomination of certain people to stand as candidates' would be required to ensure 'proportionality'. The 'proportionalists' response to this charge is to note that the practical difficulties, again, are reduced *ad absurdum*. For what seems undeniable is that the present British first-past-the-post electoral system is systematically biased *against* the representation of some groups – most particularly women and ethnic minorities (see Bogdanor 1984: 111–26; Kruthoffer 1992: 101–4; Bogdanor 1997: 63–4). At the very least, proponents argue, the institutional constrictions of the present electoral system should be lessened, and electoral reform effected, even if the result is not 'true' representativeness. *More* proportionality is the objective rather than *absolute* proportionality.

Even if the practical difficulties could be overcome, the final argument of critics is that proportionality is undesirable. Phillips Griffiths (1960: 190) regarded some deviations from proportionality to be positively bene-ficial: 'we would not want to complain that the large class of stupid or maleficent people have too few representatives in Parliament: quite the contrary'. If representation constitutes a social division of labour, in which some people develop and exercise *special* political skills on behalf of society at large, then the benefits of this specialisation would be reduced by 'proportionality'. This was the case advanced by John Stuart Mill in support of 'enlightened' decision makers; it was the case also of J.F.S. Ross, and it is still the essence of Birch's case (1993: 73) who sees the need for representatives to possess 'special talents', and of Norton who is in no doubt that the 'job of a Member of Parliament is essentially a middle class one' (1993: 141). Whilst such 'enlightenment', 'talent' and 'competence' are taken as self-evident prerequisites for representatives, it is never explained why enlightened, talented and competent Afro-Caribbeans, Asians or females are consistently under-represented in parliament. Unless, of course, 'whiteness' and 'maleness' are ultimately more important than 'special talents' and 'middle-classness'. In fairness, neither Birch nor Norton admit this, nor explicitly endorse such a posi-tion, but the logic of their own argument can ultimately be reduced to this conclusion.

Conclusion

This chapter has revealed why the claim that microcosmic representation has never taken root in either British theory or practice is misguided. On the contrary, concern over the representativeness of parliament has been at the heart of much of the discussion about representative democracy since the mid-nineteenth century. Indeed, the centrality of microcosmic notions of representation continues to be reflected, almost routinely, in standard texts:

> Strict proportionality may be unnecessary, but while gross anomalies exist and some elements of the community feel excluded from the House of Commons – which is, after all, the central representative institution of British democracy – the political process is itself far from secure.
>
> (Radice *et al.* 1990: 42)

Even Norton eventually acknowledges the significance of microcosmic notions of representation: 'the popular legitimacy of Parliament as the body for giving authoritative assent is affected by factors of *structure and composition* as well as the actions of its members' (1993: 146, added emphasis). So vital is the composition of parliament that some analysts, such as Finer, have been willing to countenance that 'representation means mathematically exact representation' (1949: 555). However, one powerful qualification preceded this statement: 'if there were no adverse consequences'. Any 'adverse consequences' of microcosmic representation identified by Finer would be upon existing notions of 'geographical representation'. And it is to these established conceptions of 'geographical representation' that we now turn.

3 Trustee theory and practice

Trustee theory is essentially a 'pre-democratic' theory. Its origins pre-date 1832, a year that was crucial to the democratisation of the franchise, as well as to the development of parliamentary government itself in Britain. After 1832 conceptions of 'who' and 'what' were to be represented changed gradually but irrevocably – as, indeed, did the 'purpose' of representation itself. The 'who' increasingly became 'all of the people', the 'what' became their opinions and the 'purpose' became *control over* decision makers. This marked a stark contrast with pre-1832 notions of trusteeship which conceived of the 'who' as 'people with economic interests', the 'what' as objective interests, and the 'purpose' as the *making* of decisions for the nation. The different bases and purposes of representation before 1832 have led many to argue that trustee theory, as outlined most famously by Edmund Burke, is outdated – it is no more than an archaeological relic from a bygone age. Yet, trustee theory cannot be dismissed so summarily as it is still alive and kicking in Britain in the 1990s.

Edmund Burke and trustee theory

Territorial and functional representation combined

Although the essence of trustee theory is remarkably simple – in that representatives should use their independent judgement in reaching decisions and should not be bound, therefore, by instructions from their electors – the premises upon which this simple conclusion is reached are in fact remarkably complex. The starting point for an analysis of Burkean trustee theory is a recognition that the basis of representation in Britain has, since medieval times, been *territorial communities*.

Medieval parliaments consisted of the three estates of the realm: the clergy, the barons and the 'commons'; or as Maitland described them, 'those who pray, those who fight and those who work' (1908: 75). However, parliament's composition at the time is best understood as 'rest[ing] securely on the representation of local communities and summoned individuals, and not on rigid divisions by estates' (Butt 1989: 153). In particular, two 'types' of community were represented in the Commons – counties and the boroughs. Vital economic interests were associated respectively with these territorial units and found representation thereby. Indeed,

> [l]and was the key resource for the medieval state, and what was more natural than to have those with a stake in it being represented through the long-standing English unit of territorial division, the county. Commerce too had to be conducted in *a place*…so that representing commercial interests by representing each borough was as self-evident as county representation.
>
> (Reeve and Ware 1992: 46)

What is important to remember, therefore, in examining Burke's ideas, and those of Whigs more generally, is that territorial representation was taken to be self-evident, and that geographical communities were believed to be inextricably linked with economic interest – be it land or commerce.

The Whig position revolved around three assumptions: first, representation was to be of particular geographical constituencies by particular Members of Parliament; second, the purpose of representation was to constitute a deliberative body, and; third, parliament was to play a leading role in the process of decision making. In essence this was a defence of the constitutional settlement of 1689, and of the 'balanced constitution' of crown-in-parliament, with parliament in the ascendant and charged with 'deliberating and pronouncing on the public interest and the common good' (Beer 1969: 13). In occupying this leading role in state policy making, Whigs contended that parliament 'should not only give expression to the various opinions, interests, and grievances within society, it should also try to reconcile them in policies which would serve the best interests of the nation' (Birch 1964: 28). Yet, here was the central conundrum of Whig thought, for if representation was territorially-based and interest-centred, how could it simultaneously secure the promotion of a wider national interest through consensual state policies? If a representative was locally elected to pursue specific territorially-linked economic interests how could he (in an era before the female franchise) be expected to articulate and advance the national interest? The answer provided by Burke was simple and to the point: there was no problem here. To understand his answer, we need to analyse Burke's conception of representation serially; to start with the relationship between individual constituency and individual represen-

tative, and then to examine the collective relationship of elected representatives within parliament.

Constituency–representative relationship

Burke's conceptualisation of the proper relationship between constituency
and representative appears, initially, to be paradoxical. On the one side,
the representative is expected to pursue the interest of his constituency;
yet, on the other, once in the confines of Westminster the representative 'is
not a member of Bristol [a constituency], but he is a member of parliament [the nation]' (Pitkin 1967: 171). If this is the case then the duty of
the representative is to the nation as a whole, and as such one 'stands in no
special relation to his constituency' (Pitkin 1967: 171). Yet, for Burke, there
is no paradox because the interest of the constituency is, ultimately,
congruent with that of the nation as a whole. How this congruence is
achieved will be examined presently, but for the moment we need to
understand how constituency interest is conceived.

Burke tends to argue that constituency interests are objective, specific
and largely economic. Moreover, each locality is seen to have a single
pervasive interest (Pitkin 1967: 174). Individual constituencies are thus
broadly defined in terms of a pre-eminent economic interest and their
prosperity is correlated closely with the promotion of that interest. In effect
this was simply a reflection of traditional notions of representation, where
Members of the Commons were returned by small, economically powerful
local electorates. In this context it made sense to associate specific
constituencies with specific interests – whether mining, agriculture, trading,
shipping, or some other commercial interest. But two corollaries stemmed
from this conception of constituency interest. First, that as this interest was
objective it was apparent to constituent and representative alike. In other
words the representative did not have to be told what the interest was, nor
did he need to receive instructions as to how best to advance that interest.
As Pitkin (1967: 174) makes clear constituency interest was thus seen to be
'unattached' – 'an objective reality…apart from any individuals it might
affect'. The second corollary was closely linked to the first in that Burke
rarely saw 'interest' linked to specific individuals. Indeed, he was fundamentally opposed to the representation of 'individuals' and their interests,
opinions and wishes. Individual opinion, especially when aggregated into
'public opinion', was invariably misguided. In which case he maintained
that only when the opinions of 'the multitude are the standard of recti-
tude, shall I think myself obliged to make those opinions the master of my
conscience' (Burke [1780a] 1801, vol. 4: 70). In the absence of such recti-
tude however, Burke was willing to inform his own constituents that his

duty was to maintain 'your interest even against your opinions' ([1780b] 1801, vol. 4: 73). And he repeatedly asserted that the representative's duty to his constituents was 'a devotion to their interests rather than to their opinions' (Canavan 1960: 155).

At the end of the eighteenth century this was a defensible position for a Whig to adopt as it simultaneously protected the existing narrow geographical franchise (which effectively excluded rapidly developing urban areas from parliamentary representation) as well as challenging radical and liberal ideas that 'individuals' should be the basis of representation. Despite the significant growth and shifts in population to urban areas the representation of counties and boroughs had remained largely unchanged. In response, the movement for parliamentary reform began to organise in the 1770s and to demand 'equal representation of the whole body of the people' (Canavan 1960: 158), annual parliaments and the redistribution of parliamentary seats. Yet, for Burke, the fact that many of the new industrial cities had no representatives in parliament was not a matter of concern: they were represented 'virtually'. In this view, as long as there were representatives from other constituencies with similar commercial, agricultural, or manufacturing interests, the interests of all other localities with these same interests could find representation in parliament – even though those localities were not directly represented therein. Hence, although there was not 'actual' representation there was 'virtual' representation. The latter occurred where 'there is a communion of interests, and a sympathy in feelings and desires between those who act in the name of any description of people, and the people in whose name they act, though the trustees are not actually chosen by them' ([1792] 1801, vol. 6: 360). 'Such a representation I think to be, in many cases, even better than the actual....Common interest and common sentiment are rarely mistaken' ([1792] 1801, vol. 6: 360). At its simplest, therefore, the representative for Bristol, in looking after the interest of Bristol, would also be looking after the same economic interest wherever it is located. The logic is that 'Birmingham is virtually represented in...parliament because both it and Bristol are of the trading interest. Bristol sees to it that a representative of the trading interest is sent to Parliament, and Birmingham thus has its spokesman' (Pitkin 1967: 178). However, for this logic to prevail two other conditions were required: first, that a representative would listen to his own constituents and be *electorally* responsible to them; and, second, that his actions in parliament should not be bound or mandated by them.

The first condition is necessary to ensure that representatives continue to promote their own constituency interests. Elections are the medium by which representatives are kept in tune with constituency interest. But elections are a reactive and not a proactive mechanism. Their purpose is not to express policy preferences but to assess the efficacy of representation and to decide how far a constituency's economic interest has been protected. In theory, 'every general election is to the representative a day of judgement, in which he appears before his constituents to account for the use of the talent with which they intrusted him, and for the improvement he has made of it for the public advantage' (Burke ([1780c] 1812, vol. 10: 79). Again, if interest is objective and if both representative and electorate alike *know* what it is, then there will be no fundamental disagreement between them. In Burke's words: 'Certainly, Gentlemen, it ought to be the happiness and glory of a representative to live in the strictest union, the closest correspondence, and the most unreserved communication with his constituents....It is his duty to sacrifice his repose, his pleasure, his satisfactions, to theirs – and above all, ever, and in all cases, to prefer their interest to his own' ([1774] 1801, vol. 3: 19). Elections are essential, however, in those cases where representatives start to prefer – whether through corruption or incompetence – their own interest to that of their constituents. If there is long-term disagreement between constituents and representative then there must be something wrong. Ultimately, this is a negative assertion on Burke's part of the value of elections, as it holds that 'a lasting discrepancy between the member and the people is *in*consistent with true representation' (Pitkin 1967: 181).

The second condition is that a representative should not be bound by instructions from their constituents, nor act as their delegate in parliament. In part, this was because Burke believed public opinion to be invariably ill-informed and unstable. In which case, he saw it as his duty as a representative 'to give them information, and not receive it from them...I should be ashamed to show my face before them, if I changed my ground as they cried up or cried down men or things or opinions – if I wavered and shifted about with every change' (Burke ([1780c] 1812, vol. 10: 76). In part also, it was because Burke believed in the superior capacities of a natural aristocracy who 'acted as the paternal guardians of the countless communities which together made up the kingdom. These men should not slavishly follow the transient whims of popular prejudice' (O'Gorman 1973: 40). Government should thus remain in the hands of this aristocracy rather than be placed in the hands of the people. An enlightened elite was to exercise power on behalf, not at the behest, of the people. (It is worth remembering at this point that the 'people' numbered, in Burke's own estimation, no more than 400,000 ([1796] 1801, vol. 8.) This did not mean that the elite was unresponsive to the electorate. Far from it, because 'the people are the masters' (Burke [1780d] 1801, vol. 3: 344). 'But', and it is a significant 'but', '[t]hey have only to express their wants at large and in gross. We [MPs] are the expert artists; we are the skilful workmen, to shape their desires into perfect form, and to fit the utensil to the use' (Burke [1780d] 1801, vol. 3: 344).

Collective relationship of elected representatives within parliament

It is at this point that our attention comes to be redirected away from the individual relationship between representative and constituency towards the collective relationship of elected representatives within parliament. But Burke's view of the collective role of parliament is predicated upon his view of society as being organic and differentiated with a paternal, aristocratic elite acting as the guardians of communities of the realm. In this sense Burke was the defender of 'aristocratic trusteeship' (O'Gorman 1973: 54). Whilst representation ensured that political power was to be exercised ultimately in the interest of the represented, the represented themselves were, for the reasons outlined above, to have little direct influence upon public policy. It is as well at this stage to underline, therefore, that Burke's ideas have little in common with modern notions of responsible government. Overall, Burke was dismissive of the view that individuals should count equally in politics and especially contemptuous of notions of popular representation. For him democracy was tyranny: 'The tyranny of the multitude is but a multiplied tyranny' (Burke [1790] 1967).

The purpose of representation instead is to allow the 'true natural aristocracy' to discover and enact the national interest. An interest, moreover, which holds paramount the defence of property against the great masses. Thus the role of representatives collectively is to identify the national interest. 'A true natural aristocracy is not a separate interest in the state, or separate from it' (Burke quoted Pitkin 1967: 171). In which case, 'a truly elite group of representatives has no interest other than the national interest' (Pitkin 1967: 171). State policy should thus reflect the interest of the whole, and, for this reason, representatives in parliament should not be mandated or bound by instructions from their constituents. Only through deliberation and the consideration of the broad range of constituency interests in the House of Commons could consensus be reached upon the national interest. The promotion of 'narrow' and 'sectional' interests by constituency delegates would not only frustrate this objective but in fact would be 'utterly unknown to the laws of this land' and would arise from a fundamental misconception 'of the whole order and tenor of our constitution' ([1774] 1801, vol. 3: 20). It is in this context that Burke's famous Speech to the Electors of Bristol should be read:

Parliament is not a *congress* of ambassadors from different and hostile interests, which interests each must maintain, as an agent and advocate, against other agents and advocates; but Parliament is a *deliberative* assembly of one nation, with one interest, that of the whole – where not local prejudices ought to guide, but the general good, resulting from the general reason of the whole. You chose a member, indeed; but when you have chosen him he is not a member of Bristol, but he is a member of *Parliament*.

([1774] 1801, vol. 3: 20)

All the different communities founded upon various forms of property thus have an ultimate interest in the well-being of the whole. The 'national interest' is conceived merely as the aggregation of the objective economic interests represented in localities. As Pitkin observes, 'The interests of the realm added together, compose the interests of the realm' (1967: 186), and so for Burke 'interests are not only broad and objective but additive'. But their 'addition' can only be achieved within parliament through a process of discussion amongst representatives of all the economic interests and communities of interest within the nation. Only parliament can discover the national interest through the articulation of constituency interests in discussion. Armed with this information, each and every representative will be able to assess the merits of each argument, and in the course of a complex process of deliberation will be able to discover the national interest. Hence, the result of parliamentary discussion is the rational formulation of the interest of the whole and consensus. But this agreement will only emerge if MPs are not bound by the opinions of their constituents. Precisely because constituents were not present at the discussions in parliament they could not know what the national interest is at any given time, and precisely because they do not have this knowledge they should give their representatives the freedom to act as they see fit to determine and promote the national interest. In which case, 'if the local constituent should have an interest or should form an hasty opinion evidently opposite to the real good of the rest of the community, the member for that place ought to be as far as any other from any endeavour to give it effect' ([1774] 1801, vol. 3: 20).

Burke's view on representation is thus complex and interweaves various ideas about the British constitution and the political balance as pivoted around the constitutional settlement of 1689; about the nature of property, and the objective nature of economic interest; about society and its organic nature, and; about the virtues of aristocratic leadership. It is within this context that his views about trusteeship have to be analysed. His was not a universal claim to 'independence' on the part of representatives. In fact, it was a specific claim made in a specific historical period to address specific problems occasioned by the rise of political parties and the demands for parliamentary reform. The irony therefore is that Burke's argument, which received little prominence at the time (O'Gorman 1973: 55), became central to the formulation of the issue of *democratic* representation in later centuries despite its *anti-democratic* premises. We will return to this irony later in this chapter, but first we need to consider the case for trusteeship advanced by John Stuart Mill in the nineteenth century, who, unlike Burke, made his case from a basic predisposition in favour of democracy.

John Stuart Mill: trusteeship in the uncertain world of democracy

John Stuart Mill's attitude to democracy has been seen to be 'deeply ambivalent' (Arblaster 1984: 280). This ambivalence has already been identified in Chapter 2 in the consideration of Mill's views on microcosmic representation. It should be recalled that he favoured a proportional electoral system in the belief that it would secure representation for an intellectually gifted minority in parliament. This elite would then be in a position to wield a disproportionate amount of political influence to offset their numerical proportionality. Indeed, Mill generally feared the uneducated masses. In his opinion, Britain in the mid-nineteenth century was far from an ideal world in which democracy could be effected.

Under ideal conditions, certainly not those in existence in mid-nineteenth century Britain, representative democracy would be based upon the principle of one-person, one-vote: 'The pure idea of democracy, according to its definition, is the government of the whole people by the whole people, equally represented' ([1861] 1910: 256). This vision may be attained at some stage in the future when each person's potential as a progressive being has been realised. In the meantime, the representative system itself could make a contribution to such development. Mill's case for democracy, therefore, was based upon its developmental capacity. If democracy was seen as the primary mechanism of moral development in the long-term (Dunn 1979: 51–3), in the short-term, in 'non-ideal' social conditions, there was a need, not only to protect the people from government in accordance with the protective model of earlier liberal theory, but also to protect the people from themselves. In making this case Mill drew a distinction between 'true and false democracy'; that is between 'representation of all and representation of the majority only' ([1861] 1910: 256). The latter would result in the 'tyranny of the majority' for, in taking people 'as they are', the masses in nineteenth century Britain were identified as generally ignorant, incapable and possessing 'insufficient mental qualifications' ([1861] 1910: 243). If a popularly elected House of Commons was to reflect these qualities it would 'impose a selfish, capricious and impulsive, a short-sighted, ignorant, and prejudicial general policy' ([1861] 1910: 248). Moreover, Mill maintained that the 'natural tendency of representative government...is towards collective mediocrity'. This tendency would only be increased by the extension of the franchise as it placed 'the principal power in the hands of classes more and more below the highest level of instruction in the community' ([1861] 1910: 265–6).

As an advocate of the universal franchise on developmental grounds, Mill was constantly troubled by the potential for the 'undeveloped' masses to promote their own short-term, class self-interest at the expense of the long-term, general interest: 'In that falsely called democracy which is really the exclusive rule of the operative classes...the only escape from class legislation in its narrowest, and political ignorance in its most dangerous, form, would lie in such disposition as the uneducated might have to choose educated representatives, and to defer to their opinions' ([1861] 1910: 342). Hence, it was important for the electors to choose as their representatives 'wiser men than themselves' and 'to consent to be governed according to that superior wisdom' ([1861] 1910: 319). And, once having chosen such competent individuals, '[i]t follows that the electors will not do wisely if they insist on absolute conformity to their opinions as the condition of his retaining his seat' ([1861] 1910: 317). Indeed, the logic of Mill's belief in 'competence' as the criterion for the choice of representatives leads to the conclusion that:

> Superior powers of mind and profound study are of no use if they do not sometimes lead a person to different conclusions from those which are formed by ordinary powers of mind without study: and if it be an object to possess representatives in any intellectual respect superior to average electors, it must be counted upon that the representative will sometimes differ in opinion from the majority of his constituents, and that when he does, his opinion will be the oftenest right of the two.
>
> (Mill [1861] 1910: 317)

The principle of trusteeship was thus self-evident for Mill. In his earlier writings he had argued that constituents should not require a representative 'to act according to their judgement, any more than they require a physician to prescribe to them according to their own notions of medicine' (Mill quoted Thompson 1976: 112). In *Considerations on Representative Government* he reaffirms his opinion that 'the delegation theory of representation seems to me false, and its practical operation hurtful' ([1861] 1910:

323), and that 'no words can exaggerate the importance in principle of leaving an unfettered discretion to the representative' ([1861] 1910: 324). In this respect Mill adopts a position not too dissimilar to that of Burke. But this is a position only in principle. For what differentiates Mill's trustee-ship from that of Burke, is that, whereas the latter believes that MPs represent objective economic interests that are known to be both repre-sented and representative, Mill is concerned with the representation of opinions and people and hence there is an uncertainty as to the reliability of political knowledge. Ultimately only individual voters can decide what their opinion is and how best it should be advanced. In which case *in prac-tice* (as opposed to 'in principle') the electors are 'the judges of the manner in which he [the representative] fulfils his trust; and how are they to judge, except by the standard of their own opinions?' ([1861] 1910: 318). Mill is willing to admit therefore that in 'some cases...it may be necessary that the representative should have his hands tied, to keep him true to their interest, or rather to the public interest as they conceive it' ([1861] 1910: 318). There are thus practical limits upon the electorate's deference to the mental superiority of their representatives. Moreover, the tension between participation and competence – between democracy and enlightened elite rule – is apparent in Mill's statement that: 'A people cannot be well governed in opposition to their primary notions of right, even though these may be in some points erroneous' ([1861] 1910: 322). This statement comes immediately after the reaffirmation of the right of a representative 'of conscience and known ability' to insist on 'full freedom to act as in his own judgement deems best'. But Mill qualifies this independence by the right of voters to know how the representative intends to act; what his opinions are; and, if these are unacceptable to the electors, it is incumbent upon the representative to 'satisfy them that he nevertheless deserves to be their representative'.

Similarly, when Mill affirms that 'actual pledges should not be required' of representatives, he then proceeds to list the occasions when pledges might be sought. First, when the choice of representative is so narrowed by 'unfavourable social circumstances or faulty institutions' that the electors are 'compelled to fix on a person presumptively under the influence of partiali-ties hostile to their interest' ([1861] 1910: 323). In practice, this meant when working class electors were obliged to choose from 'persons of a station in life widely different from theirs, and having different class-interest' ([1861] 1910: 318–9). Second, Mill concedes that electors may seek 'to make conformity to [their] own sentiments the primary requirement' ([1861] 1910: 321) when a relatively unknown person, and one without an estab-lished reputation for ability, is elected for the first time. Even in these circumstances, however, the electors would do well to remember:

that once chosen, the representative, if he devotes himself to his duty, has greater opportunities of correcting an original false judgement than fall to the lot of most of his constituents; a consideration which generally ought to prevent them...from exacting a pledge not to change his opinion, or, if he does, to resign his seat.

(Mill [1861] 1910: 321)

The opportunities to correct a 'false judgement' are particularly pronounced when representatives participate in collective deliberation within a representative assembly. As we noted in Chapter 2, Mill saw deliberation to be the legitimate function of a representative assembly. Parliament was to act as the nation's 'Congress of Opinions':

an arena in which not only the general opinion of the nation, but that of every section of it, and as far as possible of every eminent individual whom it contains, can produce itself in full light and challenge discussion; where every person in the country may count upon finding someone who speaks his mind, as well or better than he could speak it himself – not to friends and partisans exclusively, but in the face of opponents, to be tested by adverse controversy; where those whose opinion is overruled, feel satisfied that it is heard, and set aside not by a mere act of will, but what are thought superior reasons, and commend themselves as such to the representatives of the majority of the nation.

(Mill [1861] 1910: 239–40)

The role of Mill's representative in these circumstances is to voice the opinions of their constituents, to listen to all other opinions, and in the light of discussion 'to obey the dictates of his own judgement' in the determination of the national opinion. In this way 'the opinion which prevails in the nation makes itself manifest as prevailing' ([1861] 1910: 240). Parliament enables representatives to inform themselves of the changing balance of opinion and to help to shape public policy accordingly. It was only fitting therefore that 'a man of conscience and known ability should insist on full freedom to act as he in his own judgement deems best' ([1861] 1910: 322). For in so doing they would actively promote the long-term benefit of society as a whole and of their own constituents. In which case Mill's representative stands in a similar relationship to their constituents as that outlined by Burke. Whilst the starting premises, and indeed the location of ultimate political responsibility, differentiates their conceptions of representation, nonetheless, Burke and Mill are agreed that representatives should *not* be bound by instructions from the represented.

Trustee theory and modern practice

There are, of course, many commentators and politicians in the 1990s who point to the pre-democratic origins of trustee theory and argue that notions of 'trusteeship' are of little relevance to the political circumstances of modern Britain. They claim that the development of an educated citizenry, a mass electorate, political parties and party government have all served to undermine Burkean notions of representation. This case is presented most starkly in Bealey's judgement that: 'Burke is largely irrelevant, for he lived in the era of limited suffrage before there were mass parties' (1988: 40). Other academics are content simply to stress that 'the heyday of this strongly elitist view was in the nineteenth century before the rise of organised parties' (Harrop and Miller 1987: 247). Likewise, MPs, particularly Labour MPs, have argued that: 'It is time Burke was put in his place – Burke was no democrat and since he spoke a new world has been born. We do not live in Burke's world anymore' (Allaun *et al.* 1972). Conservative MPs have also been willing to acknowledge the anachronistic character of Burke's argument. Speaking in the debate on the Criminal Justice Bill in April 1987, Michael McNair-Wilson, Conservative MP for Newbury, stated:

> I suggest that the comments of an 18th century politician [Burke] are not really relevant at the end of the 20th century. He spoke when Parliament was of a different stamp, when the populace was largely illiterate and uneducated and did not possess television, radio or mass-circulation newspapers. It could scarcely claim to be informed. That society cannot be compared with our own. We now have a highly educated populace that is well informed and articulate. In these times those outside the chamber are as well equipped as we are to make a decision on their individual safety and the safety of their community.
>
> (HC Debates 1 April 1987, vol. 113: col. 1,174)

Indeed, there are now those who maintain that Burkean principles of trusteeship are a threat to the democratic process itself. This fear was articulated by Geoff Mulgan, director of the independent think-tank *Demos*:

> Edmund Burke's famous argument [was] that electorates should trust MPs to vote with their judgement, not as delegates. The principle was crucial to the rise of parliaments in the late 18th and 19th century when most 'informed opinion' viewed democracy as a road to irrational mob rule and tyranny. Yet as the decades passed, and popular pressure forced extensions of the franchise, it turned out that ordinary

people were, after all, wiser than their rulers had feared, and generally happy to leave the great decisions to their betters in Parliament.

But as politicians' public esteem has collapsed…the Burkean principle has come unstuck. Trust has been eroded and many have come to see politicians as barriers against, rather than tribunes for public opinion.

(*Guardian*, 25 February 1994)

Yet, despite these dismissals of trusteeship, Burkean ideas are still articulated and continue, selectively, to guide representatives' actions over two hundred years after they were first voiced. Indeed, the Edmund Burke Society sent every Member of the new House of Commons of May 1997 a copy of Burke's speech to the electors of Bristol, and at least one MP found that: 'it made terrifying reading in terms of the illumination that it offered to the Government's programme and our general situation because it was so deeply contemporary' (Peter Luff, HC Debates 15 May 1997, vol. 294: col. 234). Admittedly, however, the occasions upon which Burkean notions are advanced are now limited and tend to justify specific instances where representatives deem that they have a right to use their individual judgement. In other words, no British MP in the 1990s would claim to act *exclusively* as a trustee, beholden only to his or her own conception of the national interest. Instead, the reality of modern parliamentary politics is that MPs are primarily representatives of their party (see Chapter 4), increasingly attentive to their constituencies (see Chapter 7), as well as being receptive to the claims of organised interests within society (see Chapter 5). In this sense diverse conceptions of representation – party, collectivist and interest representation – coexist and contend with longer established Whig and liberal notions. The practice of representation is thus far from uni-dimensional (Judge 1981: 43).

The real significance of Burkean ideas of representation is that they preceded the dominant conceptions of party and collectivist notions, and indeed provided the frame within which later ideas had to be accommodated. Yet these later conceptions did not entirely supersede, nor totally replace notions of trusteeship; instead, new ideas were grafted onto existing theories to produce a mixture in which no single theory became hegemonic. This analytical point is well expressed by Birch when he notes that: 'As circumstances changed, so fresh theories were formulated to meet them, but it cannot be said that the fresh theories have generally replaced the older ones…the more usual development has been for the fresh theory to take its place alongside the older ones as an additional strand in the British political tradition' (1964: 227). In this respect 'old theories' still retain a legitimate place in the debate about representation. In fact, it is the legitimation afforded by such theories to MPs' actions that sustains the intensity of this debate.

The simple, but extremely important, point is that modern representatives in Britain may draw upon a range of ideas, each legitimate in their own terms, to defend or justify their actions. One example of this was provided in Nigel Forman's evidence to the Nolan Committee. In sketching the 'duties and opportunities' of MPs he provided six analytical categories of activities: four related in one sense or another to the representation of 'interests', a fifth was 'loyalty to their parties in Parliament and in the constituency' – but, 'first of all, MPs have a duty to their constituents and on certain issues to their consciences as well. One thinks, for example, of the classic issue of capital punishment...and I would say that all MPs, without exception, recognise that duty and perform it to the very best of their ability' (Cm 2850-II 1995: 71).

The fact that different conceptual bases of representation coexist enables MPs at different times to call upon different, seemingly contradictory, conceptions of representation. Burkean notions tend to be reserved for occasions when MPs find themselves in conflict with the premises of other theories – whether of individualistic, party or 'interest' representation. The idea of trusteeship can prove extremely useful to justify the actions of representatives when those actions conflict with constituency 'opinion', party policy or the wishes of interest groups. On some issues – especially 'conscience' issues – MPs may find themselves in conflict with all three simultaneously.

Conscience issues

There are a number of issues which have been treated as matters of 'conscience' in modern parliamentary politics. All recent votes in the House of Commons on, for example, abortion, capital punishment, hunting, seatbelts, and the treatment of war criminals have not been the subject of the party whip. Similarly, some, but not all, votes on the issues of homosexuality and family law reform have been unwhipped. The outcomes of these votes have been of some significance in the daily lives of many people in Britain in the 1990s.

Ultimately, however, the treatment of 'conscience issues' in the Commons raises a paradox:

> [It is] curious that on such important issues the British democratic system goes haywire: on almost all other issues, no matter how small, we have a system of party democracy. Yet on issues that actually

matter to people we revert to a system of 659 independent MPs, all
allowed to vote with their consciences.

(Cowley 1998)

This paradox becomes even more pronounced in the empirical finding
that, when MPs are freed from the constraints of the party whip on
'conscience' issues, party still remains the most powerful variable
explaining the votes of individual MPs (see Pattie *et al.* 1998). Cowley and
Stuart (1997: 123) found, for instance, that on twelve free votes on 'issues
of conscience' between 1979 and 1996, on most occasions the majority of
each of the major parties voted in opposite lobbies. On only four issues –
voluntary euthanasia, war crimes, lowering the age of consent for male
homosexual acts and legalisation of embryo research – were a majority of
Labour and Conservative MPs to be found in the same lobby. In this
respect 'conscience' issues are not 'non-party' issues. In fact, party cohesion was greater in the 1992–7 parliament on some of these supposedly
'non-party' matters than on votes with a three-line whip (Cowley 1998).

Implicit within Cowley's analysis is a criticism of the continuing practice of allowing free votes on issues of conscience when party
considerations still appear to influence the outcome in the Commons. Yet
his own findings reveal that there were internal splits, with significant
minority opinion, within the Conservative parliamentary party on five
issues and within the parliamentary Labour party (PLP) on three other
issues. These internal divisions reflected wider divisions within the parties
beyond Westminster and within the electorate at large. Given the uncer-
tainties of mobilising support, it is not too surprising to find that party
managers remain willing, on pragmatic grounds, to allow for the invocation of Burkean notions of independent judgement. More particularly,
party managers are aware of the advantages in justifying, in terms of
established representative theory and practice, what can only be called
non-democratic decisions (where a majority of the electorate are in favour
of a particular policy but the majority of party MPs are opposed, with
capital punishment providing the most clear cut example). Hence, Burkean
notions of independence retain a pragmatic utility in the legitimation of
decisions in the 1990s as well as a principled rationale for the taking of
electorally unpopular decisions.

Capital punishment

The issue of capital punishment has provided a particularly visible 'fault-
line' which has highlighted the continuing relevance of Burkean notions of
representation for MPs. This divide was evident in the debate in February

1994 on a proposed amendment to the Criminal Justice and Public Order Bill which would have reintroduced capital punishment for the murder of a police officer. On that occasion Tony Blair, then Labour frontbench spokesperson on Home Affairs, strongly defended a trustee position:

> I understand why a majority of my constituents, and perhaps a majority of people in the country, will answer yes to the question, 'Do you favour the death penalty?' They are angry and outraged at the murders and killings in our society. However, I would like…to reflect upon the fact that, in every debate on the subject that I have witnessed, the value of the debate has become obvious as it has proceeded and as we have moved from general and instantaneous reaction to the particular and the considered. Suddenly answers that appeared obvious become more complex and conclusions that seemed certain are open to doubt. Such a large majority of Members did not vote against the restoration of the death penalty on each occasion because they were unaware of their constituents' views but because, on reflection and after considered debate, they could not support those views.…
>
> I certainly do not believe that my understanding is superior to that of my constituents, but…we are representatives, not delegates, and we must act according to our conscience.
>
> (HC Debates 21 February 1994, vol. 238: col. 46)

What is of significance in Blair's statement is the emphasis placed upon deliberation and the process of rational discourse in parliament. Here is a direct echo of the emphasis placed upon deliberation in the theories of Burke and J.S. Mill. An even more direct echo of Burke, indeed almost a paraphrasing of his 1774 'Speech to the Electors of Bristol', is to be found in (MP for West Bromwich West) Betty Boothroyd's contribution to the debate on the Criminal Justice Bill in April 1987:

> My final argument…is about the democratic process, because it brings into conflict individual conscience and what I regard as majority opinion.…Since first being elected to the House, I have consistently demonstrated my opposition to judicial killing, although in all honesty I cannot say that all my constituents are aware of my views. But I take the view – I believe that my constituents share it with me – that I am not a mandated delegate, and this is not a delegated assembly. I owe respect to the people whom I represent for their point of view. I also owe them my judgement in seeking what is right and best for the country in its entirety.

It would not be wrong in itself, but wrong in the interests of the nation, to reinstate capital punishment on the basis of public opinion. That opinion I must face and convince. If I fail, my views and I can be rejected. It would be intolerable if I were to allow public perception rather than convincing argument to blow me away from the opinions that I hold.

(HC Debates 1 April 1987, vol. 113: col. 1149)

For other representatives, however, the 'democratic process' requires that MPs should 'not run too far ahead of public opinion in any matter' (Garel-Jones, HC Debates 21 February 1994, vol. 238: col. 108). For supporters of capital punishment the particular danger is that: 'Members of Parliament risk distancing themselves from the views of people outside. We are becoming less representative on this matter' (Rhodes Boyson, HC Debates 21 February 1994, vol. 238: col. 52). In which case, therefore, 'The House and we as Members should reflect public opinion....It has never been clear to me why the House continues to ignore such public opinion' (Elizabeth Peacock, HC Debates 21 February 1994, vol. 238: col. 33). But even in these latter statements the warrant of public opinion is specific and not universal. Thus, Rhodes Boyson (then MP for Brent North) offered the qualification that: 'I do not say that we should do everything that they [the people] want, but we should listen to them' (HC Debates 21 February 1994, vol. 238: col. 52). Similarly, Elizabeth Peacock (then MP for Batley and Spen) maintained that; 'I do not believe that Members of Parliament are delegates because we are not...the measure is a matter of conscience' (HC Debates 21 February 1994, vol. 238: col. 33).

The linkage between electors and elected is thus contingent rather than absolute. Burkean trusteeship confers upon the representative the discretion to choose when to heed the opinions of their constituents and when not. MPs do not dispute that they should be responsive to their party supporters and leaders and to their wider electorates; but the exact degree of responsiveness is balanced by a fine calculation of competing imperatives – party, constituency, group interest, personal morality or conviction. The very contingency of decision leads to inconsistency in the claim made on behalf of 'independence' – even by the same MP. This inconsistency was encapsulated in the exchange between Jack Straw (Secretary of State for the Home Office) and Andrew Robathan (Conservative MP for Blaby) during the second reading of the Firearms (Amendment) Bill in June 1997. This Bill sought to effect the Labour party's manifesto commitment for a complete ban on all handguns:

MR JACK STRAW: I strongly commend the Bill's proposals to the House, but I want to make it crystal clear that – as in opposition – it will be a matter for my hon. Friends' individual consciences to decide whether to support or oppose the measure tonight. But none of us should doubt the overwhelming public support for the proposed ban. For only one indication of the extent of public support for a complete handgun ban, I draw the attention of the House to the results of an opinion poll in the *Daily Telegraph* last Friday, which showed that 83 per cent of those polled approved of the Government's proposed ban on all handguns.

MR ANDREW ROBATHAN (BLABY): The opinion poll may or may not be correct, but on that logic, the Home Secretary would be introducing a Bill to reinstate capital punishment. Every time there is a poll on that subject, 75 per cent of people are in favour. That is not a good argument for the Bill.

MR STRAW: I do not accept the premise of the hon. Gentleman's argument. Of course, it is in the end a matter for the individual consciences of hon. Members, but in making our decisions, we must take account of the strength of public feeling. I do not think that anything like 83 per cent of people are in favour of capital punishment, but I am well aware that I may not have had my constituents' support when I have marched into the Lobby against it. That is a fact that I have to take into account, but it does not stop me.

(HC Debates 11 June 1997, vol. 295: col. 1,160)

Trustee versus party delegate

Despite affirmations that MPs are not delegates there is one specific sense in which they consistently act as delegates and that is in relation to their party. Although the theory of 'party representation' – and its corollaries of the electoral mandate and party cohesion within parliament – is essentially the preserve of the Labour party (see Chapter 4), the practice of collectivist representation extends to all parliamentary parties. The impact of party, even on nominally 'non-party' issues of conscience, was noted above; but the strength of party in influencing MPs' actions in parliament is indicated more powerfully in the findings of a survey, conducted by the Study of Parliament Group, of newly elected MPs in 1992. Of 79 respondents (61.4 per cent of all 127 new Members) well over four-fifths maintained that their voting decisions and parliamentary actions would 'usually', or 'nearly always' be 'strongly influenced' by their party leadership. From Labour respondents, 96 per cent believed this to be the case, as indeed did 84 per cent of new Conservative respondents.

What is equally notable, however, is that 71 per cent of Labour respondents and 85 per cent of Conservatives in the 1992 sample also said that their 'personal opinions' would be expected to influence their parliamentary actions and voting decisions. In other words, party theory coexists with trustee theories in the minds of newly elected MPs. There is, therefore, a potential for these divergent notions to come into conflict. When they do, either theory may be invoked to legitimate, or challenge, the actions of MPs. A clear illustration of this clash was provided in the battle over intra-party democracy within the Labour party in the early 1980s. On the one side, supporters of the party theory of representation chose to criticise the parliamentary Labour party because:

> Most Labour MPs appear to have the same conception of their role as do Tory and Liberal MPs. They see themselves as representatives very much as defined by Burke: they claim the right to exercise their individual judgement, and on that basis to treat the Party's Election Manifesto and Programme as little more than advisory.
>
> (Burnell 1980: 14)

What was needed, from this perspective, was to make MPs and the parliamentary leader more accountable to the wider labour movement. Not surprisingly, the reforms effected in 1980 and 1981 – the introduction of the mandatory reselection of Labour MPs, and the establishment of an electoral college for the selection of the party leader – sought to ensure just that. One consequence of adopting these constitutional changes was that the inherent tension between conceptions of parliamentary representation within the party was heightened, with three of the most vociferous opponents of the internal reforms – David Owen, Shirley Williams and William Rodgers – voicing their objections to the proposed changes in Burkean terms:

> For decades debates on policy and organisation have gone on within our party, and we have managed to find some way of working together. But this time the far left wants no compromise. It is seeking not only to dominate the party, but to destroy representative democracy itself. MPs are chosen by their constituents to exercise their conscience and judgement. MPs...who are nothing but mandated party delegates cannot be representatives of their constituencies in the true sense. They cease to be accountable to the people who elected them and become instead the rubber stamps for a party caucus, one that does not even include the majority of party members.
>
> (*Guardian*, 1 August 1980)

So great was the fear that Labour MPs would be expected to act as delegates of their constituency party activists that 28 Labour MPs chose at the time to leave the party to join the Social Democratic party (see Chapter 4). Even those MPs who were willing to remain within the Labour party expressed their concern at the possibility of being subject to the *diktat* of constituency activists 'instructing elected representatives how to behave, regardless of their electors views' (Hayter 1982).

However, invocation of Burke is not exclusively the preserve of embattled Labour MPs, as Conservative and Liberal Democratic MPs are just as likely to call upon trustee conceptions of representation when in conflict with their constituency parties, or in disagreement with party policy. Thus, for example, David Alton MP announced, in September 1992, that he would not stand as a Liberal Democrat parliamentary candidate at the next election in protest at the decision taken at the party's conference to make abortion a policy issue rather than a matter to be decided by individual conscience (*The Times*, 15 September 1992). More dramatically, in the Conservative party in the aftermath of Mrs Thatcher's resignation as party leader in 1990, eight Constituency Associations organised meetings to consider the deselection of their MPs – most notably Julian Critchley, Michael Mates and Ivor Stanbrook – who had actively sought Mrs Thatcher's replacement as party leader. On this occasion, the leader-writer of the *Independent* counselled Conservative activists to remember that:

> Members of Parliament are not delegates who can have their mandate withdrawn at the whim of local party activists. The Conservative Central Office guidance manual for intending parliamentary candidates specifically states that Tory MPs once elected, should be free to exercise their own judgement within the very wide ambit of Conservative principles.
>
> (*Independent*, 18 December 1990)

George Gardiner, Conservative MP for Reigate, felt the need to remind his local party of this freedom in his battle against deselection before the general election of 1997. His Constituency Association sought his deselection on the grounds of repeated 'disloyalty to the Prime Minister and the Cabinet'. Gardiner's response was to invoke Burke: 'An MP is not a sheep. He must follow his own convictions' (*Observer*, 23 June 1996); and, more explicitly: 'Reigate Conservatives will have to decide whether a Member of Parliament is sent to Westminster purely as lobby fodder, or whether he should exercise his own judgement on matters of supreme national importance' (*Guardian*, 28 June 1996).

Conservative MPs and Europe

Throughout the 1990s most Conservative MPs identified the issue of European integration to be of 'supreme national importance' (see Baker *et al.* 1993, 1994, Ludlam 1996). In these circumstances, the certainties of intra-party support and cohesion gave way to a contingent relationship between vertical groupings of opinion within the governing party. Not surprisingly Burke was cited in defence of the necessary 'independence' asserted by one faction in face of the other. The malleability of 'trustee-ship' and its contemporary relevance can be gauged from its deployment by those both in support of, and in opposition to, the Conservative leadership's European stance at any given moment. The respective claims revolved around who could best decipher the 'best interests of the electorate'. Both sides agreed, however, that it was not the electorate itself. Thus, those opposed to allowing the electorate to vote in a referendum on the question of a European single currency maintained that Burke was on their side:

> All of us who have been in the House for a long time have taken diffi-cult decisions on many issues. Those include moral issues, such as capital punishment and changes in the abortion laws, and constitu-tional issues such as the treaty of Maastricht, the Single European Act 1986 and, before I came here, the treaty of Rome. I agree strongly with Burke, who when speaking to the electorate of Bristol said:
> 'Your representative owes you not his industry only, but his judgment. And he betrays, instead of serving you, if he sacrifices it to your opinion'.
> That is not a popular view....If the House is to retain respect, we must have the courage at times to follow our own judgment and, having listened carefully, not to be swayed from that.
> (Tim Renton, HC Debates 13 February 1995, vol. 254: col. 692)

In the same debate, Sir Terrence Higgins (then MP for Worthing) upheld the view that MPs 'come to the House as representatives, not dele-gates':

> We are not here to function as a surrogate calculating machine, to vote the way that our constituents would if they could all press a button. We have a much greater responsibility to consult our constituents and listen to their arguments, but it is the strength of the argument and not the number of people who make it that is impor-tant. Then, we must weigh up the arguments and vote as our

constituents would if they had the advantage that we do of listening to debates and analysing the issues.

(HC Debates 13 February 1995, vol. 254: col. 703)

If Burke could be invoked against following the leadership's position on a referendum on a single currency; equally, his words could be used to rally support for a beleaguered leadership. Thus, in December 1995, Edward Heath (Father of the House and MP for Old Bexley and Sidcup) counselled his Conservative backbench colleagues not to defeat the government on a motion on EU fisheries policy. In a neat illustration of the elision between the 'interests of the country' and the 'interests of the government' he advised colleagues 'who represent the fishing industry':

> Of course my hon. Friends must take notice of the fishermen in their constituencies, but I also remind them of the remark by Burke so many centuries ago that is often repeated in the House. The purpose and responsibility of a representative is to look after the interests of his constituents, but he must also consider the interests of the country and the community. That is the basis of our work here.
>
> Every hon. Member owes his constituents not only his energy 'but his judgment'. Those were Burke's words. We can offer our fishermen our energy, but my hon. Friends have to make a judgment tonight as to whether it is an event and a matter that justifies their defeating the Government. That is the crucial question to be answered.
>
> (HC Debate 19 December 1995, vol. 268: col. 1362)

In the event the government was defeated by 299 votes to 297 with 2 Conservative MPs voting against the government and 11 others deliberately abstaining. Edward Heath's plea for Conservative MPs to use 'their judgement' in favour of the government and party loyalty was counterposed by the use of 'independent judgement' to assert the views of a broader conception of the 'interests of the country' beyond partisan considerations. On this occasion Burke and 'trusteeship' prevailed against party and 'delegate' notions of representation. That it did so to no policy effect, other than the Agriculture Minister's pronouncement that due weight would be given to the decision by the House at the next day's European Fisheries Council, did not detract from the fact that MPs were able to legitimate their 'independence' in face of collectivist notions of 'party representation'.

Conclusion

Burkean notions of the exercise of 'enlightened conscience' on the part of representatives are invariably dismissed as anachronistic in the 1990s. For some (John Lloyd, *Scotsman*, 17 November 1997), Burke is simply 'a voice from a distant past' unsuited to the age of modern party politics; for others, however, the continued invocation of Burke is more perplexing because, 'despite some 200 years of democratic advance, we appear to be content to let some of the most sensitive and important matters in society be determined in accordance with the political orthodoxy of the 18th century' (Cowley 1998). That this remains so is a reflection of the fact that the 'orthodoxy' of trusteeship has never been fully superseded by other later conceptions of representation. In turn, this reflects the fact that 'trusteeship' encapsulates the basic principles of representation: consent, authorisation, accountability and responsibility. Representatives in parliament are able to inform themselves of the changing balance of opinion in the country and to shape public policy accordingly. In using their 'enlightened conscience' or their 'full freedom to act in their own judgements' MPs do so on the understanding that their constituents expect them to promote both constituency interests and the long-term interests of society as a whole. By this view only the collective deliberation of all representatives in parliament will produce these objectives. Through the process of deliberation, representatives not only shape but also legitimise public policy. Moreover, any lasting discrepancy between MPs and their constituents would reveal a pathological condition to be rectified through the ballot box.

In this respect, 'trustee' notions provided the frame within which later collectivist ideas of representation developed. Given the potency of trustee theories in the legitimation of public policy, in that legislative outputs were deemed to be legitimate precisely because they had been subject to the process of deliberation by representatives of all sections of the 'political nation' (however defined at the time), collectivist theories could not in themselves displace these notions. Instead, as later chapters reveal, they have coexisted – often uneasily – with the continuing belief that: 'Our MPs are representatives of the people, not delegates. We expect them to exercise their own judgement, not simply to reflect ours'. What is noteworthy about this statement is that it was made at the end of the twentieth century not at the end of the eighteenth century (Tim Luckhurst, *Scotsman*, 17 October 1997). What is equally noteworthy is that 85 of 114 newly elected MPs (75 per cent) who responded to a Study of Parliament Group survey in 1997 still subscribed to the view that MPs should exercise their independent judgement, while simultaneously believing that they should also be good party members and good constituency members.

4 Party representation

Modern politics is party politics. Political parties are the main actors in the system that connects the citizenry and the governmental process....[P]olitical parties aggregate demands into coherent policy packages – a process that gives voters a choice in elections. Political parties form governments and act as opposition in legislatures....Thus they are crucial to political decision making and implementation. From this perspective, political parties...are the major actors in representative democratic systems when it comes to solving societal problems.

(Klingemann *et al.* 1994: 5)

Whereas much of the discussion of representative theory is concerned with one-to-one relationships between individual voters and individual representatives, a discussion of the practice of representation invariably, and necessarily, concerns aggregates of the represented and their representatives. As such, the practice of party representation directs attention to the multiple dimensions of aggregation: of voters into party supporters, of policies into party programmes, and of representatives into competing parliamentary parties and sets of leaders. Moreover, such practice reveals the representational transmission of power to be a *process* of responsibility: of party leaders to party members and of party governments to party voters. The congruence (or disjunction) of party promises and party performance; the articulation of promises in an electoral programme; the translation of promises into policies within the framework of the manifesto; and the correspondence of voters preferences and policy outputs all direct attention to the central concepts of 'manifesto' and 'mandate' in modern British representative government. In so doing they also reveal the essential difference between representative democracy and representative government.

A theory of party representation?

Whereas named 'theorists' of microcosmic representation and trusteeship can readily be invoked, no single theorist has been accredited with the development of a 'party theory of representation' in Britain. Instead, reviews of 'party theory' make vague references to 'British left-wing writers' (Birch 1971: 980), 'Socialist and Tory democracy' (Beer 1969: 70), or 'traditional doctrine' which is held to 'reflect the history of the party system' (Oliver 1991: 116–7). Indeed, 'party theory' is best understood as a rationale of practice rather than a theory as such. If this is so then the different interpretations of 'party theory' amongst the major British political parties can be accounted for in terms of their different patterns of development.

The core element of all interpretations, however, is the justification of party discipline within Parliament. What party theory has to justify, in essence, is a 'system in which the elected representative may be forced by his party managers to vote for a policy which is contrary to the apparent interests of his constituents, contrary to the prevailing opinion in his constituency, and contrary to his own personal judgement about what is best for the country' (Birch 1971: 97). Intertwined around this core element is the concept of the electoral mandate, and the different perspectives upon the mandate served to differentiate the variants of 'party theory' amongst the parties. What unites all parties, however, is the defence of the *idea* of party discipline based upon the *notion* of the electoral mandate. Despite routine infringements in practice this conceptual base remains largely unquestioned amongst the parliamentary elite (see Topf 1994: 150).

Disposing of the myth of the mandate?

The idea of the electoral mandate is deceptively simple and follows a logical sequence: first, each party presents to the electorate a policy programme in the form of a manifesto; second, voters make an informed choice between the competing parties on the basis of this programme; third, the successful party seeks to translate this programme into practice once in government; and, fourth, the governing party is then judged by the electorate on its success in implementing its promises at the next election. What this perspective offers, in effect, is an idealised view of responsible government – one where the actions of parliamentary elites are legitimised by the electoral choice of voters mediated through the programmes of parties. Yet it is a view which still retains a strong resonance for modern governments. Thus incoming Labour ministers after the 1997 general election repeatedly pointed to the mandate afforded by their electoral victory.

On 11 June, for example, Tony Blair reminded the House that 'we were elected on that mandate [the introduction of a windfall tax]. That was the promise we made and...we will carry through our promise' (HC Debates 11 June 1997, vol. 295: col. 1138). Gordon Brown, in his first major speech as the new Chancellor of the Exchequer, invoked the concept of the mandate with even greater vigour:

> Not since 1945 have the British people stated so clearly the need for a change of direction. The last time the British people put their trust in the Labour party with such a powerful national mandate, we created the national health service, a new education service, the welfare state and full employment for a generation. Now, in 1997, as we embark on our task of national renewal, we are conscious of the trust placed in us by the British people – the responsibilities that are imposed upon us and the will of the British people for sensible change.
>
> People voted for us because we were back again as the party of the people and this, the people's Government, will keep their promises....After 18 years, the people of this country now have a Government who are on their side. We have the people's mandate and, in government with the policies that I have suggested today, it is our determination – indeed, our task – to fulfil the people's mandate.
>
> (HC Debates 20 May 1997, vol. 294: col. 546)

While parliamentarians manifestly remain wedded to the theory of the mandate, critics argue that this perspective offers an astonishingly inaccurate view of representative practice – where the disjunction between representative *government* and representative *democracy* is starkly revealed. Whether these inaccuracies and disjunctions make the notion of the mandate mythical thus needs to be addressed.

The case against the notion of the mandate is easily stated. In the first instance, it has been questioned whether parties put forward a meaningful policy choice in their manifestos. However, this criticism can be countered at both a general and a specific level. At a general level, in terms of 'programme emphases on a left–right dimension', the major parties' programmes have been distinguishable throughout the post-war period. Thus, even on the occasions when the Labour and Conservative parties moved closer to each other (within a Keynesian welfare consensus in the 1950s and 1960s, or in the post-Thatcherite period in the 1990s) they have never completely 'leapfrogged' each other (see Klingemann *et al.* 1994: 59). At a more specific level – of detailed policy proposals – the first issue is whether parties offer specific policy pledges, and the second is whether voters are aware of these details if offered. While it is possible to maintain that manifestos are vague to the point of vacuity, empirical studies tend to support the case that they do in fact contain a series of specific proposals. As Richard Rose (1984: 61) noted: 'Beneath sloganeering headlines, a contemporary election manifesto contains much fine print detailing specific intentions to act.' More recently, Topf's content analysis of manifestos for the 1992 General Election revealed that each of the major parties offered a 'similar combination of generalised statements of the party's vision for the future, of specific election promises to subgroups within society, and of some statement of the party position on all major policy dimensions' (1994: 155). The same remained true of the 1997 manifestos.

A second defect of the mandate model is that it is generally assumed that few voters read manifestos and that 'voting choices are not made on the basis of a conscious weighting in the balance of alternative policies' (Heath *et al.* 1985: 99). As Ivor Crewe (1993: 111) puts it: 'Policy-voting is the old-fashioned liberal ideal – what most politicians understand by "voting the issues". But it is not what most voters, especially uncommitted voters do: they have neither the information nor inclination to judge the parties' specific policy proposals'. Even though there is *prima facie* evidence that issues and policies became more important in voting decisions in the 1980s, the impact of 'policy voting' remains weak in comparison with other factors influencing voting decisions (such as 'governing competence', 'performance voting' and 'leadership image' (see King 1997; Sanders 1997)). While this is not the place to follow the heated psephological debate about the influences on voting behaviour, it is sufficient to note that enough doubt has been cast upon the electoral manifesto to conclude that voters 'conduct post-mortems rather than confer mandates' (Crewe 1993: 111).

The third, and for the discussion of representation the most damning, defect of the electoral mandate doctrine is the failure of successive governments to implement their manifesto commitments. In its quintessential form the mandate theory envisages single party majority government in the House of Commons enacting the policy intentions outlined in its most recent electoral manifesto. Yet, as Birch observed in the early 1970s, 'the record of history shows that election promises are a poor guide to the actions of the successful party after it has taken government' (1971: 100). More recently, and in a more empirical vein, Klingemann *et al.* point out that 'in spite of institutional arrangements that should allow for a strong mandate in British policymaking, there is considerable evidence of a politics of accommodation' (1994: 79). The intriguing part of Klingemann *et al.*'s findings, however, is that Labour governments are subject to 'the politics of accommodation' far more than Conservative governments:

On the Labour side, apart from defence and environment, what they say before winning an election seems to bear little relationship to what actually gets done in government. This is worrisome not only for mandate theory but also for the whole focus of representative government in Britain....[It] implies a pattern of Conservative ability to see their commitments enacted, in or out of office, and of Labour's inability to do so.

(Klingemann *et al.* 1994: 71)

In part, this might explain why Labour party activists have, throughout the party's history, been preoccupied with the notion of the mandate and of ensuring that Labour governments implemented the party's programme. It might also explain why the Conservative parliamentary elite has traditionally interpreted the doctrine of the mandate as a 'mandate to govern' (Birch 1964: 116). Simply stated, if the Conservative party is more closely attuned to predominant interests in the British state then the chances of the successful implementation of policies favourable to those interests is enhanced when that party is in office. In reverse, the chances of Labour successfully implementing policies which challenge such interests are diminished.

Leaving aside these broader questions of the state, its 'interests' and the relative performance of the major parties in office, our attention needs to be focused upon the narrower issues of what are the constituent elements of a 'theory of party representation', and how has the practice of party politics approximated to this theory?

The Labour party and electoral mandate

Ultimately the issue of party representation distils into the justification of party discipline. Traditionally the Labour party, alone amongst the major parties, has espoused a simple and coherent theory of representation capable of defining the linkage between the wider party and its parliamentary representatives. But this simple theory has been built upon complex assumptions within the party about its external relations – the nature of the state and its institutional structure; and about the party's internal relations – the purposes of the party and its own organisational structure. Throughout the party's history the complexity of these wider relationships has consistently overwhelmed the simplicity of the initial theory of party representation.

It is advisable, therefore, to start by listing the essential components of this simple theory: first, that Labour supporters subscribe to the policy objectives of the party; and, second, that Labour representatives will be bound to pursue these objectives. Such a simple summary, however, begs the questions of what constitutes 'supporters', 'bound' and 'representatives'? The answers require further distinctions to be made by dividing 'supporters' into two often distinct groups – 'party members' and 'party voters'; by acknowledging that 'bound' implies a mechanism of control in the hands of both 'members' and 'voters'; and by viewing the performance of 'representative roles' in terms of 'delegation' and 'mandate'. What Labour theory does, therefore, is to prescribe a triangular relationship between members–voters–representatives. A relationship which transcends, in turn, three political dimensions: the party, the electorate and parliament. To complicate matters still further the prescription itself is based upon a description of practice. Hence, as practice changes, the relative weight afforded to each element of the triarchy also changes: occasionally reversing the direction of the representational transmission of power within the party, making representation more mediated and, ultimately, producing a far more complicated relationship than prescribed by 'party theory'.

In the beginning

The origins of the Labour party are of immense importance for the development of its 'theory' of party representation. Ernest Bevin famously claimed that the party had grown 'out of the bowels of the trade unions' (Labour Party 1935: 180). The Trade Union Congress' (TUC) resolution of 1899 in favour of the formation of a Labour Representation Committee (LRC) led directly to the formation of just such a committee in 1900. Formed in February of that year, the overwhelming majority of the LRC's membership were indeed trade unionists (Minkin 1980: 381). Moreover, trade union affiliation to the LRC increased dramatically in its first three years, as trade union rights came under judicial attack. In the same period, the number of socialists officially attached to the LRC via the Fabian Society, the Independent Labour Party and the Social Democratic Federation (SDF) actually fell with the withdrawal of the SDF from the LRC in 1901 (Callaghan 1990: 64).

In the beginning, therefore, there was a close social and organisational affinity between members, electors and representatives.

> [T]he great majority of trade unionists affiliated to the Labour Party, the majority of individual members after 1918, and the majority of trade union leaders came from manual worker backgrounds…[Moreover] in 1906 all 29 Labour MPs elected on behalf of the LRC were from working class backgrounds.
>
> (Minkin 1992: 13)

What united supporters, voters and representatives alike was thus a shared class background and a desire to protect and advance the interests of 'workers'. These interests were primarily defined by the trade union leadership and were taken to be largely synonymous with the interests of 'organised labour'.

Manifestly, what did not define the party and its supporters before 1918 was a commitment to a socialist programme (see Coates 1975: 9–12; Callaghan 1990: 65; Phillips 1992: 14). If the party subscribed to any ideology at all it was, at most, that of 'labourism'. This was an ideology with three emphases: first, a political economy which rooted labour firmly within a capitalist economy; second, an insistence that labour's interests could be advanced through social reform, and; third, the focusing of political action upon the institution of parliament (Coates 1975: 5–7; Foote 1985: 8–13; Judge 1993: 87–8). 'Labourism', in defining the party's organising principles, was a direct reflection of the predilections of the trade union leadership at the time. And it served successfully to unify the party until 1918 and the formal adoption of a 'socialist' programme in that year.

The independent representation of labour and the protection of workers' interests thus served as the 'lowest common denominator' within both the party and its electorate in the early years. Moreover, it was a denominator derived from an organisational structure bequeathed by the loose alliance of trade union and other socialist organisations. Not surprisingly, given the pre-eminence of trade unions in this alliance, the new party adopted many organisational characteristics of the trade unions themselves. In practice, therefore, the LRC, and later the Labour party, simply adopted many existing procedures of the TUC in evolving its own constitution and standing orders (see Minkin 1992: 279–80). These procedures included the 'block vote', the determination of policy by an annual conference composed of delegates from affiliated organisations and a distinct set of attitudes to leadership – where leaders were accorded no higher status than rank and file members and where each member had the right to submit resolutions to conference through their affiliated organisation. In turn, conference 'debated the various resolutions placed before it but normally most of the delegates were mandated – that is they were expected to cast their votes in accordance with the policy laid down by their own organisations' (Minkin 1980: 3). In principle at least, all party members were capable of influencing policy through conference; and, in return, were subject to the authority of conference. In this manner the sovereignty of conference came to be an accepted and integral part of Labour's organisational structure – it was both the practical embodiment and the theoretical expression of intra-party democracy. It was also to prove highly problematic for the developing party.

Conference sovereignty and parliamentary representation

The principle of conference sovereignty meant that its mandates were not only derived from party members but were also binding upon its members, including the party's representatives in parliament. The parliamentary party was thus conceived as merely the parliamentary arm of the extra-parliamentary Labour movement. Resolutions of conference were to 'instruct the Parliamentary party as to their action in the House of Commons' (Labour Party 1907a: 49). Individual MPs were to be left with little freedom of action or independent judgement on policy decisions in Westminster (Birch 1971: 98). They were expected to act simply as delegates of the wider party. Clearly, this 'party view' came into conflict with prevailing individualistic notions of representation; but there were also practical problems in the operation of the 'party view'.

It has long been held that for delegatory notions of representation to work, representatives need to be instructed, unambiguously, on specific policy decisions. Empirically, therefore, many analysts dismiss this form of representation as impracticable. Bruno Leoni, for example, argues that: 'the more numerous the people...one tries to "represent" and the more numerous the matters in which one tries to represent them, the less the word "representation" has a meaning referable to the actual will of actual people other than that of the persons named as their "representatives"' (1961: 18). In the case of the Labour party it is possible to maintain that at its inception (given the limited objectives of the infant party of 'the pursuit of trade union principles and ideals' and the close social affinity of party members and their representatives in parliament) the identity of interest within the party was sufficiently close for parliamentarians to act on the instructions of conference and to pursue the policy priorities identified in its resolutions. Thus in the early years at least there were few problems of divergence: affiliated members were largely drawn from the unions, electoral support was concentrated in heavily unionised areas, and Labour MPs were closely associated with trade unions. Within this homogeneous ideological and social framework notions of intra-party democracy and delegatory representation could take root. Once rooted they continued to serve as the defining elements of a model of party organisation for successive generations of party members.

Within a very short period, however, the practice of Party representation modified this model of party organisation to allow greater policy discretion and tactical manœuvre by Labour representatives in Westminster. This change was prompted because conference resolutions sought increasingly to instruct MPs on the introduction of specific pieces of legislation (see McKenzie 1963: 393). In response, Labour MPs complained increasingly about affiliated organisations seeking to prioritise their parliamentary activity. Indeed, within a year of adopting the name of the Labour party, the party's National Executive Committee (NEC) sought to limit the binding nature of conference resolutions. It did so by claiming that 'instructions' basically meant the expression of the 'opinions' of conference 'without prejudice to any future course of action that may be considered advisable by the party in Parliament' (Labour Party 1907b: 15). However, the NEC's proposal had to be reworded in response to intra-party hostility to any dilution of conference sovereignty. The revised proposal read:

> resolutions instructing the Parliamentary Party as to their action in the House of Commons be taken as the opinions of Conference, on the understanding that the time and method of giving effect to these instructions be left to the Party in the House.
>
> (Labour Party 1907a: 49)

The basic ambiguity of this resolution is noted by Minkin (1980: 6): conference sovereignty is asserted in the word 'instructions', but parliamentary discretion is suggested in the phrase that conference merely expresses its 'opinions'. In practice, in the period before 1918, the resolution was used to enhance the scope for policy discretion on the part of the PLP and to establish a *de facto* autonomy on the part of Labour MPs (Leys 1989: 174). Nonetheless, parliamentary independence remained limited in the short term (Minkin 1980: 7).

When the Labour party adopted a new constitution in 1918 the opportunity was taken to formalise the relationship between conference, the NEC and the party's representatives in parliament. It was firmly stated that 'the work of the Party shall be under the direction and control of the Party Conference' and it was to be conference which decided 'what specific proposals of legislative, financial or administrative reform…should be promoted, as occasion may present itself, by the National Executive and the Parliamentary Labour Party' (Labour Party 1918: 141). Furthermore, it was 'the duty of every Parliamentary representative of the Party to be guided [and]…to give effect to the decisions of the Party Conference (Labour Party 1918: 141). Hence, despite the formal restatement of conference sovereignty, the 1918 Constitution still allowed practical flexibility and discretion on the part of the PLP (see McKenzie 1963: 407–8; Minkin 1980: 8–9).

Two contradictory forces served to insulate the PLP from direct instructions from conference: one was the dominance of trade unions within the new constitutional structure, and the other was the formal commitment to socialism adopted in the new programme *Labour and the New Social Order*. The supreme irony of Labour's system of intra-party democracy was that it was founded upon the oligopolistic control of conference by the trade unions. While placing the unions in a seemingly unassailable position of influence in the party's organisation, for much of the party's history the political self-restraint, constitutional conservatism and ideological predilections of leading trade union leaders served to bolster the leadership of the PLP and to provide a realm of independence for the parliamentary wing of the labour movement from its industrial wing (see Minkin 1992; McKenzie 1963: 505; Crouch 1982: 177–82).

Equally the adoption of a socialist programme in 1918 enlarged the scope for the exercise of policy discretion by the PLP. The new constitution committed the party to:

> secure for the workers by hand or by brain the full fruits of their industry and the most equitable distribution thereof that may be possible, upon the basis of the Common Ownership of the means of production and the best obtainable system of popular administration and control of each industry and service.
>
> (Labour Party 1918: 140)

In so doing, it broadened the party's appeal beyond organised industrial labour, to include 'workers by brain' and identified a constituency beyond the manual working class. Indeed, the PLP leadership consistently conceived of the party's appeal as one based upon a 'movement of opinion' rather than one of 'class' alone. The leadership thus spoke to the electorate in terms 'of principles rather than of interests' (Minkin 1992: 17). In the immediate period after 1918 there was no immediate divergence between 'principles' and 'interests' as the new constitution and the new programme, *The New Social Order*, simply committed the party to an enhanced variant of 'labourism' (see Coates 1975: 17). What the official commitment to socialism did do, however, was to incorporate the potential for four strategic divergences within the party: first, between activists who conceived of socialism in more radical terms than labourism and the leaderships of the trade unions and the PLP who basically did not; second, between the leaderships of the industrial and political wings of the movement as to the meaning and purposes of 'public ownership'; third, between the wider electoral perspective of the PLP and the limited policy objectives of the trade unions, and; fourth, between the demands of constitutional propriety within the parliamentary state (parliamentary sovereignty) and the intra-party constitutional requirements of party democracy (conference sovereignty).

Thus, although obscured in the short-term, the 1918 constitution and programme had inherent within them a series of representational dilemmas which were to feature prominently in the subsequent history of the party. What was foreshadowed in 1918 was a widening of the representational focus of Labour MPs beyond the specific aims of organised labour, a broadening of the party's electoral appeal, and a reaffirmation of the centrality of the existing institutions of parliamentary democracy to the attainment of the party's objectives. In this process of refocusing and reaffirmation, the delegatory relationship between the labour movement and its representatives in parliament became obscured. As the party's objectives widened beyond the simple representation of labour in the political process, so the scope increased for PLP interpretation of party policy and discretion as to implementation.

With the broadening of the party's programme came an expansion of the party's electoral constituency beyond organised labour (see Phillips 1992: 39–45). With continued electoral success came too an increased prospect of forming a government. With this prospect came a strengthened strategic commitment to the parliamentary 'rules of the game' which were likely to secure that objective. In these circumstances, the simple connections specified in 'party theory' – between the wider party and the party in parliament – became ever more complex in practice. As a consequence, following the logic of Leoni (see p. 77), as the people whom Labour sought to represent became 'more numerous', and as the matters upon which the party sought to represent them also became 'more numerous', so the premises of the theory of delegation were undermined by the practice of representation at Westminster. Nevertheless, the theory remained as a conceptual frame within which that practice could be interpreted and, at times, challenged by party members.

Tensions between intra-party democracy and representative government

It should not be forgotten that Labour representatives were socialised into an existing pattern of representation at Westminster which was founded on the constitutional precepts of parliamentary sovereignty. These precepts found pragmatic reinforcement in the parliamentary procedures of privilege, and were buttressed at the level of theory by Burkean notions of trusteeship and independence (see Judge 1993: 89–92). David Coates captures the full impact of the established mode of representation in his comment that:

The Labour Party leadership spent the 1920s educating the movement in the niceties of Parliamentary politics. This education took two
principle forms. It first involved establishing the autonomy of the
Parliamentary Party from its extra-Parliamentary organisation, by
arguing that control by the latter would offend Parliamentary privilege, would tie MPs to programmes that would prevent a flexible
response to unanticipated circumstances, and would not enable the
individual Labour MP to represent adequately the constituency for
which he was elected. It also involved the education of the
Parliamentary Labour Party in the procedures of Parliament, and in
the slow pace of Parliamentary change.

(Coates 1975: 23)

Just how well these lessons had been learned by the majority of the PLP
was revealed in the experience of government, for 10 months in 1924 and
27 months from 1929 to 1931. In these periods the desire to prove that
Labour in power was 'not thinking of party; [but] of national well-being'
(Macdonald in Miliband 1972: 104) underpinned the parliamentary leadership's claim that the PLP should be free from extra-parliamentary
control by the party conference and party activists. Indeed, these early
periods in government 'were sufficient to produce an effect which tended
to manifest itself each time the party formed a government. The distribution of power would shift within the party itself....Power tended to be
redistributed once again when the party moved back into opposition'
(Minkin 1980: 13–14).

As a general rule, Labour leaders in government (with the exception of
the Attlee administrations of 1945–51 which were uniquely attuned to the
interests dominating the wider movement) emphasised their policy independence; and, in opposition, the party conference took the opportunity to
remind the PLP leaders of the error of their ways in government (see
Minkin 1980; Coates 1975: 31–41, 86–9). In conformity with this general
rule, the Wilson governments of the 1960s came to epitomise the
phenomenon of the 'grass coming away from the roots' of the party as
Labour ministers revoked manifesto commitments, ignored conference
decisions and implemented policies which ran counter to the basic principles of the wider party (see Minkin 1980: 290–1).

Not surprisingly, the electoral defeat of 1970 brought in its wake
demands for the reassertion of intra-party democracy and the restoration
of conference authority. Indeed, within months, intra-party democracy
featured as the subject of a special debate at the 1970 conference (Labour
Party 1970: 273–9). Within a few years, the party had recommitted itself in
its *Programmes* of 1973 and 1976 to the sovereignty of conference, to policy

making by 'the members' and to the determination of the 'long-term programme' by the annual conference (Minkin 1980: 330). In parallel, the *Programmes* also marked a 'turning to the left' as a reflection of the increasing strength of the new left within the party and their desire to push the PLP markedly towards democratic socialism. At the time it was argued that a radicalisation of the electorate and reform of the state were dependent upon a prior democratisation of the internal structure of the party itself. Tony Benn (1982: 177) made explicit this connection between ideological goals and party organisation in his demand 'to re-establish democracy within the party so that we can develop policies strong enough to win social justice; to be sure of the commitment of the parliamentary leadership to those policies; and to be involved directly in the implementation of those policies when Labour has a parliamentary majority'.

Mandatory reselection

What the new left proposed, and indeed had been campaigning for under the auspices of the Campaign for Labour Party Democracy (CLPD) throughout most of the 1970s (see Kogan and Kogan 1982: 23–35; Young 1983: 103–16; Rustin 1985: 63–74; Seyd 1987: 83–91), was closer control of the PLP and its leadership by the wider movement. The CLPD had been established in June 1973 to ensure that there would be no 'repetition of the sorry tale of 1964–70' (Panitch and Leys 1997: 135). In its *Statement of Aims* it sought to ensure that conference decisions in future would be binding on the parliamentary party. There was a recognition that 'under the present arrangements there is no way the Conference can effectively influence the parliamentary Labour Party'. 'Effective influence' in the CLPD's view would best be secured through 'the individual accountability of each MP to a regularly held selection conference, backed up with the possibility of replacement' (CLPD *Campaign Newsletter*, May–June 1975: 2; quoted in Seyd 1987: 85).

Although the underpinning debate in the party at this time was primarily about ideology, the need for reform was articulated in terms of the style of Labour representation in the Commons. It is within this context that the battles over the Labour party's constitution can best be understood. In these battles the new left reformers identified mandatory reselection as the priority: first, in the knowledge that constituency General Committees were predominantly left wing; and, second, in the belief that 'in the real world of parliamentary teams competing to put government in office and keep it there, the real accountability of MPs was primarily upwards to the Cabinet rather than downwards to those who nominated or elected them' (Panitch and Leys 1997: 139). This priority was later accompanied by demands for

other internal constitutional changes including the extension of the franchise for the election of the party leader beyond the PLP, and for the party's
National Executive Committee to have the final say on the contents of the
manifesto. The success of the new left can be gauged from the fact that the
reforms on reselection and the electoral college for the party leader were
accepted at successive conferences between 1979 and 1981. (NEC control
over the manifesto was approved in principle in 1981 but the amendment to
put the reform into practice was rejected.)

In adopting these constitutional changes the conflict between individualist and collectivist conceptions of parliamentary representation within
the party became apparent. As Panitch and Leys rightly note: 'What was
being put into question by the confrontation in the Labour party [over
reselection] was nothing less than the political meaning of the word
"representative"' (1997: 185). Fears that Labour MPs would now be
expected to act as delegates of their constituency activists prompted 28
social democratic Labour MPs to leave the party and to form the Social
Democratic party (see Chapter 3). Moreover, those centre-right MPs who
chose to remain in the Labour party effectively had to concede the ideological battle in the short term and to concentrate instead on countering
constitutional reform. That they chose to do so in terms of individualistic
representation was of no surprise.

One Member One Vote

What concerned centre-right members of the PLP about the new 'representational transmission of power' was that MPs would be controlled and
held accountable – not to the wider Labour electorate, or even to party
members at large – but to a small minority of activists in their constituencies. In fact, as soon as it was apparent that mandatory reselection would
occur, a proposal was made that the general membership of constituency
parties should make the final selection through the principle of One
Member One Vote. This proposal reappeared in 1984 when Neil Kinnock,
as party leader, proposed a system of 'voluntary One Member One Vote'
in which Constituency General Committees could, if they so chose, ballot
individual members on the reselection of sitting MPs (Shaw 1994: 31).
Conference rejected this proposal in 1984, but Kinnock returned to the
subject in 1987. This time he proposed a 'compromise One Member One
Vote' which took account of the sensitivities of the trade unions by
proposing local electoral colleges in which unions would have up to 40 per
cent of the vote and with individual members casting the remaining votes.
As a compromise this system satisfied no-one and in 1990 the NEC voted
for its discontinuance.

After Labour's fourth consecutive general election defeat in 1992, and the replacement of Neil Kinnock by John Smith as leader of the party, the issue of One Member One Vote was revived. The 1993 conference was persuaded to adopt One Member One Vote for candidate selection, with a minor concession to a continuing special role for the unions. Henceforth, all individual trade unionists who paid the political levy, plus a small membership fee, would be able to participate in local constituency elections. This 'levy plus' formula did not last long and was soon discarded under Tony Blair's leadership. Thereafter only ordinary individual members retained the franchise. In addition, as part of a wider programme of constitutional reform, Blair reduced the weight of the union's block vote at conference to 50 per cent (down from the 70 per cent negotiated by John Smith in 1993) and secured the agreement of trade unions, in the same year of 1996, to giving financial support to the party centrally. These funds would then be distributed to constituencies to help with running costs and election expenses rather than for sponsoring individual MPs directly.

Democratisation as emasculation

'Democratisation' within the party was advanced further in 1997 in three inter-related ways. However, this was 'democratisation as emasculation' (Webb 1994: 120) and was designed primarily to reduce the power of local party activists while simultaneously curbing criticism within the PLP. Without going into the details of these changes (see Panitch and Leys 1997: 233–6; Labour Party 1997a, 1997b), the Labour leadership extended the plebiscitary tendencies in the party; which had first been used to significant effect in 1995 in the redrafting of Clause IV. In that year Clause IV of the party's constitution was replaced by a generalised commitment to a just society, an open democracy, and a dynamic and competitive market economy. Some 470 Constituency Labour Parties (CLP), three quarters of all CLPs, chose to ballot their members on this historic change, with 467 voting in favour and only three voting against. With this level of support the leadership successfully consigned to history, at a special conference in April 1995, the party's traditional commitments to public ownership and 'equitable distribution'.

In 1996 the principle of balloting individual members was extended formally when the NEC agreed to Blair's proposal that the entire party membership should be asked to endorse a 'pre-manifesto programme' – *The Road to the Manifesto*. After approval by the 1996 annual conference, this programme was submitted to ordinary members for endorsement – which they did wholeheartedly by 95 per cent of the 61 per cent of individual party members who voted in the postal ballot. Although this ballot was grafted on to the existing decision making processes within the party, there was little doubt on the left that the intention was to ensure that 'the party conference would eventually become less important' (Panitch and Leys 1997: 233).

The second reform – launched before the general election of 1997 through the document *Labour into Power: A Framework for Partnership* (Labour Party 1997a) and endorsed at the annual conference in October 1997 as *Partnership in Power* (Labour Party 1997b) – was also seen by those on the left as a further marginalisation of conference as the sovereign policy making body within the party. Manifestly, the leadership did not openly proclaim such an objective; on the contrary, *Partnership in Power* stated that: 'Conference would remain the sovereign policy- and decision-making body of the party' (Labour Party 1997b: 2). Nonetheless, it was apparent that Conference's role was to be residualised in practice to 'agreeing' decisions taken elsewhere and to orchestrating the publicising of 'Labour's achievements and plans'. 'Annual conference should reflect all that is best about the party and its values' (1997b: 2). What had not been 'best about the party' when in government in the past was internecine ideological warfare fought out at conference. While acknowledging that there would continue to be 'debate and sometimes strong differences of opinion', *Partnership in Power* maintained that: 'It is vital that our discussions and any expressions of difference take place in a mature, informed and positive way. We need positive engagement by government and constructive debate in the party' (1997b: 5). Importantly, however, it was the leadership which was to set the parameters of the debate: 'Most of all, it needs to rest upon a clear understanding, and acceptance, of the respective roles and responsibilities of the party on the one hand and of the government on the other' (1997b: 5). If the idea of partnership was crucial it was

> a partnership based on mutual expectations, chief among which are the expectation that the party's leadership in Parliament will be accountable and responsive to the party in the country and the expectation that the party in the country will be truly representative of the communities it serves. For the government to stay in tune with the party, the party must stay in tune with the nation.
>
> (Labour Party 1997b: 5)

Here, clearly, was the assertion of the interests of the nation, determined by leaders in parliament, over the interests of the party, determined by party activists. Even supporters of modernisation within the party expressed concern that the leadership's proposals would rob conference of debate and choice. As John Edmunds of the General, Municipal and Boilermakers union commented: 'This is the Henry Ford approach to policy-making, where you can have any colour, provided that colour has been decided by the NEC' (quoted in the *Guardian*, 30 September 1997). Indeed, the membership of the NEC was to be reconstituted, with 'a strengthened role…[and] with a new focus on the strategic development of the party in order to remain an election winning organisation'. A Joint Policy Committee, to be chaired by the Prime Minister, and including equal numbers from the government and from non-government members of the NEC was to have 'strategic oversight of policy development in the party and the rolling programme. It would act as the steering group for the National Policy Forum'. The National Policy Forum was to be charged with overseeing the rolling programme of policy development. It was to have 175 members representing all sections of the party and was to establish policy commissions covering the broad areas of policy, and present an annual report to conference on progress in the rolling programme and other issues addressed by the commissions and forum during the year. In January 1998 the consultation exercise was extended further with the announcement of the creation of 45 'local policy forums' in which all party members could participate (*Guardian*, 2 January 1998).

In the view of some of the 91 critical resolutions submitted at the 1997 conference, *Partnership in Power*'s proposals constituted a direct assault on activist democracy and the ability to criticise the leadership. The fear of centralisation within the party was only heightened by a third series of reforms effected by the PLP leadership in 1997. In August 1997 each of Labour's 417 MPs received a reminder from Nick Brown, Chief Whip, of Rule 2a[8] of the party's rulebook which states that 'no member shall engage in a sustained course of conduct prejudicial, or detrimental, to the party'. There were few doubts that dissent in the PLP was to be ruthlessly curbed when the PLP rule requiring backbenchers to clear with the whips motions to be tabled in parliament was implemented in July 1997. This followed the adoption, in January 1997, of new standing orders for the PLP (based upon the recommendations of the report *PLP Review Committee: Preparing For Government*) which included the rule that MPs should 'do nothing which brings the party into disrepute'. Ken Livingstone, from the left of the PLP, reminded his PLP colleagues that 'only dictatorships insist on one line going out' (quoted in the *Guardian*, 5 December 1996). This theme was returned to in 1998 this time by Gordon Prentice MP who, having resigned as a PPS in the Blair government, repeated the accusation that the leadership of the party was 'Leninist' and that 'absolute loyalty is demanded on the grounds that we were elected as New Labour and we must govern as New Labour' (*Observer*, 11 January 1998). What concerned

Prentice was that in the New Labour party: 'Major commitments, not just proposals, bubble to the surface with nobody having any idea where they came from.' However, his suspicions echoed those of Peter Riddell that: 'Tony Blair and Gordon Brown and their small group of allies [are] operating by coup rather than consensus, and *fait accompli* rather than debate.'

Party theory in the Blair era

'Intra-party democracy', conceived in collectivist terms of the representation of CLPs, trade unions and other affiliated bodies at a sovereign annual conference, has traditionally been at the heart of the Labour theory of representation. Yet, in challenging the collectivist bases of representation within the party, successive modernising leaders have asserted their intention of re-establishing 'intra-party democracy'; but this time from an individualist base of ordinary party members. The paradox is that while the old left accused the modernisers of undermining intra-party democracy, New Labour leaders proclaimed their reforms as the reassertion of democracy within the party. Essentially, reforms throughout the 1990s have relocated the locus of authority within the party away from the *organised* party on the ground towards individual members. As Peter Mair observes in his comparative study of party organisations in Western democracies, this phenomenon is not restricted to the British Labour party but is part of a more general trend in which:

> it is not the party congress or the middle-level elite, or the activists, who are being empowered, but rather the 'ordinary' members, who are at once more docile and more likely to endorse the policies (and candidates) proposed by the party leadership and by the party in public office....[O]rdinary members often at home, and via postal ballots, are increasingly being consulted by the party leadership, and are increasingly involved in legitimising the choices of the party in public office...while the activist layer inside the party, the traditionally more troublesome layer, becomes marginalised.
>
> (Mair 1994: 16)

In this manner, the PLP leadership is granted greater control of the policy agenda as ordinary members are asked to respond to questions framed by the party's central authorities. In contradistinction to the organising principles of the Labour party, therefore, leadership is now afforded a priority over affiliated members in CLPs and the trade unions. In increasing its control over the selection of parliamentary candidates, the leadership has effectively reduced the accountability of MPs to their CLPs while, simultaneously, increasing the accountability of MPs to itself through amendment of the PLP's standing orders.

The Labour leadership has systematically exploited the organisational paradox of modern political parties – that a fully democratised party is susceptible to central control. Significantly, Labour leaders have done so while still claiming to uphold the bases of party theory: the twin pillars of intra-party democracy and party mandate (Birch 1964: 122). The seismic organisational changes of the 1990s have shaken the traditional representational foundations of intra-party democracy and its associational bases of local party activists and affiliated trade unions, and afforded a priority instead to individual members of the party. The legitimation of the party's electoral programme now flows from these ordinary members through pre-manifesto consultation and balloting exercises. The 'mandate' still derives indirectly from the intra-party processes of legitimation and directly from the sanction of the electorate at large. The 'party theory' of representation is still observable in the practice of the Labour party in the 1990s; but it is no longer the practice of the 1900s and the incipient Labour party. In other words, it is no longer the practice upon which the 'Labour theory' developed.

Party theory and the Conservative party

In twentieth-century Britain both Conservative and Labour parties enforce a fairly rigid form of discipline on their MPs, but only left-wing writers have made any serious attempt to justify this in terms of a theory of representation.

(Birch 1971: 98)

It is perhaps fitting that a party which claims to be a pragmatic party should accommodate itself to the practice of party representation without feeling the need to justify its actions. Hence, the Conservative party has subscribed pragmatically to the theory of the party mandate while traditionally eschewing intra-party democracy. As noted above, intra-party democracy in the Labour party serves both to legitimate the policy programme offered by the Labour party to the electorate and also indirectly to bind Labour representatives to pursue the programme in office. Clearly, cohesion and discipline within the PLP can be both explained and justified by this theory. But how can such cohesion and discipline be explained and justified in the Conservative party?

One route of explanation is to invoke the concept of 'Tory Democracy' (Beer 1969: 91–8). This provides a distinctive perspective on political organisation whereby older Tory ideas of authority are adapted to the conditions of the mass suffrage. In this way, 'Tory Democracy legitimizes a massive concentration of political power. It too provides a theory of party government, rationalizing tight party cohesion and stiff party discipline' (Beer 1969: 91). But it does so by emphasising the importance of political leadership. Indeed, the Tory perspective on leadership is almost tautological: 'the defining characteristic of the governing class is precisely that it has the talent to govern' (Beer 1969: 93). This is taken by Birch (1964: 116–7) to mean that the concept of the mandate for the Conservative party has traditionally entailed 'a mandate to govern'; with the party in government being 'free to pursue whatever policies it thinks appropriate'. In this sense the Conservative version of party democracy draws upon ideas of 'representative government' rather than of representative democracy (see Chapter 1) – with the emphasis placed firmly upon responsive leadership.

When wedded to the mass franchise and mass party organisation, 'Tory Democracy' endows party members and voters with the power of control rather than the power of initiative. Leaders in parliament are expected to take account of party and public opinion but are not bound by such expressions of opinion. They are not delegates. Nonetheless, Conservative leaders have been particularly sensitive to the necessity of securing the consent of party members – not least because of the latter's capacity, ultimately, to withdraw that consent. Historically, Conservative leaders have been able to count upon the support of all levels of the party – until they became clear electoral liabilities. One of the reasons why Conservative leaders were permitted such freedom of manœuvre by the party 'was the relative certainty that they would pursue the proper objectives of Conservatism' (Ingle 1997: 94). At times when these objectives were uncertain, or when the party's principles were actively redefined by the leader, then the unconstrained power of the party leader came into question (see below). Put very simply, if leaders are expected to lead from the front, they are not expected to be too far ahead of the rest of the party.

The emphasis upon leadership finds reflection in the organisation of the party. Before 1998 the leader was regarded as the 'fount of all policy' (Norton 1994: 95) as no other element within the party was vested with the formal power to determine policy. In practice, the leader had been forced to rely upon other bodies within the party to assist in policy initiation. In strict constitutional terms, however, their role remained one of offering advice. In fact the Conservative party did not have a corporate legal identity and was constituted historically in three separate organisations. First, the National Union of Conservative and Unionist Associations served as the extra-parliamentary arm of the party. It had its origins in the late nineteenth century and was created in response to the extension of the franchise and the formation of local Associations to coordinate the recruitment of members and the winning of elections. Second, Central Office, served as the professional arm of the party. Central Office was under the direct control of the party leader and provided the organisational link between party members in the country and party leaders in Westminster. The third organisation is the parliamentary party with the leader at its head. Before 1998 the Conservative parliamentary party was formally insulated from the party's professional and voluntary arms, other than through the integration of all three organisational hierarchies in the position of the party leader. Between 1965 and 1998 the Conservative parliamentary party had sole responsibility for the election of the party leader. Yet, the parliamentary leader alone was vested with responsibility for policy making.

In the absence of a formal constitution no other organisation within the party had a responsibility for the determination and implementation of party policy. Even the annual conference was officially only the conference of the National Union, and not of the party as a whole. As such it had often been portrayed as more of a 'rally for the faithful than a deliberative assembly' (Whiteley *et al.* 1994: 30) or as a 'public relations exercise' (Ingle 1989: 62). Yet this image of conference's subservience – with control from above and deference from below – has not gone unchallenged. In the revisionist analysis of Kelly (1989), for example, conference was identified as establishing the mood and receptivity of the party faithful to policy proposals. In this way it had 'considerable influence upon ministerial initiatives' (1989: 184) because conference debates provided a sounding board of wider party and public opinion. Tether develops this point further and concludes: 'A very full analysis of Conservative annual conferences this century provides so many examples of its importance to the leadership and its influence upon aspects of policy that it is difficult to sustain the view that it is of little or no importance' (1996: 107). However, it may be argued that these are examples, at best, of the 'conditional trust' under which the party leadership operated. The leader still led, but on the condition that the advice of the wider party membership was at least listened to. As Michael Trend, Deputy Chairman of the Conservative party, reminded the 1997 conference: 'the National Union is not a powerbase in the party as a whole. It is base, but it has little power' (Conservative party 1997a, Conference Speech 8 October). Trend made this statement in preface to a call for the building of a 'single, strong and unified party' and for a fundamental reorganisation of the party's structure.

The fresh future

That such a fundamental review was needed was apparent from the result of the 1 May 1997 general election. William Hague, as the new party leader, commissioned a fundamental review of the party's internal organisation, and proposals for change were presented to conference in October 1997 in the document *Our Party: Blueprint for Change*. The draftsman of this document, party Vice-Chairman Archie Norman, believed that it proposed 'a huge extension of democracy' within the party (Conservative Party 1997a, Conference Speech 8 October 1997). William Hague underlined the significance of the proposals in his opening speech to conference:

> Don't be shy because I want to give you power. The final decision on the policies on which we fight the next election will not just be mine, nor just the Shadow Cabinet's, not even just the Parliamentary Party's: it will be yours. It will be ours....We need to involve our grass roots members, to listen to our supporters and to reach out to all parts of the country, to all sections of society and to all generations....So when I say that this Party is going to involve its members much more than ever before, I mean it....When I say I am going to put our policies to the approval of the whole Party, I mean it. When I say we are going to double our Party's membership, transform our organisation and take the time and trouble to listen to millions of people, I mean it. And I mean it too when I say that once we've decided our policy we are all going to stick to it and fight for it together.
>
> (Conservative Party 1997a, Conference Speech 7 October 1997)

Following from these promises a 'White Paper' on reform of the party, entitled *The Fresh Future*, was published by Central Office in February 1998. *The Fresh Future* proposed a constitution which would create a single unified party. To oversee future constitutional change a Constitutional College, consisting primarily of a National Conservative Convention, Conservative MPs and MEPs, was to be created. But at the centre of the new unified party was to be a new governing board which was to be 'the supreme decision-making body on all matters relating to party organisation and management' (Conservative Party 1998). The largest single group on The Board was to be elected representatives from the party's membership, who would sit alongside representatives of the parliamentary party drawn from both Houses, and representatives of the professional party. The party chairman was to chair The Board on behalf of the party leader.

The declared guiding principle of reform was 'decentralisation', whereby there would be 'the fewest possible layers of communication between party members and the party leadership and that there should be a much greater degree of involvement for party members'. Constituency Associations would continue to have the autonomy to select candidates for elections 'subject to the condition that all selected candidates must be included on the party's approved list of candidates'. In pursuing the commitment to make the reformed party 'open and democratic', *The Fresh Future* proposed that, for the first time, every member would have a direct vote in the election of the party leader. The first stage in the election of the leader would involve only Conservative MPs, who could trigger the resignation of an existing party leader and who would also choose the candidates in a leadership contest. At the second stage, however, all party members would be included in the election process – with the result decided on the basis of One Member One Vote.

Not only were ordinary members to be involved directly in the choice of the party leader, but the White Paper further proposed a Policy Forum (based upon a relaunched Conservative Political Centre) to encourage political discussion throughout the party, and the creation of Regional Policy Congresses to discuss policy proposals. It was envisaged that the Conservative Policy Forum would have 'major input into the annual party conference agenda'. The annual conference itself was afforded no decision making capacity and was identified simply as 'the main party gathering of the year'. There was, however, a more specific commitment to allow party members to 'approve the outline of the next general election manifesto', as well as to endorse the shadow cabinet's position on the European single currency.

If *The Fresh Future* reflected the words of Archie Norman that 'members matter' (Conference Speech 8 October 1997), it also demonstrated that 'leadership still matters' in the Conservative party. The stated intent of the 'modernisers' in the Conservative party in October 1997 was to achieve 'in six months what took them [the Labour party] ten years' (Conservative Party 1997a, Norman, Conference Speech 8 October 1997). Certainly, by February 1998 'democratisation' was an accepted part of the lexicon of the Conservative party. Significantly, 'the launch of *The Fresh Future* was promptly criticised by grassroots Tory critics for concentrating too much power in the leaders hands' (*Guardian*, 17 February 1998). Clearly, such critics perceived the constitutional changes as part of a process of 'democratisation as emasculation'. In the case of the Conservative party it was to be the 'emasculation' of the parliamentary party through simultaneous organisational decentralisation to ordinary members and centralisation to the party leader. In pursuing these changes, Hague took full advantage of the modern paradox, noted above, that a fully democratised party is susceptible to central control. If the theory of party representation rests on two legs: a belief in intra-party democracy and the doctrine of the mandate (Birch 1964: 122), then by 1998 the Conservative party could at least claim to be hopping, on one imperfectly formed leg of 'intra-party democracy', in the general direction prescribed by the theory.

Conservatives and the mandate

As for the other leg of party theory, Birch maintained over thirty years ago that, 'Conservatives have [n]ever embraced the view that a party should go to the electorate with a set of concrete proposals which, if successful, it is thereby mandated to put into practice' (1964: 116). Even here, however, the practice of the party has gradually aligned itself in recent years more to the theory. Thus by 1970, for example, Edward Heath as party leader proclaimed in the Foreword to the Conservative manifesto, *A Better Tomorrow* (Conservative Party 1970): 'This manifesto sets out the policies of the Conservative Party for a better Britain. It provides a programme for a Parliament.' Similarly in 1983, Margaret Thatcher's Foreword proclaimed: 'This manifesto describes the achievements of four years of Conservative government and sets out our plans for our second term' (Conservative Party 1983: 5). Included in those plans were 110 statements prefaced with the words 'we will' (see Topf 1994: 54). By 1992 the number of 'we will' commitments was up to 411 (in excess of the 307 'commitments' in Labour's manifesto). Similarly, in 1997 the number of positive statements, prefaced by the words 'we will', in the Conservative manifesto outnumbered those made in Labour's *New Labour: Because Britain Deserves Better*. The former recorded 252 'commitments' while the latter recorded 182 such statements. Moreover, the manifesto, *You Can Only be Sure With the Conservatives*, specifically highlighted 98 commitments, and concluded with a 'Vision for Britain' which was organised around 25 'pledges for the nation'. Clearly, this constituted more than simply a 'mandate to govern'. In John Major's words it was 'a programme of continuing reform' (Conservative Party 1997b: 2).

Birch's view is also contradicted by daily events in Westminster – by the statements of Conservative MPs who constantly invoke manifesto commitments as legitimation of their policy proposals. In the 1992–7 parliament, party theory was corroborated repeatedly in the statements of leading Conservatives in the House of Commons. Four random ministerial pronouncements from 1995 illustrate this point. William Waldegrave, then Minister of Agriculture, Fisheries and Food, in moving the third reading of the Bill on Agriculture Tenancies, noted that: 'At the last election, the Conservative party gave a clear manifesto commitment to introduce proposals to liberalise agricultural tenancy laws. If passed by the House today, the Bill will deliver that commitment' (HC Debates 19 April 1995, vol. 258: col. 250). Brian Mahwinney, as Secretary of State for Transport, underlined in the debate on rail privatisation that: 'The Government's commitment to 'through ticketing' is absolutely clear: it has been a constant theme of our privatisation proposals. It was in our 1992 election manifesto, and in the White Paper that we published in July of that year; it was reiterated when we introduced our legislation at the beginning of 1993, and it is now in the Railways Act' (HC Debates 18 January 1995, vol. 252: col. 724). Alistair Burt, then Parliamentary Under-Secretary of State for Social Security, reassured Conservative backbenchers that: 'Child benefit remains a cornerstone of our support for families. The commitment was in the manifesto' (HC Debates 1 May 1995, vol. 259: col. 5). Similarly, Andrew Mitchell, then Parliamentary Under-Secretary of State for Social Security, in response to a question about child allowances replied: 'The Government have a clear manifesto commitment to maintaining child benefit as the cornerstone of our policy for all families with children. We will continue to honour this' (HC Debates 19 October 1995, vol. 264: col. 322).

In reverse, what did not constitute a manifesto commitment was made clear in Phil Gallie's (then Conservative MP for Ayr) statement:

> I was elected as a Conservative Member of Parliament and I will support all Conservative manifesto pledges. I do not believe that the increase in VAT was a manifesto pledge. At the last election, I argued against such taxes and feel that I cannot go the whole hog and support the Government on that issue.
>
> (HC Debates 1 December 1994, vol. 250: col. 1,399)

This view certainly contradicts Birch's belief, noted above, that Conservative MPs do not see themselves as being mandated to implement a set of 'concrete proposals' made in the manifesto. It also reveals the practical limits set by the 'party theory of representation' on Party support within Westminster.

The issue of European integration most visibly illustrated these limits in the Conservative party in the 1990s. Thus, for example, Michael Carttiss – one of the eight Conservative MPs from whom the whip was withdrawn after their failure to support the party leader on the second reading of the European Communities (Amendment) Bill in November 1994 – justified his own defiance by invoking the 1992 Conservative party manifesto:

> I could not vote for increasing our contribution in the light of the promise that I made to my electorate. That is why I did not support

the Second Reading of the European Communities (Amendment) Bill although I voted against the Labour amendment, which made good sense. In our manifesto, we pledged: 'We will redouble our efforts to reform the common agricultural policy, and we will stoutly defend the interests of British farmers and consumers'. In addition, we said: 'all member states must live up to their obligations under Community law...we secured agreement that the European Court will be able to fine any member state which fails to do so'. Those are not my words; they are quoted from page 3 of the party manifesto....There should be cries not for party unity, but for sticking to the pledges upon which we were all elected in 1992.

(HC Debates 19 December 1994, vol. 251: cols 1,440–1)

Equally significantly, John Major as Prime Minister castigated the Euro-rebels for *not* supporting manifesto commitments. In a speech in Essen, he said: 'I hope over the months to come they will show they are Conservatives [and] that they will support the Conservative Government, they will defend Conservative policy, they will defend the manifesto on which they and I were elected' (quoted HC Debates 19 December 1994, vol. 251: col. 1,440)

Conclusion

Despite the absence of identifiable 'theorists' of party representation, both major parties in the late 1990s clearly subscribe to the basic tenets of that theory: 'intra-party democracy' and the 'mandate'. In placing the emphasis upon 'democratisation', modernisers within both parties have achieved a degree of organisational symmetry in their respective parties unthinkable less than a decade before. Although organisational differences still manifest themselves in, for example, the role of conference and the electoral process for the party leader, nonetheless, the rhetoric deployed in both parties – that 'members matter' – underscores a broad-ranging commitment to intra-party democratisation. That this commitment is not necessarily altruistic is reflected in the accusations from activists and grass-roots members in both parties that the practical result of reorganisation has been a centralisation of power in the hands of the respective party leaders. Webb's (1994: 120) phrase 'democratisation as emasculation' neatly captures this activist concern and also serves to locate the process of reform within a broader European trend in party organisation.

If there has been a convergence in party organisational forms in the 1990s, there has also been a marked emphasis by both parties in office upon the importance of the manifesto and the mandate derived from electoral success. This convergence has brought the Conservative party more into line with the party theory outlined by Birch over thirty years ago and its associated doctrines of the mandate and of intra-party democracy. Significantly, both parties invoke a theory of representation to justify the practice of disciplined party government. But the precise meaning of the theory has been open to interpretation in both parties throughout their respective histories. If an existing practice of representation – of delegation within the trade unions – came to be articulated as the theory of representation in the infant Labour party; then the 'theory', so defined, subsequently served as a touchstone by which later practice could be assessed. Hence, the 'meaning' of representation has always been an integral part of the 'meaning' and the definition of the purpose of the Labour party itself. While the Conservative party has been less introspective about its purpose, and traditionally sceptical of the role of the mass membership, nonetheless, it has pragmatically subscribed to the notion of the mandate, including specific manifesto pledges, and has recently accommodated itself, with a vengeance, to 'intra-party democracy'.

The representational practice of both major British parties now conforms with the basic outline of 'party theory' provided by Birch. The irony is that the tenets of the theory have moved away from collectivist notions of participation and associational forms of organisation within parties, to individualistic conceptions of One Member One Vote. Critics argue that in this process the organisational balance has been tipped in favour of the party leaderships. The charge is that the rhetoric of 'democratisation' within the parties has been used to reverse the flow of decision making power between leaders and party members from that initially stipulated in the original Labour theory of 'intra-party democracy'. Hence, the form of party representation remains but its substance has changed.

5 Representation of interests in Westminster

A recurrent theme of this book is that 'theory' often reflects the political practice of representation at any given time. Indeed, political practice might usefully be likened to geological sedimentary layers stacked-up on top of each other with veins of 'theory' – indicating waves, rifts and fissures – permeating successive deposits of practice. One notable feature of the 'geology' of British representative practice since medieval times has been the 'representation of interests'. If, as argued in Chapter 1, representation is conceived in part as the legitimation of the power of decision making, then material or functional interests were long regarded as the source of that legitimation in British politics. Only with the rise of the mass franchise and the emphasis upon legitimation derived from 'the people' was the primary focus of representation redirected away from the representation of 'particular interests' to the 'general will'. Yet, in practice, the former mode of representation continued alongside the latter. On the one side, this allowed proponents to advance the case that the representation of specific material interests enhanced the determination of the general/national interest. On the other side, it allowed opponents to advance the counter case – that the general interest was undermined by the *specific* representation of functional interests.

At its heart, this was a debate as much about practice as theory. It was about the accommodation of different representative practices to prevailing theories and vice versa. The starting point of the debate was that there was nothing improper in an explicit linkage between specific material interests and representatives in parliament. Its recent end-point, in the mid-1990s, entailed accusations of parliamentary 'sleaze', heightened public disquiet about the representation of material interests, and enforced regulation of the linkages between MPs and 'outside interests'. In between times, there was a complex and changing debate about the interconnections between the nature of 'interests' and the nature of 'representation'.

Starting point: a brief history of interest representation in the House of Commons

> It is usually assumed by writers upon constitutional matters that the British House of Commons is an institution built upon geographical areas....However, any correct appreciation of the political process necessarily involves a realistic analysis of political institutions. A mere clinging to theories, even though these are hoary with age, does not bring us one step nearer our goal. It may be the intention to set up a political organ which represents men as citizens; in practice the House of Commons…is a body in which property and function are represented.
>
> (Thomas 1939: 1)

This statement reflects the historical fact that the House of Commons accepted from medieval times, that interests – most particularly propertied interests – had the right to be represented in parliament (Beer 1969: 6–32; Alderman 1984: 6–16; Judge 1993: 7–27). Thus, even before parliaments were convened on a regular basis, and before the principle of the sovereignty of the 'crown in parliament' had been secured (*de facto* at least by 1603 (see Loades 1997: 16)), MPs were developing a role not only in petitioning against malpractices of government but also in promoting local economic interests. Certainly by the time of the Reformation Parliament in the sixteenth century the processing of legislation dealing with economic and social development was an accepted function of parliament. The corollaries of this were that the 'majority of members never took their noses off that humdrum grindstone' and 'private lobbying groups took up an increasing proportion of session time' (Loades 1997: 46). Significant numbers of private bills were promoted, and opposed, on behalf of boroughs, crafts, companies and individuals, often in the context of intensive lobbying. This increased role in the 'low politics' of the Tudor period underpinned the more portentous demand of MPs – made on the basis of the Commons' representative nature – to secure an entitlement to advise the monarch on matters of 'high politics'.

Yet 'low politics' mattered for economic interests outside parliament, to the extent that organisations would often provide expenses for MPs to assist in the introduction of private legislation to promote their interests. The City of London provides a very clear example of a corporate body that was well organised and active in the promotion of its interests at this time. From the fifteenth century onwards, it had a paid agent to look after its interests in parliament, and provided 'money for lobbying, briefing, and

even feeing Members of Parliament' (Beer 1969: 7). However, the dominant interest at the time, which was to remain so well into the nineteenth
century, was that of 'land'. Representation of the 'landed interest' in
parliament took several forms: by Lords who were great landowners, by
MPs who were substantial landowners but not part of the aristocracy, and
by MPs who had 'patrons'. Indeed, it is estimated that half of all MPs at
the end of the eighteenth century were there because of the support of
patrons (Evans 1996: 18). These members were effectively 'sponsored
MPs'. They had their election expenses paid as well as receiving other
forms of assistance in return for advancing the interests of their patrons.
The clear expectation was that if an MP failed to promote the interests of
his patron he would be expected to resign. Butt summarises the position
thus: 'A member was honourably bound to pursue a policy which his
patron...approved and much of the private legislation was on behalf of
outside interests with which the Member was personally linked' (1969: 56).
It is no surprise to find, therefore, that in a period when some three-quar-
ters of MPs had land as their primary economic interest, there was a close
and transparent connection between the enclosure movement and 'interested' MPs in the House of Commons (Beer 1969: 27).

Other blocs of MPs also gradually coalesced to promote the cause of
developing economic interests. 'New men' from trade, commerce and,
eventually, manufacturing were able to buy themselves into parliament and
so promote their interests. Thus, for example, from the seventeenth
century on, merchants, most notably in the corporate form of the East and
West India Companies, pressed for legislation to protect their special interests. So successful were they that by the eighteenth century complaints
were frequently voiced about 'the growing influence of oceanic mercantile
interests in parliament, specifically of "nabobs", men who had made their
fortunes trading with India and returned to buy up pocket boroughs (seats
where the representation was effectively controlled)' (Black 1993: 21).

In parallel, the canal interest, and later the railway and shipping interests, promoted their interests to great effect through the direct
representation of MPs in parliament. Invariably such MPs were themselves
members of the interests they defended. In this manner, the legislative
framework of the Industrial Revolution in Britain came to be fuelled not
by any grand design of government but out of the clash of local interests
in parliament (see Black 1993: 39; Walkland 1968: 13–14). Cumulatively
great social and economic changes were effected in piecemeal fashion by
private legislation introduced on behalf of specific economic interests. The
increased importance of private legislation can be gauged from the simple
statistics that in 1760 68 private bills were passed by the Commons, but by
1800 the number had grown to 210 (Black 1993: 77). As Walkland points

out: 'Private Bill procedure gave the country enclosures of agricultural land, railways, docks and harbours, river improvements, water supplies, and many local authority services' (1968: 13). In this process there was a clear expectation that those best qualified to decide on these matters were MPs 'who had some personal local or professional knowledge of the matter, and who represented interests likely to be affected. It was held to be not only a duty, but a right of such members to speak and to vote in committee on matters on which, through local or personal interest, they had special knowledge and decided, if biased, views' (Millar cited Beer 1969: 26). There was no doubt that the House of Commons represented the various kinds of property effectively, if not in equal proportions. There was equally no doubt that there was seen to be nothing wrong or scandalous about such 'interested' representation. Indeed, it was held to be in accord with what Beer calls the 'Old Whig theory of interest representation' (1969: 28).

Theories of interest

Burke and the 'old Whig' theory of interest representation

As we saw in Chapter 3, the essence of Burke's views on parliamentary representation was that parliament provided a forum in which discrete and identifiable interests could be voiced by MPs and reconciled with one another to produce a common good. The focus of the discussion in Chapter 3 was upon how representation allowed for the discovery of the national interest through a complex process of parliamentary deliberation. An essential part of that discussion was how the 'national interest' was conceived as the aggregation of the objective economic interests represented in localities; and how parliament alone was deemed capable of discovering the national interest through the articulation of constituency interests. It was held that, because constituents were not present in parliament during these discussions, they could not know what the national interest was at any given time. Burke believed that in the absence of this wider knowledge derived from parliamentary deliberation the represented should not seek to bind their representatives to their own opinions. The representative's primary duty to their constituents was thus conceived as 'a devotion to their interests rather than to their opinions'. From this premise Burke maintained that constituents should not seek to enforce their own policy preferences on their MPs but, through the medium of elections, could expect to assess the efficacy of representation and to decide how far constituency economic interests had been protected. In sum, this explains how Burke came to conceive of the role of the representative as that of a 'trustee' who should exercise independent judgement in identifying the common good. What concerns us here, however, is how Burke conceived of 'interest' and how 'interests' find representation in parliament.

Virtual representation

Burke tends to argue that constituency interests are objective, specific and largely economic. Moreover, each locality is seen to have a single pervasive interest (Pitkin 1967: 174). Individual constituencies are thus broadly defined in terms of a pre-eminent economic interest and their prosperity is correlated closely with the promotion of that interest. In effect this was simply a reflection of the practice of representation described above, where members of the Commons were returned by small, economically powerful local electorates. In this context it made sense to associate specific constituencies with specific interests – whether mining, agriculture, trading, shipping, or some other commercial interest. For this reason Burke rarely saw 'interest' linked to specific individuals. Indeed, as seen in Chapter 3, he was fundamentally opposed to the representation of 'individuals' and maintained that individual opinion, especially when aggregated into 'public opinion', was invariably misguided.

Since it is 'interest' that is represented and not individuals, Burke is able to argue that it is not necessary for all groups of people, aggregated into constituencies, to elect an MP – as long as their 'interest' is represented in parliament. This notion revolves around a distinction between 'actual' and 'virtual' representation. Actual representation entails electors voting directly for an MP to represent their constituency interest. Virtual representation on the other hand is where

> there is a communion of interests and a sympathy in feelings and desires between those who act in the name of any description of people and the people in whose name they act, though the trustees are not actually chosen by them.
>
> (Burke [1792] 1801: 360)

In this view, as long as there are representatives from other constituencies with similar commercial, agricultural, or manufacturing interests, the interests of all other localities with these same interests could find representation in parliament – even though those localities were not directly represented therein.

Virtual representation is thus based on a commonality between a representative and an 'interest', rather than on the actual choice of a representative for a specific constituency. Even so, virtual representation must have some basis in direct representation. In Burke's words: 'The Member must have some relation to the constituents' (Burke [1792] 1801: 360). Hence, some MPs have to be elected by, and for, some constituencies. Pitkin makes this point through example: 'Birmingham is virtually represented in...parliament because both it and Bristol are of the trading interest. Bristol sees to it that a representative of the trading interest is sent to Parliament, and Birmingham thus has its spokesman' (1967: 178). In which case it is immaterial to Burke whether every commercial city is represented at Westminster just so long as some commercial cities are represented.

Burke's view of representation was clearly influenced by representative practice in the eighteenth century and was a defensible position for a Whig to adopt, as it simultaneously protected the existing narrow geographical franchise (which effectively excluded rapidly developing urban areas from parliamentary representation) as well as challenging the radical and liberal ideas that 'individuals' should be the basis of representation. The fact that many of the new industrial cities had no representatives in parliament was not a matter of concern: they were represented 'virtually'.

J.S. Mill and 'sinister interests'

In the 1820s James Mill attacked the Whig idea of virtual representation as a recipe for 'misgovernment, corruption, and the triumph of the aristocratic or 'sinister interests' of the few over the many' (Ball 1992: xx). 'Sinister interests' were associated in James Mill's thought with the selfish interests of a 'class' – a group of people united by shared, usually economic, interests. Similarly, his son, John Stuart Mill attacked aristocratic and monarchical government on the grounds that their interest is to 'assume to themselves an endless variety of unjust privileges, sometimes benefiting their pockets at the expense of the people, sometimes merely to exalt them above others' ([1861] 1910: 249). If these 'evils' were 'superabundantly evident in the case of a monarchy or an aristocracy;...it is sometimes rather gratuitously assumed that the same kind of injurious influences do not operate in a democracy' ([1861] 1910: 249). But Mill was at pains to point out that:

> One of the greatest dangers,...of democracy, as of all other forms of government, lies in the sinister interest of the holders of power: it is the danger of class legislation: of government intended for...the immediate benefit of the dominant class, to the lasting detriment of the whole.
>
> ([1861] 1910: 254)

A class is defined as 'any number of persons who have the same sinister interest – that is, whose direct and apparent interest points towards the same description of bad measures' ([1861] 1910: 254–5). While conceiving of 'class' primarily in socioeconomic terms – 'labourers on the one hand, employers of labour on the other' ([1861] 1910: 255) – Mill also allows for a plurality of other 'various sectional interests' ([1861] 1910: 256; see Thompson 1976: 118; Judge 1990a: 22). His prime concern in advancing the cause of representative government was thus to ensure that 'it ought not to allow any of the various sectional interests to be so powerful as to be capable of prevailing against truth and justice and the other sectional interests combined' ([1861] 1910: 256). The great virtue of representative government, therefore, is that it allows 'the whole people, or some numerous portion of them, [to] exercise through deputies periodically elected by themselves the ultimate controlling power' ([1861] 1910: 228). Manifestly this was an attack on the practice of representation in mid-nineteenth century Britain, on the limited franchise, and on the Whig notion of virtual representation.

While promoting the extension of the franchise, and the defensive idea of 'individual interests' (whereby the individual was deemed to be the best judge of his or her interests), Mill was also willing to accept a legitimate realm for the representation of material interest in parliament. This acceptance is most explicit when Mill considers schemes for electoral reform. Thus, in supporting Thomas Hare's proposals for a voting system approximating to the single transferable vote, he notes how 'it unites the good points of class representation and the good points of numerical representation' ([1861] 1910: 275). In noting the objections of the opponents to franchise reform, Mill explicitly concedes a continuing role for the 'representation of interests' in the reformed Commons:

> Not many years ago it was the favourite argument in support of the then existing system of representation, that under it all 'interests' or 'classes' were represented. *And certainly, all interests or classes of any importance ought to be represented, that is ought to have spokesmen, or advocates, in Parliament.* But from thence it was argued that a system ought to be supported which gave to the partial interests not advocates merely, but the tribunal itself. Now behold the change. Mr Hare's system makes it impossible for partial interests to have the command of the tribunal, but it ensures them advocates, and for doing even this it is reproached.
> (Mill [1861] 1910: 274–5, emphasis added)

Ultimately, while opposed to the promotion of 'sinister interests', Mill acknowledged the legitimate advocacy of 'partial interests' in parliamentary deliberations upon public policy. What had to be guarded against, however, was the domination of these interests over those of a general, wider public interest.

In this manner Mill sought to resolve the issue of the 'representation of interest' within a broader theory of representative government. Not surprisingly, attempts to resolve this issue have featured in the practice of parliamentary representation throughout the late-nineteenth and twentieth centuries.

The practice of interest representation

The gradual arrival of 'democracy', with successive extensions of the franchise in the late-nineteenth century, did not see the departure of interest representation from the Commons. Instead, 'interested MPs' now had to be more sensitive to attune their activities to the changing political framework provided by 'public opinion', mass political parties, and party government. A good example of the changed context of interest representation is provided in the activities of 'the railway interest' in the nineteenth century.

Railways were big business, accounting for almost a quarter of the expansion of national income between 1840 and 1865 (Evans 1996: 125). The parliamentary strength of this interest can be gauged from the numbers of MPs who had directorships in railway companies: 145 in 1841, 179 in 1867, and 90 in 1886 (Beer 1969: 65). Of these, a hard core of MPs actively promoted private legislation to create the necessary railway infrastructure. From a standing start in 1825, with the opening of the Stockton to Darlington railway, over 13,000 miles of track had been laid within fifty years, each new line requiring parliamentary authorisation. In the fifty years after 1830 some 4,000 private railway bills passed through Westminster. Significant sums of money were expended by railway companies on 'parliamentary expenses' – primarily for lobbying. For example, the passage of legislation authorising the Liverpool and Manchester Railway between 1824–6 cost some £80,000 in parliamentary expenses, and the promoters of the Great Western Railway bill spent £40,000 in seeking the support of MPs – unsuccessfully as it transpired (Beer 1969: 66).

Concern about the activities of interested railway MPs prompted regulation of their activities in the House of Commons. Thus in 1844 the House required members serving on private bill committees dealing with competing railway lines to sign declarations of non-interest. In the same year, MPs with direct pecuniary interests in a private bill were forbidden from voting in committee on that legislation. In 1855 the House decided further to abolish local representation on opposed private bill committees.

Subsequently, each member dealing with an opposed private bill was required to sign a declaration that neither he nor his constituents respectively had a personal or constituency interest in the bill.

Gradually, the number of private bills decreased as the number of public bills increased. In the specific case of the railways, governments began to seek through general public acts a more orderly development of railway policy to take account of the interests of consumers as well as of the railway companies themselves (Beer 1969: 67–8). More broadly in the second-half of the nineteenth century, governments were increasingly pressed into introducing public bills to regulate economic and social relations in a rapidly industrialising state. As such, public bills came to 'engage almost the entire attention of an increasingly representative parliament' (Walkland 1968: 16). As government became more interventionist and regulatory so more organisations developed to defend or promote their interests in the face of state activity. By the mid-1880s, therefore, numerous organisations were readily identifiable as representing the commercial interests of traders, manufacturers and agriculturalists; or the interests of professions; or the promotion of 'worthy causes' (see Beer 1969: 67–8; Alderman 1984: 8–14; Judge 1990a: 12–13). A common characteristic of these diverse groups was that they often maintained close links with MPs in the Commons. In this specific sense they all had their own 'interested' MPs – whose 'interest' stemmed from either direct financial, commercial or occupational involvement, or through membership of a profession, or support for some 'cause', or other form of 'sponsorship' – most visibly that by trade unions. While the organisation of functional groups beyond Westminster was to have significant consequences for the representation of interests in public policy making (see Chapter 6), our concern here is simply to monitor how MPs have continued to represent interests within the Commons, and how they have sought to reconcile this mode of representation with established notions of representation associated with 'trusteeship'.

Interests and influence

Although the representation of 'interests' in parliament has been a recurring feature throughout the history of representative government in Britain a distinction has traditionally been made between 'proper' and 'improper' influence associated with outside interests. In practice, the reconciliation of interest representation with the representation of geographical constituencies has been left largely to the personal judgement of individual MPs (in accordance with parliamentary privilege). However, MPs have been assisted in making this judgement by at least three resolutions of the House of Commons. In 1695 it was resolved that:

the offer of any money, or other advantage, to any Member of Parliament for promoting of any matter whatsoever depending, or to be transacted in Parliament, is high crime and misdemeanour and tends to the subversion of the English Constitution.

(CJ 11 1693–97: 331 cited HC 108 1991: x)

In the same tradition of independence the House of Commons further resolved in 1858 that:

it is contrary to the usage and derogatory to the dignity of this House that any of its Members should bring forward, promote or advocate in this House any proceeding or measure in which he may have acted or been concerned for or in consideration of any pecuniary fee or reward.

(Erskine May 1989: 120)

More recently the resolution of 1947 held that:

it is inconsistent with the dignity of the House, with the duty of a Member to his constituents, and with the maintenance of the privilege of freedom of speech, for any Member of this House to enter into a contractual agreement with an outside body, controlling or limiting the Member's complete independence and freedom of action in Parliament or stipulating that he shall act in any way as the representative of such outside body in regard of any matters transacted in Parliament; the duty of a Member being to his constituents and to the country as a whole, rather than to any particular section thereof.

(CJ 202 1946–7: 310 in HC 108 1991: x)

Each of these resolutions was passed to deal with specific problems at the time – a bribe to the Speaker by the City of London in connection with the passage of a bill in 1695, restriction of the activities of barristers in 1858 and prevention of an attempt to instruct an MP by a trade union in 1947 – but each resolution had a broader significance in regulating the representation of outside interests. Significantly, none of the resolutions adopted by the House banned outright the payment of MPs to represent outside interests. In fact, the resolutions leave open the possibility that MPs may enter into contractual relationships with outside bodies which do not limit their freedom of action in the Commons. Equally, they do not prohibit MPs from entering into a binding obligation to advise an outside client on parliamentary matters. Nor do they prevent MPs from *voluntarily* promoting the interest of an outside organisation – an MP may have no contractual or direct pecuniary relationship with an outside interest yet still lobby on behalf of that sectional interest in parliament.

The advantages of interest representation

There is a basic consensus that an MP should maintain contact with 'interests' beyond Westminster (and by implication beyond their party and the representation of opinion in their constituency). This consensus is built upon two propositions: first that such contact enhances the efficacy of decision making, and; second, that it is compatible with established conceptions of representation in Britain. In the first case, even critics of the paid advocacy of outside interests in Westminster, willingly concede that 'Members of Parliament having outside jobs and interests...adds to the experience and authority of the House ' (Peter Shore, HC Debates 18 May 1995, vol. 260: col. 510); and that 'Parliament is helped by the direct knowledge that Members can bring to it from their personal involvement with the outside world' (Robert Maclennan, HC Debates 18 May 1995, vol. 260: col. 524). Other MPs maintain that: 'we will do this House and the country a grave disservice by any suggestion that all outside interests should be banned' (Sainsbury, HC Debates 6 November 1995, vol. 265: col. 645). Yet such a complete ban has not been contemplated seriously in any recent discussion of the representation of interests in the Commons.

Part of the defence of the 'interested MP' is that 'full-time' MPs would lead a disembodied existence cut off from the immediate daily concerns of their constituents and the wider country as a whole. This point is exemplified in Tony Newton's statement to the Nolan Committee:

> None of us would gain from a House of Commons made up of 651 people who were completely cut off from the rest of life, except on the basis of representations they received rather than of experience of contacts they continued to have in various walks of life.
>
> (Cm 2850-I 1995: 23)

But this is not a view held exclusively by MPs, academics such as Hugh Berrington (1995: 443) have argued that there would be a 'crucial defect' in a chamber consisting solely of full-timers and that is 'the cast of mind of such members'. By this Berrington means that the sheer mechanics of politics 'will assume a reality in the minds of such members far distant from the outlook of their constituents'. What makes this prospect even more daunting for many is the rise of the 'career politician', who before entering the Commons served as party researcher, special adviser, or general party apparatchik or political consultant and so had only limited experience outside of politics. Dame Angela Rumbold, Conservative Deputy party chairperson with responsibility for candidate selection for the 1997 election, characterised such candidates as political 'clones' (Criddle 1997: 195). Given this development, proponents of the continued representation of outside interests by MPs believe that it mitigates the effects of the trend towards representation by full-time, career politicians.

The nature of interests

If it is conceded that there is a case for the representation of outside interests, questions then arise about the nature of the interests to be represented, and how these interests are to be represented. At this point 'microcosmic' notions of representation are frequently invoked to legitimate a role for continued interest representation in the Commons. If interest representation allows for 'informed and equally weighted argument' then even reform groups such as Charter 88 would be willing to countenance its continuance (Power 1997). But, as Chapter 2 revealed, the Commons has never been a microcosm of the wider British social structure, let alone of economic interests. Indeed, if the pre-entry occupation of MPs is taken as one indicator of the breadth of interest 'represented' in the House, then it is apparent that the professions – most particularly the legal and educational professions – and business have dominated post-war parliaments. In particular, as manufacturing industry declined rapidly in the 1980s, there was a pervasive feeling that the limited number of MPs with direct experience of manufacturing contributed to a lack of understanding within Westminster of the practical requirements of productive industry (see Judge 1990a: 226–8). More generally, manual occupations have traditionally been under-represented in the House, and after the 1997 general election less than 10 per cent of MPs came from manual backgrounds. This decline of working class representation was symbolised most vividly in the return of only 12 miners in 1997, down in numbers from 39 in 1945. The danger in this pattern is that the lack of occupational proportionality in the House has given the 'talking classes' 'too big a share in controlling our destinies, by comparison with the people who *do* things instead of holding forth about them' (Ross 1948: 77, original emphasis).

If the disproportionality of the pre-entry occupational experience of MPs gives rise to concern, these concerns are only heightened by examining the post-entry occupational profiles of MPs. A general problem is captured in the comments of one experienced MP:

> For all that an MP might bring knowledge [from his or her former occupation] into the House when [s]he is first elected such knowledge

is, if you like, 'date stamped' – it can become stale, even outdated as technology advances or as the competitive environment changes. In which case we need to be kept up-to-date on what's happening in the field.

(quoted in Judge 1990a: 232)

One way of 'keeping up to date' is for MPs to continue with their previous occupations in parallel with the performance of their parliamentary duties. The capacity to do so, however, is restricted mainly to those occupations which can be fitted around the parliamentary day – traditionally law and business. Moreover, as Bob Cryer MP pointed out, it was difficult to find

any instance of an MP having, let us say, manual jobs, where they go out in order to obtain expertise in cleaning out wards in a hospital for elderly people or the mentally handicapped, or working on an engineering shop floor to gain some knowledge of manufacturing industry.

(HC 326 1992: 4 para 11)

Linkages between MPs and outside interests

Beyond direct engagement in an occupation there are, however, a series of other linkage mechanisms whereby MPs can be kept informed of developments affecting specific interests. There is, for example, a long history of MPs being appointed as non-executive directors of companies. Unpaid directorships have not aroused great controversy. Neither has much heat been generated by MPs holding other honorary appointments for commercial organisations, charities or 'cause' groups. A number of examples of such appointments are provided in the October 1997 Register of Members' Interests: in the first category, for instance, John Butterfill was listed as Honorary President of European Property Associations; Clive Efford as a member of the London Taxi Board, which represents the licensed taxi trade in London, and John Gunnell as Honorary President of both the Yorkshire and Humberside Development Association and the North of England Regional Consortium. In the second category, Tom Fox was listed as parliamentary adviser to the Ancient Order of Foresters Friendly Society, Peter Emery as a Trustee of the National Asthma Campaign, and Llin Golding as a Trustee of the NSPCC, SAFE (a children's charity) and Second Chance. In the third category, Vernon Coaker listed his membership of the League Against Cruel Sports and Friends of the Earth; Michael Colvin listed membership of National Rifle Association, Edward O'Hara served as Vice-Chairman of the National

Wild Flower Club, and Chris Pond as Honorary Associate Director of the Low Pay Unit. MPs with unremunerated links to outside groups usually declare their interest when speaking in debate of direct relevance to the outside organisation.

Much more heat and concern has been generated by MPs holding remunerated directorships. Over a century ago the *Economist* noted: 'Notoriously, men are often placed upon boards of directors simply and solely because they are Members of Parliament and are, therefore, believed to be able to exercise useful influence' (18 April 1896). In October 1997, 78 MPs held 148 remunerated directorships (in 1992, 287 director-ships were held by 135 Conservative MPs alone). This prompts the question of why MPs 'need to be on the board of several companies to have experience of the real world. And it does not explain why they need to be paid jobs' (Hollingsworth 1991: 161). The conventional response is that there is no impropriety in MPs acting as paid directors, as the nature of the contractual linkage is openly declared both in individual company reports and in the Register of Members' Interests in the House of Commons (see pp. 116–19). Some go further and maintain that any suggestion that MPs can be 'bought' by outside interests in this manner is 'nonsense' (Berry 1993: 24).

Equally, on the other side of industry, it has traditionally been deemed to be 'nonsense' that MPs sponsored by trade unions could be 'bought' by the small financial sums involved in such a relationship. As Roy Hattersley informed the Nolan Committee:

> I do not believe that the small sums, which they [trade unions] provide to subsidise some MPs' constituency activities and re-election, are a threat to democracy....If you take the obvious case, the archetypal trade union MP, Mr Dennis Skinner...fairly obviously [his] loyalty to the miners is hardly anything to do with £500 a year. It is to do with his background, beliefs, emotions and convictions.
>
> (Cm 2850-II 1995: 19–21 para 99, 110)

Before the introduction of parliamentary salaries in 1911, trade unions did assist individual MPs directly by making contributions towards their electoral expenses and providing maintenance payments. However, since 1933, the Labour party and the unions have regulated sponsorship arrangements under the 'Hastings Agreement'. This agreement set a maximum limit on a trade union's contributions to the election expenses of a sponsored candidate, as well as to contributions made to the constituency party, and to the salary of a full time agent in that constituency. Before the system was abandoned in 1996 the respective totals were 80 per cent of a candidate's election expenses; £600 or £750 in total to a constituency party (depending on the nature of the constituency); and no more than 70 per cent of an agent's salary. The important point to note is that under this arrangement no payment was made to an MP directly by the trade union.

Indeed, it was the indirect nature of this association which led Labour MPs to distinguish trade union sponsorship from other forms of sponsorship. Conservative MPs have been less convinced by this distinction and have persistently drawn direct parallels with other forms of sponsorship. For example, Nigel Evans, Conservative MP for Ribble Valley, pointed out in the House on 6 November 1995 that:

> Some 167 Opposition Members are sponsored by single-interest groups such as trade unions. Earlier this year, I participated in a debate on the railways. Only five Opposition Members were present, all of whom were sponsored by railway trade unions.
>
> (HC Debates 6 November 1995, vol. 265: col. 625)

Reflected in this statement was the common assumption that sponsored MPs would speak for the functional interests of their unions.

In practice, however, this linkage has never been so clear cut and so direct. Historically, one complication arose from the fact that, given the nature of many of the safe Labour seats for which trade union MPs sat, the specific functional concerns of the sponsoring trade union tended to merge with the wider concerns of the constituency. This was most clearly the case with area-specific industries such as coalmining and shipbuilding. In these circumstances, the conjunction of relatively homogeneous sectoral and territorial interests allowed sponsored MPs to promote the functional interests of their unions while simultaneously promoting the interests of their constituencies. However, expectations as to what constituted 'typical' behaviour on the part of sponsored MPs was further complicated by the growing practice of some trade unions, most notably the TGWU and UNISON, to extend sponsorship to sitting MPs without a prior occupational link with the union. In 1992 143 sponsored MPs were returned to the Labour benches, most of whom had no direct pre-entry occupational link with their sponsoring trade union. The last cohort of MPs sponsored under the Hastings Agreement was thus characterised by the 'parliamentarist' ambitions of their sponsoring unions – the achievement of frontbench status by their sponsored Members – rather than 'actual representation' of industrial experience and skills in the House (the distinction between 'parliamentarist' and 'actualist' representation is made by Ellis and Johnson 1974). Effectively, these unions sought to 'co-opt' candidates who possessed the general attributes of educational attainment, oratorical skills and a dynamic image to pursue a successful parliamentary career. In 'backing winners' and in choosing 'careerists' the unions proved willing to sever the link between first-hand occupational experience and parliamentary representation of the 'labour interest'.

In so doing, the trade unions perhaps reaped the whirlwind of their own ambition. After 1992 the 'parliamentarist' strategy was so successful that all but one of Labour's frontbench spokespersons were trade union sponsored MPs, including successive party leaders John Smith and Tony Blair. Ironically, it was precisely this new leadership which sought a decoupling of the Labour party from the wider trade union movement (see Chapter 4). One step towards this separation was the formal discontinuance of the sponsorship of individual MPs by trade unions. A move which led Ann Taylor to declare in July 1996 that 'there is no such thing as a sponsored Member of Parliament' (HC Debates 24 July 1996, vol. 282: col. 398). Indeed, after the ending of the Hastings Agreement the initial intention was for unions to continue to contribute to election expenses, but through a central financial pool managed by the party. This would enable the party to redirect election contributions towards local parties in marginal constituencies rather than to individual candidates in safe seats. As a result, the link between TU sponsors and individual Labour candidates was to be broken.

Another objective of the revised funding arrangement, however, was to remove the 'natural' suspicion, recorded in the Nolan Report, that sponsorship gave rise 'to feelings of obligation which have the potential to influence the Member's conduct in the House' (Cm 2850-I 1995: 22). Nonetheless, some unions continued to make donations linked to the promotion of particular candidates in particular constituencies at the general election of 1997. As a result, 35 Labour MPs recorded in the 1997 Register of Members' Interests that they had received contributions in excess of 25 per cent of their election expenses from a trade union. Five Labour MPs also recorded that their constituency party had received trade union donations. However, the assumption of the Parliamentary Commissioner for Standards (HC 181 1997) was that by the next election all financial support from the unions would be paid into the central party pool. In this manner, the direct link between donor trade union and individual parliamentary candidate would be broken and, hence, the contribution would no longer be registerable under the House's rules.

'Instructions' and advocacy

Trade union sponsorship

The indirect nature of the linkage between sponsoring union and spon-sored MP, in combination with the protection afforded by the resolutions of the Commons, have tended to militate against unions seeking overtly to 'instruct' 'their MPs' as to their conduct in the House of Commons. As noted above, the 1947 resolution defining the limits of propriety in the relationship between MPs and sponsoring organisations was prompted by the specific case of W.J. Brown. The issue at stake in that case was that Brown, who acted as the paid Political General Secretary of the Civil Service Clerical Association, had his sponsorship terminated following a disagreement with the Association's Executive Committee. The Committee of Privileges was asked to rule on the matter, and reported that, while it accepted the legitimacy of sponsoring arrangements, and even that action 'calculated and intended to bring pressure on a member to take or refrain from taking a particular course' was not in itself a breach of privilege, nonetheless, sponsorships or other such arrangements were not to be used 'to seek to control the conduct of a Member or to punish him for what he has done as a Member' (HC 118 1947: paras 11–15).

Following the Brown case, trade union leaders were particularly anxious not to be seen to be attaching any sanctions to sponsorship arrangements with MPs, and, in 1967, the TUC made it clear that they accepted that 'the responsibility of a Member of Parliament is primarily to his party and his constituents' (quoted in Minkin 1992: 261). However, the subsequent actions of the Yorkshire Area of the NUM revealed that not all sections of the union movement fully subscribed to the TUC's view. For example, in June 1975 the Yorkshire Area Council passed a resolution which was openly critical of five Yorkshire NUM MPs who had campaigned, against union policy, for continued membership of the European Community. The resolution threatened a withdrawal of sponsorship if an MP infringed 'guidelines' which stipulated: 'no Miners MP shall vote or speak against Union policy on any issue which affects the coal mining industry...or actively campaign or work against Union policy on any other major issue' (HC 634 1975: vii). The NUM's national leadership was quick to dissociate itself from the Yorkshire Area's actions by nullifying the resolution and assuring the Privileges Committee that 'this Union would never seek to interfere with the freedom of speech or actions of Members of Parliament' (HC 634 1975: v). Nonetheless, the Committee found that the resolution had 'constituted a serious contempt, which represented a continuing threat to Members' freedom of speech and action' (HC 634 1975: iv).

In December 1990 the issue of the 1975 'guidelines' re-emerged. On this occasion, a copy of the guidelines was sent by the General Secretary of the Yorkshire Area Council to Kevin Barron (NUM sponsored candidate for Rother Valley). In an accompanying letter Barron was reminded that: 'the policy of the Yorkshire Area Council regarding sponsored Members…is clear and enclosed for your information'. The event that triggered this correspondence was Barron's decision to publicise, against the wishes of the Area Council, the critical findings of the Lightman Report (an enquiry into the use of NUM funds during the 1984–5 miners' strike). In October 1991 the Privileges Committee ruled that the actions of the Area Council: 'bore a clear implication of a threat to Mr Barron's freedom of speech in Parliament', but equally that the union was free to withdraw its sponsorship. While noting that the sending of the guidelines was in itself an 'ill-considered and empty' threat (as they had already been withdrawn by the national union in 1975), the Committee took the opportunity to reiterate the fundamental point that sponsorship should not be used to seek to control MPs (HC 420 1991: v).

Such explicit attempts to control the actions of MPs are atypical, however. Traditionally, conflicts of opinion between sponsored MP and sponsoring union have been resolved in favour of the MP (see Muller 1977). Confirmation that this tradition continued in the 1990s was willingly provided to the Nolan Committee by Roy Hattersley and Stuart Bell. Hattersley reassured the Committee:

> I have never had any pressure brought to bear on me; I have had recommendations about what I should do but if you take an issue very sensitive to USDAW, Sunday trading, to which USDAW are profoundly opposed and to which I was strongly in favour, there was no attempt to be unpleasant to me or threaten me about that.
>
> (Cm 2850-II 1995: 20–1)

Similarly, Stuart Bell recalled that his sponsoring union, the GMB,

> were in favour of Sunday trading and I was opposed to it; I spoke and voted accordingly. Lately, the union was opposed to the abolition of Cleveland County Council, which I felt very strongly about and I spoke in favour of abolition. On neither occasion did my union ever suggest to me that this was improper conduct…I certainly felt no inhibition about the action I would take, nor would I, under any circumstances.
>
> (Cm 2850-II 1995: 135)

Advocacy versus advice: are some paid outside interests less acceptable than others?

Labour MPs have consistently drawn attention to the fact that under the provisions of the Hastings Agreement there was only an indirect linkage between sponsoring unions and 'their MPs'. In their view, sponsored MPs did not receive 'instructions' from the unions; and, hence, sponsorship was different from other forms of 'paid' representation of sectional interests. However, opponents of the Labour party have not been convinced by this distinction. Likewise, the Nolan Report, in recording the 'very substantial increase in the number of Members of Parliament employed as consultants and advisers to companies, trade associations and the like', went on to acknowledge 'a similar, though by no means identical, relationship...between Members and trade unions' (Cm 2850-I 1995: 22). In the view of the Committee, both constituted financial relationships with outside bodies relating directly to an MP's membership of the House of Commons.

Any examination of these broader pecuniary interests rapidly reveals two contrasting positions. The first is that MPs should be banned altogether from holding remunerated posts outside of Parliament. This case was forcibly presented to the Nolan Committee by Harry Barnes:

> A rule banning MPs from taking outside jobs would do more than anything else to advance the case [of democracy]...I believe that generally if people are taking paid employment, consultancies etc., then they are liable to be concentrating a great deal upon the areas that they are receiving the payments for. This in fact restricts the areas that they should be involved with in Parliament. An MP...will be something of a generalist, turning into all sorts of areas that interest constituents and are before the country.
>
> (Cm 2850-II 1995: 67)

Barnes' view was supported by 48 per cent of respondents to a public opinion poll conducted by MORI in June 1995 (reported in Dunleavy *et al.* 1995: 609); and by nearly two-thirds of those surveyed by the SCPR in 1997 (Curtice and Jowell 1997: 105) who agreed that there should be a total ban on 'MPs having any paid job outside parliament'. Notably, the Nolan Committee itself did not agree with a total ban; in part on the pragmatic grounds that, 'many able people would not wish to enter Parliament if they...had to take a substantial drop in income'; and, in part also, because of an associated worry 'about the possibility of a narrowing in the range of able men and women who would be attracted to stand for

Parliament if Members were barred from having paid outside interests' (Cm 2850-I 1995: 23).

The second position on pecuniary interests, therefore, is the one adopted by the Nolan Committee, and, ultimately by the House of Commons in its code of conduct 1995. This position holds that MPs should remain free to pursue paid employment which is *'unrelated to their role as MP'* (Cm 2850-I 1995: 24). This draws upon the distinction between 'advocacy' and 'interest representation'. A distinction initially made by the first inquiry of the Select Committee on Members' Interests (HC 57 1969). The Committee proposed banning the former – where MPs promoted specific interests primarily or solely for payment, and regulating the latter – where MPs promoted interests on the basis of direct knowledge or involvement with the interest (even if also receiving payment from the interest concerned) (see HC 57 1969; Doig and Wilson 1995: 567). In the event, this distinction was dropped when a Register of Members' Interests was hurriedly introduced in 1975 (in an attempt to reassure the public that corruption among MPs was not widespread in the aftermath of the Poulson affair). The purpose of the Register was to subject the personal pecuniary interests of MPs to public scrutiny (HC 326 1992: xxiii).

The reason why such a Register was needed was restated in 1992 by the Select Committee on Members' Interests:

> to provide information of any pecuniary interest or other material benefit which a Member receives which might reasonably be thought by others to influence his or her actions, speeches or votes in Parliament, or actions taken in his or her capacity as a Member of Parliament.
>
> (HC 326 1992: xiii)

The problem with the concept of registration so defined is that some Members may be under the 'false impression that any interest is acceptable once it has been registered' (Cm 2850-I 1995: 27). In other words, anything that was not legally prohibited was acceptable. The danger was exacerbated further by leaving the judgement of the 'relevance' of any financial interest, and hence the need for declaration, to the MP himself or herself. The danger was variously spelled out in the debate on the introduction of the Register (HC Debates 22 May 1974, vol. 874: cols 391–522), by the Speaker (HC 326 1992: 85–6), and by academics (Williams 1985; Mancuso 1995: 172–3). The danger became increasingly manifest in the 1990s in the activities of a number of MPs whose activities came under investigation by the Select Committee on Members' Interests: Harry Greenway, Michael Grylls, Michael Mates, and John Browne in

1990, through to David Tredinnick's and Graham Riddick's involvement in the 'cash for questions' episode (where each was accused of accepting £1,000 to table parliamentary questions), and, most spectacularly of all, Neil Hamilton's promotion of the interests of Mohammed al-Fayed which culminated in, what journalists Leigh and Vulliamy called, 'the Westminster scandal of the decade' (1997: xvii).

At the heart of these investigations, and the rising public unease about the representation of interests in the 1990s, was the changing nature of the mode of interest representation within Westminster. Writing in 1995 Mancuso noted: 'The rise and increase of...new types of outside employment represent a threat that the British parliamentary system is not equipped to defend itself against.' Of particular concern was the development of the practice for MPs to act as parliamentary or political consultants. Two types of consultancy were easily identifiable: one saw MPs hiring themselves out to lobbying firms; the other saw MPs establishing their own consultancy businesses and offering their services directly to clients. In the case of multi-client or general consultancies the actual relationship between MP and specific client was easily obscured, whether intentionally or not. In 1992 the Select Committee on Members' Interests noted that MPs were increasingly accepting positions 'which involve advice or consultancy deriving from their knowledge or expertise as parliamentarians or in other ways related to their parliamentary activities' (HC 326 1992: xvi), and that the clients or indirect recipients of this advice were not always fully identified. By 1995 the Nolan Committee (Cm 2850-I 1995: 27) was concerned at the 'very significant level' of the proportion of MPs whose outside employment arose directly out of their membership of the House of Commons. In fact the number of MPs who recorded paid consultancies rose from 35 in 1991 (Hollingsworth 1991: 119) to 168 in 1995 (holding 356 consultancies among them (Cm 2850-I 1995: 22)).

Norton crystallises the problem by drawing a distinction between the representation of interests as a process designed to 'acquire knowledge for the purpose of being an MP', and as an activity designed to 'sell one's knowledge as an MP' (1997: 366). In accumulating paid consultancies on a large scale the latter activity left MPs open to the accusation that 'not only advice but also advocacy have been bought by the client' (Cm 2850-I 1995: 29). This infringed what the Nolan Committee believed was a basic principle of representative government in Britain: 'A Member who believes in a cause should be prepared to promote it without payment: equally a Member ought not to pursue a cause more forcefully than might otherwise have been the case as a result of financial interest' (Cm 2850-I 1995: 29). The extent to which the debate about MPs acting as consultants and advocates was underpinned by an implicit acceptance of 'trustee' theories of representation was manifest not only in the Nolan report itself but also in academic commentary upon the report. One example is provided by Oliver who concludes: 'In sum the objections to the various activities [including advocacy of a cause in parliament for payment] were that they affected the exercise by MPs of their judgement in various ways that were contrary to the Burkean theory of representation' (1997: 547).

Nolan and after

The starting point for Nolan's recommendations was the 1947 resolution of the House and, by implication, a reaffirmation of 'trustee' notions of representation. The 1947 resolution, as noted earlier, prohibited any restrictions on the freedom of MPs to act and speak as they wish, or which caused them to act as representatives of outside bodies. The Nolan Committee recommended a restatement of this resolution, and, in November 1995, the House amended the 1947 resolution to include the words:

> no Member of the House shall, in consideration of any remuneration, fee, payment, reward or benefit in kind, direct or indirect, which the Member or any member of his or her family has received is receiving or expects to receive –

(i)   advocate or initiate any cause or matter on behalf of any outside body or individual, or
(ii)   urge any other Member of either House of Parliament, including ministers, to do so,
       by means of any speech, Question, Motion, introduction of a Bill or amendment to a Motion or Bill.

Whereas Nolan had proposed only a limited ban on MPs entering into agreements with multi-client consultancies, the amended resolution adopted by the House in November 1995 specifically prohibited paid advocacy for any cause. Despite the reservations of some MPs about the practicalities of drawing a distinction between advice and advocacy, the House agreed to bring greater transparency to the former and to ban the latter. The House also agreed to accept Nolan's recommendations on a Code of Conduct for MPs, the appointment of a Parliamentary Commissioner for Standards, the creation of a new Select Committee on Standards and Privileges (to replace the existing Committees on Privileges and Members Interests), and for the disclosure of income derived from services offered by MPs as parliamentarians. The Code of Conduct is notable in that it seeks to 'provide a framework within which acceptable conduct should be judged' (HC 688 1996: 1). At the heart of that framework is the Burkean belief that 'Members have a general duty to act in the interests of the nation as a whole; and a special duty to their constituents' and that to perform this duty Members must have 'complete independence in Parliament' (HC 688 1996: 1).

An immediate consequence of the adoption of the Code of Conduct and the new procedures for the registration of interests was to increase the length of the Register from 144 pages in 1995 (HC 186 1995), to 148 in 1996 (HC 345 1996) and to 149 in January 1997 (HC 259 1997). It also allowed for a more accurate assessment of the total amount of money associated with consultancies, adviserships and work related to MPs' parliamentary activities. The *Observer* estimated this to be £2 million in 1996 (*Observer*, 12 May 1996); but this was regarded as a conservative estimate, as, for instance, some MPs did not declare income derived from consultancies and directorships as they claimed that the contracts did not arise from their work as MPs. By October 1997 the number of declared consultancies listed in the Register was down to 80 from 240 in January 1997 (and the total number of pages in the Register was down to 112 [HC 291 1997]). This was not only reflection of the impact of the Nolan reforms but also recognition of the changed composition of the House after the 1997 election.

Conclusion

Clearly, public concern about 'sleaze' has led to a clarification and codification of the standards of conduct expected of MPs. However, it still remains true that MPs continue to determine and regulate their own standards, but now this is done within a tighter ethical framework and with the assistance of a semi-independent Officer of the House – the Parliamentary Commissioner for Standards.

Underpinning the concern about 'sleaze', and the remedial measures taken by the Commons since 1995, has been a fundamental perception that the legitimacy of parliamentary representation was being eroded. In turn, this perception stemmed from a conception of representation rooted in 'trustee' notions of independence and the belief that MPs represented the nation generally and their constituencies specifically. In the words of Peter Shore: 'The country has a gut feeling that Members of Parliament are here above all to serve them and the nation, and that anything that interferes with that must be justified rather than taken for granted' (HC Debates 6 November 1995, vol. 265: col. 635). This belief shone through the successive resolutions of the House, the Nolan Report, and the Code of Conduct adopted by the House in July 1996. In this sense, Oliver is correct to state that

> standards of conduct required of British MPs rest on a number of often unspoken assumptions which reflect the underlying theory of representative democracy....The established basic theory of representation in the UK is that expressed by Edmund Burke in his Letter to the Electors of Bristol in 1774.
>
> (1997: 544)

But this basic theory has always been qualified in practice by an acceptance that 'specific interests' constitute a part of a wider national interest and, therefore, a legitimate part of the process of representation. Even in the post-Nolan world this remains so. Indeed, the Nolan report considered it 'desirable for the House of Commons to contain Members with a wide variety of continuing outside interests' (Cm 2850-I 1995: 23). What was undesirable, and remains so, is for MPs to promote outside interests in parliament in return for payment and in conflict with their responsibilities to wider public and constituency interests. Where MPs advance sectional interests voluntarily, openly and in symmetry with these wider interests then the representation of specific interests continues as a supplementary theme to the 'established basic theory of representation'. This is as true at the end of the twentieth century as it was at the end of the nineteenth century. In which case, to return to the geological analogy in the introduction to this chapter, the accumulated sediments of political practice in the intervening period have had running throughout them a visible vein of 'theory' justifying and legitimising the representation of specific material interests in parliament.

6 Representation and 'post-parliamentary' governance

It is commonplace to argue that parliamentary institutions in Western liberal democracies are undergoing systematic erosion – and that traditional models of representative government, let alone representative democracy, are no longer accurately descriptive, if ever they were, of the complex form of modern government. Indeed, it is now fashionable to talk of *governance* rather than government. Whereas the model of 'representative government' mapped out fairly simple, serial flows of power between the represented and their representatives, the defining characteristics of 'governance' is the differentiation of the 'represented' and the complexity of their relations with the institutions of government. As Andersen and Burns argue:

> Modern governance is increasingly divided into semi-autonomous, specialised segments or sectors; that is, it is multi-polar with the inter-penetration of state agencies and agents of civil society. In everyday policy-making, there is no single centre. The complex differentiation of society is reflected in the differentiation and complexity of governance, the differentiation of representation, the differentiation of systems of knowledge and expertise, and the spectrum of values and lifestyles of ordinary citizens.
>
> (1996: 228)

The incorporation of 'private' organisations into public policy making and regulation – into the direct representation of these interests in sub-governmental systems – is held to contrast sharply with the established tenets of the territorial representation of citizens in representative democracy. The academic consensus is that fragmentation and 'sectorisation' characterise the reality of public policy making in Britain today. We live in what Rhodes (1997: 7) calls a 'differentiated polity' where functional and institutional specialisation is accompanied by organisational interdependence between public organisations and private interests. There is an institutionalisation of outside interests in government. As this institutionalisation has progressed so have fears grown about the marginalisation of established modes of representation through the parliamentary system. 'The conflicts between representative democracy, and the differentiated polity, between functional and territorial politics, plays a central role in [the new] interpretation of British government' (Rhodes 1997: 22). Indeed, what is taken as axiomatic in this interpretation is that Britain had become a 'post-parliamentary democracy'.

The long road to 'post-parliamentary democracy'

> It is this opposition between highly specialised expertise and the principle of democratic participation that appears as the central structural problem of all western parliamentary democracies. To be sure this dilemma is also by no means new, however sharply it confronts us today on all sides.
>
> (Bracher 1967: 251)

At the beginning of the twentieth century Max Weber identified the problem which was to be deemed endemic to legislatures at the end of that century. In noting the development of functional expertise within state bureaucracies, Weber argued that the elected politician – the 'political master' – 'finds himself in the position of the "dilettante" who stands opposite the "expert"' (Weber in Gerth and Mills 1970: 234–5). As the scope of governmental activity expanded and as the issues requiring decision by governments became ever more complex, so the premium placed upon specialist expertise increased almost exponentially. In these circumstances the linkage between the state bureaucracy and organised interests trading on their possession of functional expertise became ever closer and routinised (see Alderman 1984: 8–16; Judge 1990a: 12–16). British civil servants became dependent on groups for specialist advice, and from the late Victorian period onwards consultation became a defining feature of the policy style of British government. Even groups lacking in economic power were able to gain credibility with, and hence access to, policy makers through their possession of 'technical expertise or political sophistication' (Maloney *et al.* 1994: 21). Equally, governments came to depend on groups for compliance and the implementation of public policies. Against this background of mutual accommodation between organised interests and governments, commentators noted the disjunction between the political practice of decision making and established theories of representative government in Britain.

In examining the extent of the disjunction between theory and practice, the following discussion will focus upon three related issues: first, the extent to which different variants of interest representation are deemed compatible with territorially-based theories of representation; second, the differing bases for the legitimation of 'public' policies; and, third, the tension between efficiency in decision making and the wider requirement of public consent. The discussion will also concentrate primarily upon interest *representation* rather than the broader concerns of the role of interests within systems of governance; and in so doing will analyse six models which have predominated in the British discussion of interest representation: old-style associationalism, functional representation, corporatism, pluralism, networks and new associationalism. What links all six is the belief that individualistic representation in parliament is neither descriptively nor normatively an accurate reflection of the complexity of public policy making in the twentieth century. All six maintain that greater descriptive accuracy or normative saliency is to be found in some variant of 'functional representation' (as defined by Beer [1969: 71] as 'any theory that finds the community divided into various strata, regards each of these strata as having a certain corporate unity, and holds that they ought to be represented in government').

Old-style associationalism

Associationalism is both the oldest and newest theory of representation to be considered in this chapter. According to one of its leading modern proponents, Paul Hirst: 'the late twentieth century offers new conditions in which ideas marginalised for many decades can be redefined and developed to serve as an alternative, radical means of reforming and reorganising...governance in Western societies' (1994: 2). However, before examining this modern reformulation it is advisable to sketch an earlier version of associationalism, that proposed by G.D.H. Cole who was, in Hirst's (1994: 16) opinion, one of the two major English associationalist writers of this century (the other being H.J. Laski).

Guild Socialism

It has been claimed that Guild Socialism for Cole was essentially a theory of democracy, and that Cole's greatest contribution to that theory was his analysis of the concept of representation (Wright 1979: 50). The problem with conceiving of the Guild Socialist critique as essentially concerned with the inadequate current *form* of parliamentary representation – that it is general rather than specific, exclusive rather than inclusive – is that it assumes that a change in the form of representation will permit the 'real representation of actual interests and will solve the problem of the gap between representatives and represented' (Hirst 1994: 34). In reality, however, Cole's critique of the liberal representative state was far more elaborate than a simple refutation of the democratic credentials of the existing form of territorial representation (see Judge 1993: 51–5). Nonetheless, for present purposes, we will focus exclusively upon his ideas on representation.

It is important to remember from the outset, therefore, that Cole's ideas were not 'an anarchic attack on the concept of representation itself, but an attack on the current misuse of the concept contained in the doctrine that in one single and general act man as a whole could be "represented"' (Wright 1979: 58). Cole's theory was, at heart, a critique of liberal democracy in that it was a 'reaction against two related ideas: that society was atomistic, simply a collection of discrete individuals; and that it was ruled by an absolute state power by which alone those individuals were wedded together in a community' (Greenleaf 1983: 422).

> The omnicompetent State, with its omnicompetent Parliament, is…utterly unsuitable to any really democratic community, and must be destroyed or painlessly extinguished as it has destroyed or painlessly extinguished its rivals in the sphere of communal organisation. Whatever the structure of the new Society may be, the Guildsman is sure that it will have no place for the survival of the *factotum* State of today.
>
> (Cole 1920b: 32)

Cole's attack was upon liberal individualistic conceptions of representation. In his view, existing forms of representation were misrepresentation 'based upon a totally false theory of representation' (1920a: 103). Two reasons were adduced: first, the theory was false in assuming that it was possible for an individual to be represented as a whole, for all purposes, and; second, the elector was unable to exercise control over the representative. In which case, 'having chosen his representative, the ordinary man has, according to that theory, nothing left to do except let other people govern him' (1920a: 114). In stark contrast, however, functional representation and organisation (as theory and practice) offer 'the constant participation of the ordinary man in the conduct of those parts of the structure of society with which he is directly concerned, and which he has therefore the best chance of understanding' (1920a: 114). For Cole, 'all true representation and democratic representation is therefore *functional* representation' (1920b: 33). 'True representation…like true association, is always specific and functional, and never general and inclusive' (1920a: 106).

The result is a double-edged critique of parliamentary democracy. On the one side, the territorial and individualistic bases of representation are questioned; on the other, the claimed omnicompetence of parliament and the impossibility of representing all citizens in all things is attacked. Parliament was 'chosen to deal with anything that may turn up, quite irrespective of the fact that the different things that do turn up require different types of persons to deal with them. This is not the fault of the actual Members of Parliament; they muddle because they are set the impossible task of being good at everything, and representing everybody in relation to every purpose' (1920a: 108). Consequently, Cole argued that 'real democracy' would only be achieved when parliament was replaced by a system of coordinated functional representative bodies.

The central feature of Cole's future socialist society and state, therefore, was to be a decentralised Guild system. 'The factory, or place of work, will be the natural unit of Guild life. It will be, to a great extent, internally self-governing, and it will be the unit and basis of the wider local and national government of the Guild' (1920b: 48–9). The claim of existing capitalist states to sovereignty, to superior obligation, was thus denied. Instead, the state was simply one association among others (Cole 1917: 11). In which case, political authority was to be diffused throughout society through a multiplex of functional organisations, with the community – as constituted in the totality of groups – claiming sovereignty rather than a single omnipotent parliament. Subsequently, much of Cole's attention was devoted to 'system-building'; to the construction of practical organisational forms to be derived from associationalist theory. Whilst the results of this system-building have been described as 'impossibly Byzantine' (Wright 1979: 39) their importance for present purposes is in the starting premise of the critique of territorially based representation. In essence, Cole saw liberal individualistic conceptions of representation to be incompatible with functional representation. The latter had to *replace* the former.

In answer to the first question raised above – the extent to which different variants of interest representation are deemed compatible with territorially based theories of representation – Cole's Guild Socialist scheme is clear: the two are incompatible. The second issue – the bases for the legitimation of 'public' policies – is addressed in the fact that there are 'as many separately elected groups of representatives as there are distinct essential groups of functions to be performed' (1920b: 33). These groups, in a future socialist society, would have 'no real divergence of interests between them' (1920b: 39) because, ultimately, the 'whole body of consumers and the whole body of producers are practically the same people, only ranged in the two cases in different formations' (1920b: 39). Public policies would derive legitimation from the simple fact that these 'different formations' were concerned with 'doing a definite job' and their members were members of different associations precisely because they knew what the job was and could initiate and criticise action within the appropriate association. As a result, the tension between efficiency in decision making and the wider requirement of public consent – the third issue raised above – would be resolved in the coordination of the activities of self-governing functional organisations.

Functional representation in the inter-war period

Whereas Cole (1920a: 108) was adamant that existing forms of representation had to be replaced, other inter-war advocates of functional representation in Britain believed that it could be grafted onto, and act as a supplement to, parliamentary representation. Thus Herman Finer, for example, in *Representative Government and a Parliament of Industry* (1923), examined the work of the German Federal Economic Council in order 'to help towards a better perception of our own problems and towards their solution' (Finer 1923: 34). Following Cole, Finer located the problem of representative government within the context of the increased scope and technical complexity of policy making in the twentieth-century industrial state. If the diagnosis is much the same as that of Cole – the incapacity of a miscellaneous representative assembly to discharge the modern interventions required in the late-capitalist state – the prescription is significantly different. It is also more attuned to later calls for the institutionalisation of a functional element of representation alongside territorial representation.

Finer maintained that the stark realities of the industrial system in Britain called for 'something in the nature of an Industrial Parliament' (1923: 32), in fact, something like a permanent Economic Council based on the German model. Hence, he proposed an English Economic Council composed of employers and employees, in parity, with minority representation for consumer and local authority interests, and a limited number of technocrats who were used 'to the handling and the objective analysis of sociological and economic argument' (Finer 1923: 216).

Any contradiction between functional and parliamentary modes of representation is subsumed away by Finer. There 'would be no division of authority' within the state, as parliament would remain the locus of sovereign power. The Economic Council would 'advise', 'scrutinise' and 'carefully comment' on policy, drawing upon its 'representative and expert character' (1923: 217) – *but*, and it is a vitally important qualification: 'In all of these activities it resolves what the nation *ought* to do, but to the political parliament is reserved the power to say what the nation *shall* do' (Finer 1923: 219). Advice of the Economic Council would thus not detract from the 'sole and indivisible responsibility' of the House of Commons. This might be the case in theory but it asserts away the whole contradiction in practice between the bases of 'authority' and 'legitimation' of functional and parliamentary representation. The initial problematic is simply defined out of existence in the stipulation of a *fusion* of functional and parliamentary modes; and thus their essentially *contradictory* nature is denied.

In the 1930s, Winston Churchill, given his status within the Conservative party, attracted more attention for his call for the creation of an Economic Sub-Parliament. Initially his schema was proposed during the course of his Romanes lecture at Oxford University in 1930 (Churchill 1930), and then elaborated in his evidence to the Procedure Committee in 1931 (HC 161 1931). His underpinning premise was that parliament had 'shown itself incapable of dealing with...fundamental and imperative economic need' (Churchill 1930: 15) and there was thus 'grave doubt...whether institutions based on adult suffrage could possibly arrive at the right decisions upon the intricate propositions of modern business and finance' (1930: 9). Churchill based his argument upon a fundamental separation of the economic and political dimensions of the liberal democratic state. Yet he exaggerated this separation arguing that the major issues confronting the British state since 1918 had been economic and not political, and that 'the nation is not interested in politics, it is interested in economics' (Churchill 1930: 7). However, when the nation 'turn[ed] to parliament asking for guidance', although voluble in so many matters, parliament was 'on this one paramount topic dumb' (1930: 7).

If the House of Commons, and the executive therein, was thus unsuited to the effective management of the economy then the solution for Churchill was to 'build another storey upon [traditional representative institutions] equally well-proportioned, symmetrical and unified' (1930: 12). This was to take the form of an Economic Sub-Parliament, to consist of some 120 Members: 40 MPs with experience of economic matters, and 80 representatives drawn from both sides of industry or who were themselves 'economic authorities'. The envisaged remit of this body was essentially advisory and deliberative, with all bills dealing with trade and industry referred to it after they had been given a second reading in the Commons (Butt 1969: 139). This certainly would be an innovation, with the Economic Sub-Parliament 'debating day after day with fearless detachment from public opinion all the most disputed questions of finance and trade, and reaching conclusions by voting' but in Churchill's (1930: 16) view it would be 'an innovation easily to be embraced by our flexible constitutional system'.

Whilst Churchill saw no reason why 'the new system should be at vari-
ance with the old' (1930: 12), given his assertion that parliament's
sovereignty would not be questioned in the new arrangement, there are
manifest problems as to how functional representation could be reconciled
with individualistic bases of representation. In fact, several contradictions
are inherent within Churchill's schema, not the least of which is the ability
of a 'political' parliament – based upon territorial/individualistic principles of representation with representatives pledged to reflect the diversity
of public opinion on the miscellany of public policy – controlling or
reversing the 'advice' of a functionally constituted sub-parliament based
upon expertise and reflecting the industrial power of its own representatives (for others see Butt 1969: 139; Smith 1979: 19–21; Judge 1981: 30–2).

Exactly the same contradiction is to be found in other contemporary
proposals made by Percy (1931) and Macmillan (1933). Indeed, the latter
provided, in the opinion of Carpenter, 'one of the most comprehensive
corporatist models produced in [Britain]' (1976: 11). In each scheme some
form of functional representation was to be introduced in parallel with
existing modes of parliamentary representation. However, in proposing,
respectively, the creation of a Ministry of Economic Development alongside a new functionally-based 'deliberative body' (Percy 1931: 61), or a
Central Economic Council dominated by industrial interests (Macmillan
1933), these bodies would move beyond being merely advisory and
become endowed with 'executive authority' (Carpenter 1976: 11). In
which case the tension between legitimation derived from a territorially-
based 'sovereign' parliament and a functionally-based expert 'executive'
would be brought into stark relief.

'Early' pluralism

The problem with pluralist theory is that, although it has dominated much
of the analysis of the interaction between groups and governments, especially in the US, there is often little agreement upon its defining
characteristics given the many variants identified by political scientists (see
Judge 1995: 14–15; Grant 1995: 28–30). Moreover, pluralism has attracted
ferocious criticism in its time, as well as being denounced as ideologically
unsound in its 'complacent defence of the status quo' (Phillips 1993: 139).
Yet pluralists have consistently maintained that theirs is at best an 'empirical descriptive' analysis of decision making rather than a 'theory' as such.
They have proclaimed their basic task to be the bringing of greater empirical precision to the understanding of how decisions are made (see Dahl
1961: vi; 1984: 240).

Certainly, the early analyses of British pressure groups in the 1950s and

1960s were located firmly in an empirical descriptive frame. Thus, for example, the opening sentence of Stewart's *British Pressure Groups* states: 'This book is an attempt to describe the activities of various unions, associations and societies in relation to the House of Commons' (1958: 1). In being empirically grounded, Stewart's study – along with other British studies of the time (see Finer [1958] 1966; Potter 1961) – came to many of the same conclusions as American pluralists about the centrality of organised interests within the policy making process, but did so without the theoretical framework which helped the Americans to define the essence of pluralist democracy. Whilst it is now commonplace to describe such British works as 'pluralist', what is remarkable is the limited reference to the contemporary American pluralist literature within such works (see Jordan and Richardson 1987b: 53–4). In fact, Jordan maintains that the stunted theoretical roots of many successive British empirical studies reflected the fact that pluralism was adopted merely as 'a theoretical window-dressing' because 'it better accords with their findings than does the picture-book account of policy-making through party manifestos and Parliament' (1990a: 293).

As part of a 'general pluralist model' Jordan (1990a: 293) identifies a common core of ideas: first, that power is fragmented and decentralised, with inequalities dispersed in Western societies; second, that all groups would be heard at some stage even if all groups could not be 'winners' in the policy process; third, that the dispersion of power was a 'desirable feature in any system approaching the status of a democracy'; fourth, that an understanding of political practice should be based upon observation of the process of policy development, and; fifth, that political outcomes in different policy sectors will reflect different processes, different actors and distributions of power within those sectors. However, of more immediate importance for the present discussion are the sixth and seventh elements of the general model identified by Jordan: sixth, 'the formal process of political choice through elections and parliamentary activity are likely to mislead about the actual distribution of power', and, seventh, the interaction of interests was assumed 'to supply a practical alternative to the 'general will' as the source of legitimate authority' (Jordan 1990a: 293).

The sixth and seventh elements clearly reflect Jordan's own critical perspective on the traditional models of representative government in Britain (see pp. 138–9) but before examining his position it is necessary to outline the views of earlier British 'pluralist' analysts. What distinguishes the empirical investigations of pressure group activity in Britain in the 1950s and 1960s from Jordan's later investigations was that the necessary contribution of representative institutions to the process of policy making was largely taken for granted. Hence, Stewart believed that 'the British system of government might appear to have found a satisfactory balance' between parliamentary and group representation (1958: 240). He identified as a 'special feature' of modern British government the fact that governments were led to consult 'various representative organisations' in the formulation of policy affecting their specific interests. But, importantly, this did not mean that 'Parliament's position is undermined. It merely means that consultation with groups at all points is essential to the administrative system, and that without it Parliament would be presented with unworkable bills' (Stewart 1958: 17). Stewart was clear that in the process of decision making 'it was desirable that...there be brought into play considerations deriving from a wider view of the political scene than is possible to individual groups' (1958: 239). Indeed, the process of territorial representation endowed governments with 'the authority to resist the groups'. Similarly, Allan Potter emphasised the importance of the derivative nature of consent to government actions in Britain:

> the Government derives its political authority from the House of Commons, which derives its authority from the electorate. This theory is important in providing the common framework of assumptions within which the relations between Government and organised groups are set.
>
> (Potter 1961: 228)

And, in what is perhaps the quintessential British version of pluralism in the 1950s, Finer ([1958] 1966: 22) identified parliament as 'being the repository of the public interest' (Finer [1958] 1966: 23). As such it is one of the political institutions which 'counter the centrifugal demands of the sectional groups' (Finer [1958] 1966: 101). The end result of the dual process of parliamentary and group representation was, for Finer, the 'domestication' and 'amalgamation' of sectional interests to 'produce government which, all in all, is still honest, humane and just' (Finer [1958] 1966: 101).

What British pluralists accepted implicitly in the 1950s and 1960s was what the American pluralist theorist David Truman had accepted explicitly in *The Governmental Process*, and that was that an 'objective description' (1951: 47) of policy making entailed the inclusion of group activity *alongside* established representative institutions. For Truman the legislature was not relegated to being 'just a sounding-board or passive registering device for the demands of organised political interest groups' (1951: 350). Instead:

> The legislature as a part of the institution of government embodies, albeit incompletely, the expectations, understandings, and values

prevailing in the society concerning how the government should operate. These expectations may cover now a wide and now a relatively narrow range of behavior; they may be fairly explicit or highly ambiguous...[but, partly because of these norms, a legislator] cannot behave simply and completely as a vehicle for organised group demands.

(Truman 1951: 350)

The existence of representative institutions based upon territorial representation was thus identified as a prerequisite of group politics (Judge 1990b: 29). In the words of Robert Dahl, there was clearly a need in a pluralist process for 'a more or less representative body to legitimize basic decisions by some process of assent' (1956: 136). While this view was clearly shared by British analysts in the 1950s, nonetheless, their own empirical studies cast doubts upon the efficacy of parliament in the policy process as well as upon its capacity to articulate a broader 'public interest'.

In particular, Finer's study revealed dark shadows cast by important tendencies within the group process in Britain. He observed that as lobbying became more extensive, as consultation became routinised in close links between central departments and affected interests, so 'to put the matter crudely, a close relationship became a *closed* one' (Finer [1958] 1966: 38). From this closed relationship two consequences flowed. First, the negotiated deals worked out behind closed doors between groups and civil servants in Whitehall effectively excluded the wider public and, notably, parliament (Finer [1958] 1966: 42). Second, there was what Finer termed a 'law of inverse proportion' whereby 'the closer and snugger the Lobby's consultative status, the more exclusive its relationship with its ministry, the less use will it care to make of parliamentary methods' (Finer [1958] 1966: 43). The practical result was a residualisation of parliament in the policy process. Ultimately, therefore, Finer was led to conclude that his initial description (and indeed general predilection in favour) of parliament as the custodian of the general public interest was inaccurate: 'This custodianship Parliament finds itself incapable of exercising' (Finer [1958] 1966: 141–2).

The mismatch between constitutional theory and political practice was left unresolved in Finer's own work, but the tension between the bases of parliamentary and group representation was apparent nonetheless. Indeed, this analytical tension became more pronounced with each passing empirical study. In the British context of centralised executive control, founded upon party government and the hierarchical structuring of authority relations within Westminster itself, the classical pluralist theory of Truman and Dahl – developed in the fragmented institutional structure of the United

States – seemed less than appropriate (see Grant 1995: 30). In describing policy making in Britain the analytical picture became increasingly obscure; at its centre groups could readily be identified, but the exact number – and their exact relationship with each other and with the executive – was to divide empirical studies into two broad but related categories – of corporatism and policy networks.

Corporatism: dead but not forgotten?

'Neo-corporatism' was the term used in the 1960s and 1970s to describe a 'relatively institutionalised and permanent relationship between government, business and labour interests at the policy making level of the state' (Cox 1988a: 28). Whilst agreement was easily reached that something new was happening in this period, neo-corporatist theorists, spread across most Western industrialised countries, had considerably more difficulty in explaining exactly what was happening. In Britain alone, corporatism was identified variously as a new political economy (Pahl and Winkler 1974; Winkler 1976; 1977), a system of industrial relations (Crouch 1977; Panitch 1979; 1980; Strinati 1979; 1982), a new state form (Jessop 1978) or a system of interest intermediation (Cawson 1982; 1989). To expect an unambiguous definition of corporatism to arise from such diversity is perhaps unrealistic, but there was one common element, however, which unified the British variants of neo-corporatist theory – and that was a belief in the progressive displacement of traditional parliamentary modes of representation by tripartite (or bipartite) interest intermediation.

One particularly influential exposition of this argument was made by Keith Middlemas in 1979. His starting premise was that the practical experience of British government had made accepted liberal versions of the constitution at best inadequate and at worst erroneous. Hence he sought to discover a 'hidden code' which would more realistically explain political institutional behaviour. The 'code' deciphered by Middlemas was one of 'corporate bias' (1979: 20). By this he meant a process whereby a 'triangular pattern of cooperation between government and the two sides of industry…led to the elevation of trade unions and employers' associations to a new sort of status: from interest groups they became "governing institutions"'. These institutions were differentiated from 'pressure groups' as they became 'partners' of governments with permanent rights of access and accorded devolved powers by the state (1979: 381). Middlemas was adamant that the British political system reflected a corporate *bias* but that the system itself was not corporatism. Too many fluctuations in the central relationship amongst the tripartite partners existed to ensure a stable system. In which case Middlemas concluded: 'like the bias of a wood at bowls [corporate bias] is in itself no more than a tendency always to run to one side' (1979: 380) and that this description must suffice given the tentative, even fragile nature of its development.

Nonetheless, this bias had ramifications for the representation of interests both through parliament and through established interest groups. The pervasiveness of corporate bias at all levels of political activity was such that it reduced, on the one hand, the power of interests and organisations beyond the 'threshold' of tripartism, whilst, on the other, simultaneously it replaced 'for all practical purposes, classical democratic theory' as it had been understood for most of the twentieth century (Middlemas 1979: 374). Middlemas was insistent that the British state was, in 1979, composed of governing institutions alongside the formal state apparatus and that crisis avoidance and the maintenance of political harmony could only be achieved through their incorporation (1979: 460). Revealingly, he argued that governments in the 1960s and 1970s had 'no other model' (1979: 429) upon which to base their actions.

This insistence upon the displacement of parliamentary representation is also evident in the industrial relations literature on corporatism. From this perspective Panitch (1980) and Strinati (1982) identified neo-corporatism as a state-induced form of collaboration designed to incorporate organised labour more closely into the capitalist economy. Descriptively, corporatism was identified as being both specific and partial: pertaining to specific tripartite structures and to partial modes of representation – one that neither encompassed all forms of interest nor displaced representation itself. Nonetheless, corporatism as a system of representation was contrasted with, and was seen to be 'clearly inimical' to, parliamentarism (see Strinati 1979: 202; 1982: 23–4; MacInnes 1987: 45). The representative institutions of liberal democracy were seen to be marginalised by the progressive expansion of a tripartite process of decision making. Extra-parliamentary bodies of functional representatives came to constitute the major institutions for the articulation and resolution of economic demands. Parliament was thus further undermined in the process of representation.

Corporatism in its macro-form of tripartism – of the incorporation of organised labour and industrial capital into the process of executive decision making – was presented therefore as an extension of the tendency towards functional representation endemic within British industrialism. As such it was claimed that there was little need for the development of a theory of corporatism:

In Britain the tradition of secret 'efficient' government developing through *ad hoc* pragmatic adjustments and legitimated by a 'dignified' parliamentarism reduces the need for participants in the process to have any sort of theory of corporatism.

(Harden 1988: 43)

Yet, others clearly maintained that there was a need to 'theorise' corporatism. In this respect the developing ideas of Bob Jessop were of particular importance. Initially, Jessop conceptualised corporatism as a discrete 'state form' distinct from parliamentarism. In trying to link the contemporary discussion of corporatism to Marxist political economy Jessop arrived at the position that:

> corporatist institutions are *displacing* parliamentary institutions as the dominant state apparatus in Britain and that these constitute a *contradictory unity*. Both corporatist and parliamentary representation are necessary to the reproduction of capital in the present situation.
>
> (Jessop 1978: 44, original emphasis)

Corporatism was seen to be the highest form of social democracy, particularly appropriate to the interventionist state in the 'post-Keynesian period' of the mixed economy and welfare state. There was, however, the manifest problem that corporatism did not constitute a complete system of representation. At best it took a hybrid form. Whilst corporatism merged representation and intervention in functionally-based institutions, it also necessarily institutionalised at the centre of the state conflicts based upon the economic division between labour and capital. This interaction of the functional representatives of labour and capital at the level of the state was the central contradiction pointed to by Marxists (see Jessop 1978, 1979; Panitch 1980). Corporatism with its emphasis upon consensual and cooperative modes of decision making was based upon the representation of divergent socioeconomic interests. What was distinctive about corporatism, therefore, was that the functional groups at the heart of the system were 'constituted in terms of a contradictory relation to one another' (Panitch 1980: 176), and that this relationship was focused upon the very economic interests that divide them in the first instance.

Jessop (1978: 49; 1980: 51) repeatedly stated that the transition from parliamentarism was not automatic but was dependent upon the specific conjunction of political forces at any period. Throughout, Jessop recognised that corporatism in itself was incapable of providing the necessary legitimation for policies derived from tripartite bargaining without the existence of a 'determinate (although pluralist and non-unitary) sovereign authority' (1979: 195). Although not linked analytically, he refers elsewhere to the legitimation and flexibility afforded by 'electoral politics' (1978: 43).

What was vitally important was the very strength of the 'parliamentary tradition in Britain' (1978: 43). Consequently, 'the most that can be expected is the displacement of the dominant position within the hierarchy of state apparatuses of representation from parliament to tripartite institutions' (1978: 43). In this manner Jessop reached the position that there was a 'contradictory unity', where a fusion of corporatist and parliamentary representation was required but is unsustainable. An inherent conflict was identified between the social bases of representation in the two systems (see Jessop 1978: 44–5; 1979: 205); between organised labour and capital and their preference for centralisation and concentration of state power, and the unorganised, the jobless, small capital, petit bourgeois interests, wider social movements, and what Jessop called 'popular-democratic forces' for whom parliament still remained a favourable political terrain for the mobilisation and articulation of interest. By this point, however, it is apparent that corporatism was no longer seen to be a discrete state-form distinct from parliamentarism: at its most developed it was at best a hybrid form (which is the essence of Jessop's argument), at its least developed stage it was simply a variant of functional representation within parliamentarism.

When attention is focused upon the conception of liberal-corporatism as a system of interest representation, commentators upon corporatist theory were prone to oversimplify the position. Thus, for example, Cox (1988b: 198) stated: 'The corporatist form is straightforward. It involves the state in creating a privileged policy making role for key interest groups at the expense of the legislature and individual representation on a territorial basis.' Yet, the neo-corporatist theorists themselves were more circumspect with Lehmbruch (1979: 181) maintaining, for example, that it is 'unrealistic to consider corporatism as a realistic alternative to representative government'. This was because of its limited capacity for consensus-building. Similarly, whilst Schmitter (1979: 64), in examining the coexistence of corporatist modes of interest intermediation alongside parliamentary representation, noted the radical alteration that the former had brought to the 'liberal-bourgeois-parliamentary-democratic mode of political domination', nevertheless, he speculated that this alteration could be reversed as professional politicians 'no matter how beholden they may be to special interests, might...resist the progressive short-circuiting and bypassing of party channels, territorial constituencies and legislative processes that, after all, constitute their reason for being' (Schmitter 1982: 274). In future, Schmitter (1982: 274) argued, more explicit attention would have to be paid to traditional modes of representation in the praxis of neo-corporatism. In large part this was because neo-corporatism in practice had been 'very weakly legitimated by the political cultures in which it is embedded', generally lacking 'the socialised normative support and explicit ideological justification' necessary to sustain its claims to legitimacy (Schmitter 1982: 266–7). Thus, although corporatist intermediation might be necessary, it was seen to be neither a complete system of representation nor one capable of dominating the procedural democratic norms of parliamentarism.

This was certainly to prove the case in Britain after 1979. The significant point for the present discussion is that the 'contradictory unity' identified by Jessop was resolved through the reassertion of the primacy of 'authority' derived from parliamentary representation over that derived from functional representation and corporatism (see Judge and Dickson 1987: 24–6, Grant 1995: 38–9; Judge 1990a: 47–50; Judge 1993: 118–20). The political success of Mrs Thatcher in the 1980s was to evoke the powerful legitimatory symbolism of parliamentary representation to defuse the potency of corporatist modes of representation in the national policy making process.

However, if as Wyn Grant concludes, 'Thatcherism and corporatism proved to be incompatible' (1995: 38), other forms of interest representation were to prove more compatible with the style of successive Conservative governments in the 1980s and 1990s. Indeed, as the practice of government continued to accommodate organised groups in the process of policy making, the response of British political scientists was to search for a more appropriate empirical-descriptive theory: this time focusing upon policy communities and policy networks.

Policy communities and networks

> The first problem is to provide an organising format for the literature on networks.
>
> (Rhodes 1990: 293)

This problem arises because so much is included in this literature. Basically at least three discrete, but often interlinked, approaches to networks can be discerned. The first treats networks as an analytical model which helps to describe, and understand, the processes of policy making and implementation. A central feature of this model is the 'multi-organizational character of action' in the modern policy process (Hanf and O'Toole 1992: 165; Bressers *et al.* 1994: 8). The second approach constitutes a typology of interest representation or intermediation. Rhodes, for example, in defining a policy network as a cluster or complex of organisations connected to one another by resource dependencies, produces a typology of five network variants ranging along a continuum from tightly integrated 'policy communities' to loosely formed 'issue networks'. This typology treats networks and communities as types of relationships between groups and government (Rhodes 1997: 43). The third approach conceives of policy networks as a particular form of governance. Thus, for example, Hanf and O'Toole note that in a functionally interdependent world of public and private actors 'modern governance is characterised by decision systems in which territorial and functional differentiation disaggregate effective problem-solving capacity into a collection of sub-systems of actors with specialised tasks and limited competence and resources' (1992: 166). This finds reflection in Rhodes' (1997: 45) view that governance emerged in Britain as an unplanned, unheralded governing structure as a result of the fragmentation of the state, institutional differentiation, institutional pluralisation in the multiplication of organisational types, and the sheer complexities facing modern government.

For present purposes we only have to skirt the voluminous network literature – sidestepping the definitional convolutions, the methodological disputes, the debate about whether networks analysis is a model or a metaphor, the attempts to discover whether policy networks affect policy outcomes, and explanations of changing relationships within and between networks – and concentrate instead on 'the thorny and perennial problems of the relationship between parliamentary and functional representation and between political responsibility and private government by interest groups' (Rhodes and Marsh 1992a: 200).

Certainly in the early British analyses, networks were identified unambiguously as a challenge to traditional notions of representative government. At one end of the network continuum, policy communities were defined in terms of their distance from established modes of parliamentary representation. Rod Rhodes relentlessly repeated this point (1985: 15; 1988: 78; 1990: 204; Rhodes and Marsh 1992a: 182; Rhodes and Marsh 1992b: 13) in defining policy communities as:

> networks characterised by stability of relationships, continuity of a highly restrictive membership, vertical interdependence based upon shared delivery responsibilities and insulation from other networks and invariably from the general public (including Parliament).

The very stability of relationships was deemed to influence the process of policy making itself. The internal characteristics of the process were characterised as: bargaining; consensus, based upon shared understandings of the nature of a problem; dependency, in the form of the exchange of information and professional expertise; and compromise. 'Sectorisation'

(Jordan and Richardson 1982: 82) was seen as an essential ingredient in the development of policy communities, with communities organised around individual government departments and their client groups. In this compartmentalisation consensus within communities was facilitated through the exclusion of groups and political institutions 'outside' of its own specialist professional or ideological norms. Ultimately, therefore, the process of policy making came to be conceived of as 'a series of vertical compartments or segments – each segment inhabited by a different set of organised groups and generally impenetrable by "unrecognised groups" or by the general public' (Richardson and Jordan 1979: 174). The term 'bureaucratic accommodation' was used to typify the 'normal' policy style in Britain and to identify a system in which the 'prominent actors are groups and government departments and the mode is bargaining rather than imposition' (Jordan and Richardson 1982: 81). One consequence of the 'notion that policies are the product of sectoral bargaining in which ministries have clientelistic orientations to the major groups' was a reduction in the importance of legislatures, parties and the formal institutions of government (Jordan 1990b: 473).

Confirmation of this 'closed' world of communities was seemingly found in the case studies examined by Rhodes and Marsh (1992a: 200) which 'describe a system of *private* government subject only to the most tenuous forms of accountability'. However, the most insistent proponents of the view that the British policy process was now best conceived as being 'non-parliamentary' were Jordan and Richardson. They repeatedly pointed out that there was 'little opportunity for participation by Parliament', that the agenda of the group-government world is not that of Parliament' (1987b: 7), and 'an important factor in the decline of the House of Commons…is the 'leakage' of power to the myriad of policy communities surrounding the executive' (1982: 102). Their description of the segmentation of policy making and the development of policy communities residualised the involvement of the legislature and led them to conclude that 'the traditional model of cabinet and party government is a travesty of reality' (Richardson and Jordan 1979: 191). In successive studies they found it increasingly difficult to reconcile the 'empirical world of government-group relations' (Jordan and Richardson 1987b: 287–8) with the prescriptions of the British liberal democratic constitution. Indeed, so profound was their scepticism of accepted notions of parliamentary representation that they found it hard to answer the question 'of whether the House contributes more to the policy process or to the tourist trade?' (Jordan and Richardson 1987a: 57).

Throughout their joint work, therefore, Jordan and Richardson contrasted the 'clear-cut and traditional principles of parliamentary and party government' (Richardson and Jordan 1979: 74), 'traditional notions of democracy, accountability and parliamentary sovereignty' (Jordan and Richardson 1987b: 288), and 'traditional notions of parliamentary and electoral democracy' (1987b: 289) with the reality and practice of group politics in Britain. In so setting the practice of groups against the theory of parliamentary democracy Richardson and Jordan characterised the British system of government as 'post-parliamentary'. Indeed, for over a decade this characterisation remained largely unquestioned and came to find reflection in other important commentaries (see for example Marquand 1988: 182–6).

The challenge posed by networks to existing modes of representation was also starkly identified by Rhodes and Marsh:

> The legitimacy of networks is not political but resides in the claims to superior expertise and/or to increased effectiveness of service provision....Professional expertise and effective service delivery legitimise the oligarchy of the policy network...[and] also to strengthen the networks' claim to make policy free from the 'irritating' constraint of political, especially electoral, legitimacy.
>
> (1992a: 200)

From a broader European perspective, Andersen and Burns elaborate on this theme:

> One of the main reasons that parliamentary systems are increasingly marginalized in modern politics and governance is that western societies have become highly differentiated and far too complex for parliament or its government to monitor, acquire sufficient knowledge and competence, and to deliberate on....Each specific policy area requires specialised technical and often scientific expertise and engage multiple interests and groups with special concern or interest in the particular, specialised policy matter. They represent themselves, *self-representation*. Such patterns contrast sharply with the territorial representation of citizens in parliamentary democracy.
>
> (1996: 229, original emphasis)

Later Andersen and Burns argue that the new forms of governance 'are more technically effective and flexible than the forms of representative democracy, and that they tend *to replace and crowd out* the latter' (1996: 231, emphasis added).

Clearly, therefore, a tension between functional and territorial forms of representation is identified in the 'post-parliamentary' thesis. But what needs to be considered is the extent to which the former can in fact *replace* the latter; or the extent to which 'self-representation' of groups can *supplant* 'general' representation through parliament; or the degree to which networks can legitimate their own activities *independently* of 'electoral' legitimacy. Without denying the descriptive accuracy of network analysis or a trend towards complex 'governance' the claims on behalf of new functional forms of representation – that they are replacing, supplanting and operating independently of parliamentary representation – need careful examination.

At an empirical level there are numerous examples where issues have 'escaped' the closed world of networks and placed themselves firmly on the public and parliamentary agenda (see Judge 1990a: 34–8; Judge 1990b: 61–6; Smith 1991: 243–51; Judge 1993: 126–30; Maloney and Richardson 1994: 121–34). At a conceptual level, network analysts have minimised the symbolic and legitimating functions of parliamentary representation. In so doing, they have tended to de-emphasise a prerequisite of functional representation, one that had been integral to earlier pluralist theory, namely, the very existence of elections and representative institutions themselves. Certainly, proponents of network analysis and governance are aware of the legitimation to be derived from territorial representation (see Judge 1993: 106–13). Thus, Andersen and Burns (1996: 228) are at pains to point out that their characterisation of governance 'does not claim that parliamentary democracy has become largely meaningless, or has no future role to play. It still remains the major basis for legitimising political authority and government in modern Western societies'. However, having recognised this vital point, they then redirect their argument towards the legislative and policy making roles of parliaments. In finding parliaments deficient in these latter roles the conclusion is reached that we have moved into a post-parliamentary era. But it was ever thus! Throughout its recent history the British parliament has been criticised for its restricted legislative and policy making role (see Judge 1983a: 1; Norton 1993: 2–11). To conclude that parliament's substantive contribution to law-making is limited, even peripheral in the case of detailed formulation and implementation, does not mean that parliament is peripheral to the process of policy making itself. Often the contribution of parliaments are indirect (see Daugbjerg and Marsh 1998: 62; Olsen *et al.* 1982: 65), or perform a 'climate setting' role, or, through oversight of policy implementation, contribute to the 'next round' of policy development (Pross 1986: 259; see also Judge 1990b: 38–9; Norton 1993: 109–12). But, even if it is conceded that, despite all of this, parliament's practical contribution to policy making is relatively restricted, the crucial point remains that parliamentary representation is still of *paramount importance* in the legitimation of public policy outputs.

In making this case, what also needs to be considered are the 'supports', in the language of systems theory, which enable demands to be processed and outputs to be implemented (see Easton 1966: 272–3, Kornberg and Clarke 1992: 19–23). The general belief, whether based on reason or not, that parliament is authoritative – that public policy should be sanctioned and authorised by a representative body – still pervades the British polity. There might be scepticism about the individual motivations of MPs and concern about individual policy outputs, but overriding this scepticism is a fundamental perception that the representative *system* is legitimate. As Norton (1993: 134) puts it: 'The power of Parliament derives from the fact that it is seen as authoritative – the legitimate – body for conferring legitimacy on measures of public policy.' Indeed, this point is conceded by Andersen and Burns when they note: 'A further weakening [of group-based governance] is that the specialised organic forms are not particularly effective at legitimising the system of modern governance. Typically, the formal democratic arrangements, in particular parliament, still remain essential in this respect' (1996: 246). It is reinforced implicitly in their recognition that 'organic governance' cannot in its own right deal with 'general legal and administrative functions' or cope with 'the fragmentation of policy making or the multitude of piecemeal developments' (1996: 246). Ultimately, they admit that there are serious problems – of legitimation and integration – with 'organic governance'. In other words, despite their earlier declaration that the 'robustness of these forms of governance is based in part on their effectiveness, but also on their democratic legitimacy' (1996: 240) there is no comprehensive source, no general fount, of legitimation for group-based governance. Indeed, Andersen and Burns are forced into an immediate qualification of their assertion of 'democratic legitimacy' on behalf of 'organic governance' as in the very next sentence they note: 'this legitimacy is, however, weaker or more open to criticism than that of popular sovereignty/representation, which is part of the sacred core of the west' (1996: 240).

Recent academic works have been willing to afford some greater recognition to the legitimating frame of representative democracy within which policy networks and structures of governance have to operate. Richardson, for example, acknowledges that 'a useful qualification to the post-parliamentary thesis…is [that it is] important to note the symbolic and legitimating functions of parliament' (1993: 90). Similarly, Daugbjerg and Marsh maintain that: 'Since representative democracy is the major form of governance in Western societies, it does not make sense simply to argue that parliaments are excluded from influence because we cannot observe the direct effects upon the policy outcome' (1998: 62). They conclude that: 'Overlooking the role of parliaments in analyses of policy making is, therefore, a great mistake' (Daugbjerg and Marsh 1998: 63). There is, thus, a growing recognition of the importance of the legitimation afforded by the representative process to network outputs. Exactly how this legitimation is bestowed on public policies remains an under-researched phenomenon, but the following statement serves as a starting hypothesis for future empirical research:

> For 'political' legitimacy to be conferred upon the outputs of the group process requires them to be translated into 'government' outputs and so to gain legitimacy from the authorisation derived from the electoral process and parliamentary representation. This has been recognised by classical pluralists (including Dahl) and Marxists alike. Hence, in the latter camp Miliband (1982: 20) is convinced that the importance of the House of Commons stems from the fact that 'it enshrines the elective principle and thus provides the absolutely indispensable legitimation for the government of the country; nothing...could be more important than that'.
>
> (Judge 1993: 131)

British analysts in focusing upon the routines and stability of policy communities, or the complex interlinkages of 'organic governance', initially at least, took for granted, or simply overlooked, the elemental fact that the outputs of this process – no matter how necessary in terms of efficiency – could not be legitimised simply in functional terms.

Associative democracy in the 1990s

The essential analytical points to be drawn from the preceding discussion are: first, that the theory and practice of functional or interest representation has constituted a normative challenge to established notions of representative government; and, second, that the practice of interest representation – in its 'non-parliamentary', limited participatory forms – reveals the extent to which that practice has reflected the configuration of political power resulting from established notions of representative government.

At first sight, therefore, it appears somewhat strange for a respected social theorist, Paul Hirst, and a practising politician, Antony Wright, to advocate the *supplementation* of territorial representation with a developed system of functional representation. It has to be admitted from the outset, however, that their concern is not with the mere supplementation of existing representative democracy but with the creation of a 'developed structure of functional representation alongside a *reformed* structure of territorial representation' (Wright 1994: 97, emphasis added). Nor are they concerned with the wholesale replacement of representative democracy, as was the case with Cole's version of Guild Socialism.

Unlike Cole, Hirst's starting premise is 'to reason from existing political institutions and contemporary political problems towards possible alternatives' (1997: 2). He argues, therefore, that a response to the new institutional architecture of 'governance' needs to address 'the powers of all organizations and not just to confine their remedies to government and the state' (Hirst 1997: 12–13). From this starting point he rapidly reaches the conclusion that 'the old liberal architecture is obsolete and that we need to develop democratic practices across the whole of society, considering it an ensemble of forms of governance' (1997: 13). The new model of governance identified by Hirst is that of 'associative democracy'.

This new model would not abolish representative government (Hirst 1997: 17). Indeed, 'modern associative democracy can only be a more or less extensive supplement to liberal representative democracy, it cannot seek to abolish the individual right to vote on a territorial basis, nor to abolish the state as a public power' (Hirst 1994: 19). The same point is made by Wright who maintains that reform 'does not mean a devaluation of territorial and electoral representation' (1994: 97). Instead, what it does mean is that 'territorial representation is not enough' (Wright 1994: 97). What is also required is 'a developed structure of functional representation alongside a reformed structure of territorial representation' (Wright 1994: 97). But it is left to Hirst to sketch the details of this new disaggregated form of representation.

The essence of Hirst's argument is that there is a 'deep and widespread dissatisfaction about both economic performance and the health of democracy' (Hirst 1993: 116; Hirst 1997: 28–30). In this respect his concern is identical to that of inter-war functional theorists considered above. Yet, he is adamant that the experience of the 1980s and 1990s has heightened awareness of the lack of citizen control over decision makers and the increased centralisation of power within liberal democracies. Moreover, in the absence of an alternative, viable soviet model of 'democracy' – given the collapse of the USSR – Western liberal democracy can no longer present itself as a flawed, but still superior system to state socialism. In other words, 'western societies now have to be judged by their own standards and on their own merits' (Hirst 1994: 3). In these circumstances the deficiencies of representative government become apparent in their own right, and the remedy is to make 'accountable representative democracy possible again' through the development of 'associationalism' (Hirst 1994: 12).

Associationalism is based upon three basic principles of political organisation: first, that voluntary self-governing associations should be the primary means of democratic governance; second, that power should be decentralised to the lowest level consistent with effective governance of economic and social affairs – in other words that the principles of 'state pluralism and federation' should prevail, and; third, that there should be a continuous flow of information between governors and the governed (Hirst 1994: 20; 1997: 31–2. (By 1997 Hirst identifies the third proposition as the organisation of the economy along 'mutualist lines')). Whilst power should be decentralised as far as possible, Hirst still believes that there is a need for a 'common public power'. This power would be based on representative democratic principles and would take the institutional form of a legislature elected on a territorial basis by universal suffrage, and an independent judiciary. 'Such a public power would be, in effect, a liberal constitutional state, but with limited functions' (Hirst 1994: 33).

Associationalism and liberalism, for Hirst, are not in conflict. In which case 'the associational principle can democratize and reinvigorate societies as a supplement to and a healthy competitor for, the currently dominant forms of social organization: representative mass democracy, bureaucratic state welfare and the big corporation' (Hirst 1994: 42; 1997: 56). Having made this stipulation, Hirst is preoccupied thereafter with 'working out the detail of credible models of associational governance' (1994: 43). Without being drawn into the details of Hirst's scheme it is possible to identify the central characteristics of the new model. The first is that territorially-based representative institutions would continue to provide a framework of basic rules and fiscal organisation within which associations could provide services for their members. The second is that there would be 'subsidiary governments' – voluntary self-governing associations in which individuals would participate. Associations would have their own rules and 'their own forms of accountability'. 'The affairs of such governments in civil society could thus be specific to them for most matters concerned with providing services to their members and need not directly concern the public power' (Hirst 1997: 18). The benefits claimed for the new models are those of both 'representative and direct democracy, whilst minimizing the costs of both' (1997: 19).

Hirst is aware that 'these are large claims' but is adamant that the new form of associative democracy is sustainable. However, such sustainability is dependent upon fundamental reforms in economic and social organisation in parallel with those to be effected in the political domain. To function effectively as 'agencies of supervision and accountability' (1997: 33), the institutions of representative democracy would require voluntary self-governing associations to accept responsibility for service delivery in primary areas of welfare – such as education and health. The underlying assumption is that voluntarism would make social provision and social governance less conflictual (1997: 33), though it may be argued that this has as much the status of an article of faith as an analytically sound prognostication. Similarly, fundamental changes in the organisation of the economy appear to be an essential underpinning proposition for effective associational governance. An economy organised on mutualist lines, as proposed by Hirst (1997: 18), would be based on 'non-profit financial institutions and co-operative firms in which both investors and workers have a significant say in their governance'. Such a transformation would be long-term and would involve the transformation of companies and welfare agencies into self-governing associations (Hirst 1997: 50). For Hirst such a transformation would not be utopian and a new societal model of associationalism would be 'administratively and organizationally feasible' (1997: 66). Fortunately for our purposes we do not have to make a judgement on Hirst's proposals for economic and social reform. Instead, we need simply to consider the relationship between associationalism and representative democracy.

Hirst openly acknowledges the crucial legitimatory capacity of representative democracy. Indeed, he is critical of leftist reformers who wish to replace representative democracy with some other form of democracy, claiming that this 'is not only dangerous, it is suicidal' (1997: 83). He also recognises that despite the defects associated with the modern British state 'the legitimacy of representative government remains unshaken and people are terrified by the advocacy of alternatives to it' (1997: 83). This then prompts the question of how can democratisation of the state take place without a frontal attack on existing forms of representative democracy? The answer, for Hirst, is to avoid the question by asserting from the outset that 'modern representative institutions cannot be supplanted, they can only be supplemented' (1997: 87). Democratisation, if it is to be successful, must entail building an effective pluralist system of political competition which embraces both associationalism and territorial representation.

The fundamental difficulty of achieving this synthesis of different modes of representation – one based on the specific principles of function, the other on the general principles of territory – is precisely that identified throughout this chapter: while the latter provides an overarching legitimating frame the former can only legitimate specific outputs relating to specific groups. Hence, in assessing Hirst's scheme, at least two dimensions of representation have to be considered, first the viability of representation at the level of associations and second the interrelationship between associational and parliamentary representation.

On the first dimension, in Hirst's scheme, if groups are to be considered 'democratic' then there is a basic requirement for them to be 'more inclusive of their potential memberships and impelled, by bargaining, to take heed of other organizations and interests' (1997: 87). Groups would not necessarily be organised on the principle of extensive membership participation. Individuals who choose to be active may be active, but it is assumed that 'even the most active will choose a small range of organizations to be active in' (1997: 19). What associationalism offers in terms of participation, therefore, is basically 'choice and voice' (1997: 19). It offers the opportunity for individuals to choose to participate in associations offering specific services, as well as the opportunity to exit from unsatisfactory service providers.

What associationalism offers in terms of decision making is a process 'of concession and intermediation of interests in which a common course of action or a mutually agreed objective is the result' (1997: 88). In this second dimension it is assumed that plural and competitive interests can be accommodated in a course of action that enjoys common consent. Throughout, Hirst assumes that associations would be 'lightly regulated' (1997: 18) and that the public power would serve primarily to protect the 'autonomy of groups from predation by other groups, through the defence of group and individual rights' (1997: 45). His ultimate objective is to secure the conditions under which 'outside of irreconcilable and competing claims to rights and moral regulation, the parallel and socially competitive social governance by associations would be possible more often than not' (1997: 44).

The difficulty in effecting such a 'voluntary membership representative government' (1997: 18) alongside existing territorially-based representative government, is that the realm of 'consensus' and 'democratic legitimation' is dependent upon a 'public power' defining this consensus and the scope of legitimation. Groups, in and of themselves, cannot sustain a broad policy consensus in a competitive process of service delivery. In this respect Hirst encounters a basic problem commonly identified with pluralism: the crucial role ascribed to consensus.

The problem for Hirst is thus, that despite identifying a process of policy making and of service delivery which is competitive, ultimately the process is deemed capable of producing consensual outputs. Yet, other than through the mere assertion of a pre-existing consensus, it is unclear how consensual and 'democratically legitimated' (1997: 19) policies will emerge in an increasingly heterogenous society in which 'distinct communities have very different and often conflicting standards' (1997: 29). While Hirst believes that 'groups and associations would compete non-politically' (1997: 33), this simply assumes away conflict, and fails to address the thorny problem of how the preferred policy outputs of any specific group could be translated into binding policies – other than through the involve-

ment of the 'public power' and the invocation of the legislative authority
and accountability derived from the wider electoral process and territorial
representation. Only by stipulating the existence of 'commonly agreed
community standards of service provision' (1997: 44), in direct contradiction of the countervailing trend identified earlier, can Hirst sustain the
notion of consensus. Only by stipulating that self-governing and accountable organisations would be 'the *primary* means of organizing social life'
(1997: 42, original emphasis) can their practical subservience to representative democracy – which Hirst holds responsible for inspecting and
overseeing associations, ensuring their compliance with democratic norms,
and providing services in conformity with 'commonly agreed' standards –
be sidestepped. Implicitly Hirst's argument depends upon a fact which
other associational theorists make explicit: 'First and all-important, our
scheme assumes that final authority continues to rest with more traditional,
encompassing, territorially-based systems of representation' (Cohen and
Rodgers 1995: 69). Without such explicit acknowledgement of the primacy
of the legitimation derived from territorial representation, Hirst's argument encounters similar obstacles to those confronting earlier functional
theorists and other associational theorists. Whereas these theorists posit
complementarity between existing representative institutions and associational life, it can just as easily be argued that interaction rather than
complementarity would result. As Immergut notes, the institutions of
representative democracy 'are important not just for establishing the
contours of associational representation, but they also affect the behavior
of associations during negotiation processes'. In which case, 'these interactions should be explored in more depth because they could inadvertently
undermine associative democracy in practice' (1995: 202).

Conclusion

The examination of six major models of interest representation has
revealed inherent empirical and normative tensions between them and
existing territorial, individualistic conceptions of representation. One way
of resolving these tensions, prescribed by Guild Socialism, would have
been the simple replacement of territorial representation with a comprehensive and integrated scheme of functional representation in a new
socialist society. However, the other models examined in this chapter have
operated within the context of capitalist liberal democratic society. In
various ways they have confronted the issue of the compatibility of territorially-based representation through parliament with functionally-based
representation through organised groups or self-governing associations.

Schemes for the supplementation of parliamentary representation with some form of functional representation (in some new institutional form, in the inter-war period, or through the competitive group process of early 'pluralism' in the 1950s, or in the new associationalism of the 1990s) have recognised the necessary contribution of territorial representation to the conferring of legitimacy on public policies, but have also recognised its empirical limitations in the practical process of policy making. These practical limitations, and the mismatch between established representative theories and political practice, have been at the centre of the new British political science orthodoxies of 'networks' and 'governance'. Parliamentary institutions, based upon the principles of territorial representation, have been seen to have been marginalised in the new forms of governance. Policy outputs are now considered to be legitimised by the claims to superior expertise and/or to increased effectiveness in service delivery on the part of networks (Rhodes and Marsh 1992a: 200). The conclusion reached is that the 'mismatch between theory and practice will erode the legitimating role of parliament' (Rhodes 1997: 2). By this view, 'governance' poses a clear and apparent normative danger to representative democracy.

We will return to this normative challenge in Chapter 8, in the meantime, however, we need to identify the 'levels' of territorial representation in Britain, and the extent to which the issues identified in this chapter recur at those levels to constitute a sustained challenge to traditional notions of territorial representation.

7   Territory and levels of representation

The simple overriding fact about parliamentary representation in Britain is that it is based upon territory. This statement might seem to fly in the face of earlier pronouncements in this book that representation is not uni-dimensional and that MPs in practice may represent different foci of representation – 'party', 'organised interests', 'social identities' and 'the nation' – serially or even simultaneously. Nonetheless, the primary basis of representation remains territorial. A Member of Parliament is formally the representative of a designated geographical area and by convention can expect, if not a minister or other office holder, to be addressed in debate in the House of Commons simply as the Honourable Member for Tatton or wherever. The Committee examining the modernisation of the House of Commons had cause to explain the contemporary importance of this convention:

> There are some who feel that the need to refer to other Members by their constituencies is both difficult and unnecessary, and that use of names would be more fitting in a modern Parliament....Quite apart from the practicalities there is, however, a much more important point of principle. Members do not sit in the House as individual citizens, they are there as representatives of their constituencies: and it is in that capacity that they should be addressed.
>
> (HC 600 1998: paras 38–9)

It is important, therefore, to start our discussion of territorial representation by acknowledging that the core principles of representation in Britain – of consent, legitimation and the authorisation of decision making (considered in Chapter 1) – were built upon territorial foundations. This point is neatly summarised by Reeve and Ware:

> one of the most interesting features of the representation of counties and boroughs in the medieval Parliament is that important socio-

economic interests were being represented on a territorial basis. Nor was there any other way to do this. Land was the key resource for the medieval state, and what was more natural than to have those with a stake in it being represented through the long-standing English unit of territorial divisions, the county. Commerce too had to be conducted in *a place* – as, indeed, it largely has been until the 'computer revolution' of the 1970s – so that representing commercial interests by representing each borough was as self-evident as county representation.

(1992: 46, original emphasis)

In granting consent to the raising of additional taxation, representatives in medieval parliaments not only conferred the assent of their local communities and associated economic interests, but also used the monarch's dependency upon that consent to promote the welfare of their constituents through the presentation of public petitions and the redress of individual grievances (see Butt 1989: 272–354; Judge 1993: 7–12). In this respect, as Searing points out, 'the modern role of the Constituency Member is, in fact, a new version of a very old role which has been neglected for some time' (1994: 123).

This modern constituency role is examined in the first part of this chapter. Then, broader analysis of territorial representation in Britain beyond Westminster is examined through other *levels of representation*. Other representative institutions and processes of representation have developed, and continue to develop, at local, sub-national and European levels. The first level is local government. Traditionally, local representative institutions in Britain, in the form of elected local councils, have coexisted with a sovereign representative parliament. In part, this very coexistence has been posited upon the constitutional proposition that local councils are 'subordinate units, subject to the sovereignty of the state' (Hill 1974: 25). But from this subordinate position many of the arguments about local government have reflected the discussions about parliamentary representation – about representative democracy and government; microcosmic representation; party representation; functional representation; and issues of 'governance'.

The development of a directly elected European Parliament since 1979 has also prompted further consideration of the territorial dimensions of representation in Britain. Unlike locally elected councils, the European Parliament is not subordinate to the UK parliament and exercises its representative functions in parallel with those exercised by the UK parliament. This has led to a belief that the Westminster parliament and its Members face a challenge from the Strasbourg parliament and the assertion of its own representative legitimacy in the European policy process. Since the referenda of September 1997, similar fears have also been expressed about the creation of a Scottish parliament and Welsh assembly (see Chapter 8).

Constituency representation

The simple statement that 'parliamentary representation involves a territory' (Hibbing and Patterson 1986: 992) raises a series of complex research questions. For the sake of simplicity these questions can be grouped into those dealing with the 'style' of representation and those dealing with the 'focus' of representation. Those dealing with 'style' direct attention towards how representatives act (Wahlke *et al.* 1962). Typically the answer has been to locate the actions of MPs on a continuum from the position of 'independent trustee' through 'politico' to 'mandated delegate'. At the respective ends of this continuum the representative is held either to act independently of constituency opinion or interest; or, alternatively, to take instructions from his or her constituents. In between, a representative who acts as a 'politico' may adopt trustee and delegate styles at different times on different policy issues. Indeed, most of the literature on representational 'style' is concerned with determining the extent of the 'policy responsiveness' of representatives to the known policy preferences of their constituents. Although this is a remarkably complex issue (not least because of the difficulty of ascertaining, through aggregation, the policy preferences of 70,000 constituents and the extent of congruence between such policy preferences and the activities of representatives in parliament), empirical studies have tended to simplify this relationship into linear form. While the deficiencies of research strategies and findings on representational style need not detain us here (for a discussion see Jewell 1983: 321–9; McCrone and Stone 1986: 956–74; Studlar and McAlistair 1996: 70–2), the broader issue needs to be addressed of how appropriate is the discussion of policy responsiveness in a parliamentary system in which 'party representation' predominates. In Britain, as Norton and Wood (1993: 26) note: 'fidelity to party "instructions" complicates the relationship between MP and constituents'. The expectation is that very rarely will an MP afford priority to constituency opinion ahead of party policy in deciding how to vote in parliament.

The second set of questions relating to constituency raise the issue of the 'focus' of representation. As originally conceived by Wahlke *et al.* (1962) the 'focus' of representation referred to the 'what' of representation. 'What' was to be represented could be conceived of not only as a geographical constituency but also in terms of other spatial areas such as 'the nation', or other organisations such as parties or functional groups. The notion of 'representational focus' thus encompassed 'areal' conceptions alongside functional and ideological groupings. In Britain, as seen in chapters 4 and 5, functional and party foci have tended to engage MPs' attention over and above areal foci. Even when geographical area has featured in the performance of representational roles, 'the nation' has been afforded pre-eminence over constituency in representative theory. Thus Searing observes that 'when political opinions are represented in Britain, the process typically has a national rather than a constituency focus: it is national views and moods which are considered by British Governments' (1985: 370). In which case, Searing is led to speculate that: 'the role of the Constituency Member, which immerses backbenchers in the small disputes and difficulties of their constituents, must seem a peculiar occupation for members of a parliament that is so nationally oriented' (Searing 1994: 121). As we will soon see, however, constituency service is not as peculiar as initially predicted, but, before examining the role of the 'Constituency MP', we need to clarify what 'constituency' means to most MPs. In this task Richard Fenno's (1978) work on 'homestyle' proves to be of considerable help.

Of particular value is Fenno's conception of constituency as a series of concentric circles which embrace successively smaller subsets of voters in a geographical electoral district. Indeed, successive studies of constituency representation in Britain have drawn upon Fenno's four-fold distinction between geographical, re-election, primary and personal constituencies (see Cain *et al.* 1979: 520–2; Judge 1981: 29; Norton and Wood 1993: 27–8). The innermost circle is the 'personal constituency' which can be identified as an MP's agent, secretary, spouse or partner, and close personal friends. The 'primary constituency' approximates to party activists and 'local party opinion leaders' – who might include local councillors, and respectively local trade unionists or officers of local Chambers of Commerce. The third circle is the 're-election' constituency which consists of voters who voted for the MP; and the fourth, and widest, circle is the geographical boundary of the constituency itself.

The importance of this conceptualisation of constituency is that it provides an analytical tool for discovering 'what' representatives think they are representing in their constituencies and how various sub-sets of constituents can provide 'voting cues' for their representative in parliament (see Judge 1981: 34). In the British context it helps to re-incorporate constituency preferences back into a model of policy responsiveness based largely on party premises. This is evident in Norton and Wood's study, *Back from Westminster*, which conceives of

a triadic relationship among the legislator, the legislator's parliamentary party, and his primary constituency. The legislator will be most unlikely to vote against the coincident preferences of both the parliamentary party leaders and the primary constituency. When these do not coincide, the legislator may have more leeway to vote with the preferences of one or the other....In Britain, the leadership of the parliamentary party carries the greatest weight with most back-benchers most of the time. Nevertheless, the MP must be attentive to the policy wishes of that subset of constituents who 'count'.

(Norton and Wood 1993: 28)

How far MPs are attentive to their primary constituency, to the extent of cross-voting in the House of Commons, is revealed in the findings of Searing (1994: 136–40; see also Cain *et al.* 1979: 520). Instances of open backbench revolt against government policy are often linked by dissenters to the expression of unfavourable constituency opinion, and certainly the opinions of party activists in the constituency weigh heavily in any intra-party policy disputes. Thus, for example, in December 1997 several of the 47 Labour MPs who defied a three-line whip over reductions in lone parent benefits made direct reference to their primary and re-election constituencies in defence of their actions. The strength of constituency support for one of the rebels, Ann Clwyd MP for Cynon, was such that she could report a message from a local party supporter which threatened that, should the Labour Chief Whip dare 'come to Aberdare to try to reselect you...he'll be tarred and feathered and thrown in the river' (*Observer*, 14 December 1997). In contrast, one Labour MP who voted in support of the benefit cut was reported to have turned up at his constituency after the vote to find his party staff refusing to speak to him (*Guardian*, 20 December 1997).

Constituency service

The above discussion reflects the academic concern (particularly pronounced in the US) with policy advocacy and the strategies adopted by representatives in identifying, interpreting and incorporating constituency opinion into their legislative activities. Yet, the conceptual and method-ological shortcomings of the 'policy congruence' approach (for overviews see Jewell 1983: 322–4; Norton and Wood 1993: 29) have led to a more recent research concern with 'constituency service' undertaken by repre-sentatives. In part, this concern is prompted by 'the puzzle of constituency service' – why British MPs faced with overloaded schedules and conflicting priorities spend so much time on constituency service (Norris 1997a: 29). But, in part also, it is a pragmatic recognition that what interests political scientists about constituency representation – policy advocacy and policy congruence – is not necessarily what interests constituents themselves. As Norton and Wood (1993: 29) observe: 'carrying out constituents' wishes will more often mean raising a matter of personal concern to a constituent or group – particularly at the level of detail, amenable to administrative redress – than expressing views on grand issues of national policy'.

One thing is clear, however, British MPs are spending an increased proportion of their time on constituency 'service responsiveness'. Throughout the post-war period, but especially since the mid-1960s, the average amount of time spent by MPs on constituency matters has increased significantly. Estimates vary as to the exact amount of time expended on such matters but various indicators suggest that 'constituency work has more than doubled in the last two decades' (Norris 1997a: 30), and that (in the intervening period between surveys of MPs for pay reviews in 1983 and 1996) 'work related to the constituency, often initiated by individuals in some form of trouble, has become more burdensome' (Cm 3330-II 1996: 4). Data from the British Candidate Study revealed that in 1992 MPs estimated that they spent 25 hours per week on constituency work, representing one-third of their workload (Norris 1997a: 30). A survey conducted by the Review Body on Senior Salaries in early 1996 found that respondent MPs estimated that they spent 31 hours a week, or 38 per cent of their time, on constituency work (Cm 3330-II 1996: 30). However, these aggregate figures conceal substantial variations in the amount of time expended on constituency work. These variations reflect differences in MPs' pre-parliamentary backgrounds, career aspirations, and role orientations; as well as differences in constituency demographics and socioeconomic profiles (see Norton and Wood 1993; Searing 1994: 121–60; Norris 1997a). If anything, junior MPs are prone to spend more time on constituency service than their more established colleagues. Wood and Young (1997: 221) report, from their interviews with relatively inexperienced MPs in 1995, that new MPs estimated that they spent around 35 hours a week on constituency matters, with up to 47 per cent of their total working hours devoted to constituency service. Perhaps it is not surprising to find, therefore, that, in view of the increased importance attached to constituency service in recent years by MPs, local political parties, individual constituents and the local media (see Cm 3330-II 1996: 5), the 1997 cohort of newly elected MPs prioritised 'representing their constituents' above even 'advancing the party cause' (Norton and Mitchell 1997: 13). The exact motivations for this prioritisation still remain the cause of academic dispute: whether to maximise the 'personal vote' associated with 'the good constituency Member' (see Cain *et al.* 1984: 110–25; Cain *et al.* 1987: 77–88; Norton and Wood 1994: 126–42; Norris 1997a: 30–2), or to derive 'psychological reward' for the successful redress of grievance or for enhancing service delivery (Norris 1997a: 41–3) or simply because welfare provision constitutes the major part of state expenditure and assumes an immediate and overarching part of constituents' daily lives.

What is not in dispute, however, is that 'constituency service' forms a significant part of the generic job description of a British MP in the 1990s (see Cm 3330-II 1996: 24). This 'service activity' on behalf of constituents encompasses at least two, often discrete, roles. One is commonly referred to as the 'welfare officer role', with MPs carrying out 'casework' on behalf of aggrieved constituents, the other is concerned with the 'promotion' of collective constituency projects, such as local industrial and economic development, environmental improvement or some other social project.

Local promotion: territorial advocacy

What is particularly important about 'project work' (Norton and Wood 1993) or 'local promotion' (Searing 1994), for present purposes, is that it 'involves promotion and defence of interests found within a particular part of the country' (Norton and Wood 1993: 58). In other words, it is a form of 'territorial advocacy'. MPs promote constituency interests by 'lobbying' on their behalf, by making representations to ministers and other decision makers such as managers and chief executives of commercial and industrial organisations located in the constituency (or of enterprises which constituents would like to be located in their area). Indeed, a detailed study of the activities of MPs on industrial policy concluded that: 'overall, it was apparent that spatial foci, where backbenchers had as their primary concern the geographical area of constituency or region, proportionally outweighed most other individual 'functional' concerns' (Judge 1990a: 123).

Findings which reveal that MPs place as much, if not more, emphasis upon territory as upon function in their promotion of the material interests of their constituents do challenge, however, at least one academic orthodoxy of the 1980s – as well as reflecting a practical paradox confronting representatives themselves. In the 1980s Richard Rose championed the view that territory did not play an important role in national policy making, and that MPs must be more functionally than territorially oriented in their attempts to influence policy (see Rose 1982: 88). The identification of a 'territorial advocacy' role in successive studies (see Wood 1987; Judge 1990a; Norton and Wood 1993) clearly challenged Rose's view. These studies also highlighted the paradox that party representatives who were mandated to a national electoral programme might also seek to promote dissonant policies in the process of representing constituency interests. This leads Wood and Norton (1993: 62–3) to argue that MPs must effectively compartmentalise the areal dimensions of their representative roles. What this means in practice is that MPs 'must be prepared to act as if there is no connection between national policy commitments and local needs for policy to be delivered in certain ways'. They must find, therefore, 'some means of subdividing the two parts of their world [constituency and Westminster]…[they] must find ways of reconciling their functional with their territorial concerns'. Empirical illustration of this subdivision was provided by neo-liberal Conservative MPs in the 1980s – who were strongly anti-interventionist in their pronouncements on industrial policy at the national level at Westminster – but who wore 'at least moderately interventionist' faces in their constituencies (Wood 1987: 407–9; Judge 1990a: 127–9).

Welfare officer: casework

The second dimension of the constituency 'service delivery' role is that associated with 'casework' and 'representing constituents against the bureaucracy' (Cain *et al.* 1984: 114). There is widespread agreement that this part of the representative's job has increased enormously in the last two decades (see Rawlings 1990: 22–4; Norton 1993: 147–53; Norton and Wood 1993: 42–6; Norris 1997a: 30). Correspondingly, there has been an increased expectation on the part of constituents that 'the most important part of an MP's job is to deal with their problems' (*The Times*, 25 August 1997), and that MPs will have close personal links with the constituency (Curtice and Jowell 1997: 96).

MPs receive a substantial number of requests from individual constituents to intervene on their behalf to resolve some administrative problem. Typical problems relate to social security provision, housing, schooling, the National Health Service, immigration services and policing matters, and reflect the mix of institutions that MPs are expected to mediate with – local government, central government departments and agencies, and private utilities and institutions. Yet, there is a fundamental ambiguity about the status of MPs in dealing with these matters: as the responsibility for service delivery is often in the hands of local officials who are responsible to locally elected councillors (see below) or to private companies which are responsible to their shareholders. Nonetheless, MPs are willing to act as intermediaries, literally to 're-present' the grievances of individual constituents to service providers, and, in reverse, to inform the complainant of the response. In many ways the constituency MP acts as a sorting mechanism in the process of the redress of grievances. Individual constituents when confronted with a maze of administrative agencies in an era of rapid change in jurisdictional boundaries – occasioned by privatisation, agencification and local government reform – often turn to an MP to act as 'their representative'. In this capacity, the MP provides not only a point of access into the complicated system of 'governance' but also serves to educate both the individual complainant and the MP himself or herself about the wider process of governance.

Often what the constituent is seeking is information about, or an explanation of, a decision taken; or reassurance that some action is being taken on their particular case. Rawlings (1990: 42) found, for example, that nearly two-thirds of the constituency cases he studied sought further information or confirmation that the matter was in hand. Equally, MPs gain valuable information in dealing with service delivery cases: not the least of which is a clearer understanding of the problems and issues confronting their constituents in their daily routines. In the words of one MP: 'the cases are often a useful reminder of how awful government can be' (quoted in Radice *et al.* 1990: 106–7; see also Norton 1993: 158).

If the 'majority of MPs – especially the more recently elected – regard [the welfare officer] role as one of the most important things they do' (Cm 3330-II 1996: 24), there are those who now believe that this role has assumed too great a prominence in the process of representation. Thus Peter Riddell argues: 'the constituency welfare officer role is valuable…but MPs should not let it undermine their national work at Westminster. This means that MPs should take a decision no longer to deal with matters which are properly the responsibility of those elected at local level, or to a Scottish parliament' (*The Times*, 25 August 1997). While the inconsistencies of Riddell's argument need not detain us – the assumption that the national focus of representation should be paramount, the failure to appreciate the historical importance of the redress of local grievances by Westminster MPs, the close connection between policy advocacy and the administration of public services, and the informatory dimension of dealing with casework – his statement does highlight the importance of other levels of representation in Britain and the need to consider these other levels in any discussion of the modern practice of representation.

Local government and governance

One of the problems with Riddell's belief that MPs should leave well alone 'matters which are properly the responsibility of those elected at local level', is that over the past two decades the traditional responsibilities of local authorities have been diminished as non-elected or indirectly elected bodies have assumed responsibility for service delivery. In education, local authorities have lost direct responsibility for polytechnics, further education colleges, school budgets and opted-out schools; in housing, housing action trusts and housing associations have challenged local authority provision and administration; urban development corporations have assumed important responsibilities for inner city regeneration; partnerships with private and voluntary agencies have developed in the provision of welfare services, while direct provision of such services as cleansing, street cleaning and catering have been undermined by the process of competitive tendering. In other words, an important element of the trend towards the 'differentiated polity' and the development of 'governance' (see Chapter 6) is 'local governance' which implies a reduced role for local authorities as direct service providers (Wilson and Game 1998: 83). One ironic consequence of this increased fragmentation of local service provision might well be the possible expansion of the 'service delivery' role of MPs. In the face of such diversity, MPs may come to serve as a single identifiable beacon for constituents in search of redress of grievance. The constituency MP may increasingly become identified as the point of connection, even if only in the limited sense of redirecting enquiries, between constituents and a multitude of public and quasi-public agencies and organisations.

Nonetheless, despite the challenges of recent years, local authorities in Britain still remain major service providers. Such service provision has traditionally been justified and defended on grounds of efficiency and effectiveness (see Sharpe 1970: 166–74; Stoker 1996: 190), but a parallel and persistent concern has been to ensure that these services are publicly accountable. In this respect, the debate has been not simply about the local *administration* of services but about local *government* – with a special emphasis upon *representative* government and the legitimacy to be derived from local elections. As Loughlin (1996: 39) observes: 'local councils, being the only governmental institutions outside of Parliament which are subject to direct periodic election [not withstanding the European Parliament], are accorded a degree of political legitimacy which other agencies of government do not possess'. For many, following in the tradition of J.S. Mill ([1861] 1910: 346–59), local government has constituted an essential component of 'democratic society' – in that it has provided 'elected representatives who are close to those they serve, and who form an easy channel of communication between public opinion and the council. No other body does this' (Hill 1974: 15). The 'degree of legitimacy' of local authorities, and their 'unique contribution' to democratic government, is contingent, however, upon a grant of authorisation from Westminster and the national representative process. As the Widdicombe Report on *The Conduct of Local Authority Business* noted: 'All current local authorities are the statutory creations of Parliament and have no independent status or right to exist' (Cmnd 9797-I 1986: 45). Successive reorganisations of the structure of local authorities in the constituent parts of the UK have visibly underlined the contingent nature of local government.

Slipping 'n sliding between local representative democracy and local representative government

The tendency to slide between notions of representative democracy and representative government, noted in Chapter 1, is also prevalent in the discussion of local government. For example, the Widdicombe Report in talking of the 'essential currency of representative democracy' conceived of this in terms of 'an organisational basis through which citizens can achieve the type of government and type of services they want without themselves needing to participate directly in the process of government. If the political party for which they vote fails to deliver, that party can be held accountable through the ballot box at the next election' (Cmnd 9797-I 1986: 60). Here the claim of local government to be 'representative' entails the implicit assumption that the local political executive will be 'responsible' to the electorate. The condition of executive responsiveness overrides notions of active citizen participation.

More perspicacious commentators, however, make a distinction between the concepts of 'representative democracy' and 'representative government' (see Beetham 1996: 30–4) and in looking to the future of local government, and in 'rethinking local democracy' (see King and Stoker 1996), place the emphasis firmly on 'democratising' the processes of decision making. Significantly, much of the argument about enhancing local democracy is based on the premise that 'there is no point in arguing against representative democracy *per se*' (Phillips 1996a: 28; see Chapter 8). There is a recognition that electing representatives to act on behalf of the represented has to remain a major component of local democracy (Phillips 1996a: 28). There is a further acknowledgement that without the legitimacy conferred through popular election, the necessary general consent for, and authorisation of, local decisions would be difficult to generate. Hence, and not surprisingly, the basic features of representation identified at the national level – consent, legitimation, authorisation – reappear in the discussion of local democracy and government. Equally, most other issues examined in preceding chapters – of microcosmic representation, independent trusteeship, party representation, associative democracy – reappear at the local level.

Microcosmic representation at the local level

There are some 23,000 elected local politicians in the UK (Wilson and Game 1998: 218) who are each elected by the residents of a defined geographical area. (There are also an estimated 80,000 members of parish, town and community councils, but these councils have only limited, discretionary service responsibilities at best; or act in an advisory capacity.) Indeed, 'the existence of local interests and local people's identification with, and commitment to, their area can be seen as the focus of local government and the basis of its legitimacy' (Fraser 1996: 103). Yet, although far outnumbering MPs, there are fewer elected councillors in the UK than in most other Western European states. Each elected local politician in the UK represents an average of 2,605 constituents, whereas in France the corresponding figure is 116 and in Germany the figure is 250 (Wilson and Game 1998: 228). But these average statistics conceal the fact that in some large urban conurbations in the UK individual councillors may represent up to 25,000 constituents. The corollaries of this scale 'are that we citizens have fewer councillors to represent us, and we are less likely to know or be known by them' (Wilson and Game 1998: 228).

If the 'scale' of local representation gives rise for concern, so too does the social composition of local councils. In trying to answer the question 'why local government matters?' Phillips argues that, 'if democratic representation is conceived in terms of the different needs and concerns of the electorate, this demands closer attention to the characteristics of the people elected' (1996a: 31). Thus the same microcosmic arguments examined in Chapter 2 resurface in the discussion of local representation. If anything, the concern with the under-representation of some segments of society is heightened at the local level. Again the position of women and ethnic minorities attracts most attention.

Local government has proved itself significantly more open to women than representation at the national level. Women have had a considerably longer history of involvement, and proportionally higher success rates, in local participation and elections than at Westminster. In part, this reflects the congruence between 'women's issues' and the nature of the services provided by local authorities (see Phillips 1996b: 113–4). In which case, 'women's relatively high profile in local government hardly needs to have any further explanation: what is odd is that men still remain dominant' (Phillips 1996b: 114). The extent of this dominance is such that, even though the proportion of female councillors has doubled in the past thirty years and stands at over 25 per cent of locally elected representatives, and so is substantially higher than the proportion of women MPs even after May 1997, the figures remain 'dispiriting' for many commentators (Wilson and Game 1998: 222). For others of a more sceptical nature, the very openness of local government to women is because of its relative lack of power: 'One might argue that the relative (if mild) feminisation of local government has coincided with its most marked period of impotence and decline, and that if the power of local councils were later restored (or even increased), this might well remove women's relative advantage' (Phillips 1996b: 116).

Ultimately, the basic question raised in Chapter 2 – 'does it matter or make a difference?' – is exactly the same question that drives the debate about female representation at the local level. Not surprisingly, the same neo-Benthamite concerns emerge. Under-representation of women is regarded as a problem precisely because 'there is a growing conviction that people's interests are not adequately expressed when their "representatives" are so different from themselves' (Phillips 1996a: 30). Hence, in common with the debate outlined in Chapter 2, observers of the local scene find it 'difficult to believe that councils on which 75 per cent of members are men pursue the same priorities and arrive in the same way at the same decisions as would councils on which 40 per cent, let alone 75 per cent, of members were female' (Wilson and Game 1998: 222). The concern with the under-representation of women is only heightened by the fact that women are presently the main users and consumers of council services. More speculatively, some observers are willing to argue that local democracy is crucial for feminism both because of the past experience of local councils in introducing innovative policies favourable to women, and also because of its potential for developing new possibilities for public action and for redefining political agendas (Phillips 1996b: 126–8).

Similarly, the under-representation of ethnic minorities in local government also prompts microcosmic concerns. In 1996 there were approximately 600 black councillors in England and Wales, over half of whom served on London councils. A quarter of these councillors were African-Caribbean, and some two-thirds were Asian (Sophal and Muir 1996). Overall, therefore, some 3 per cent of councillors came from ethnic minorities, again a higher proportion than among Westminster MPs. Still these aggregate figures conceal the problem of the specificity of microcosmic representation. This problem is best illustrated by Wilson and Game's observations about Birmingham :

> there are some 20 ethnic minority members on the 117-seat City Council. This 17 per cent might seem like a not unreasonable representation of the city's approximately 25 per cent ethnic minority population – until you consider the sheer diversity of that population: The African-Caribbeans; the Khamiris...the Punjab Sikhs...the Gujuratis...the smaller Chinese and Vietnamese communities. Several of these groups are bound to regard themselves as unrepresented – not merely under-represented – on the City Council in any racial,

religious or cultural sense, and if this is true in Birmingham, it is even more so in most other towns and cities.

(Wilson and Game 1998: 223)

Clearly, as British society becomes more diverse, the neo-Benthamite critique of existing patterns of representation is likely to become more pronounced. The Widdicombe Report made this point explicitly in its conclusion that: 'Councillors should not only be representatives of the community, but should be representative of it' (Cmnd 9797-I 1986: 105). The danger was that as 'society is becoming increasingly sectionalised...this poses problems for the councillors' representative role' (Cmnd 9797-I 1986: 104–5).

Party representation and local councils

In 1986 the Widdicombe Report (Cmnd 9797-I 1986: 59) noted that: 'our research shows that the great majority of councillors and councils are now elected and organised on party lines'. In 1997 Peter John (1997: 271) recorded that the system of party control of local government had, if anything, been strengthened since the 1980s. In 1998 Wilson and Game again confirmed the dominance of party politics and went on to note that: 'the majority groups' manifesto becomes the council's agenda, to be translated into practical policy proposals' (1998: 267). Hence, the trend towards pervasive group discipline and a 'Westminster style' approach to party discipline clearly has been manifest in local government in the 1990s (Game and Leach 1996: 128–31); so too have been the tensions between party representatives, party activists and party leaders (Wilson and Game 1998: 271–2).

Notions of 'party representation' prompt consideration of the extent to which councillors are expected to act as 'party delegates', or spokespersons for their constituents, or independent 'trustees' for the locality as a whole. The most extensive survey of councillors' representational roles was published by Newton in 1976, before the entrenchment of 'party government' in local authorities. He found that in his sample of elected councillors in Birmingham, 32 per cent saw themselves as 'delegates', 43 per cent regarded themselves as 'trustees', and 25 per cent identified themselves as 'politicos' (Newton 1976: 120). From Newton's study it is not entirely clear that those councillors who classified themselves as 'delegates' saw themselves exclusively as 'party delegates', but Newton does note that 64 out of the 66 respondents took party organisation on the council as given (1976: 122). Clearer evidence of the existence of the 'party delegate' role is to be found in Gyford's research for the Widdicombe Committee

(Cmnd 9801 1986: 129). 'Delegate democracy' was identified by Gyford as an attempt to fuse together representative and participatory forms of government. This form of democracy prompted the expectation that the local representative would (in accordance with the model outlined in Chapter 4):

> reflect the express wishes of his constituents and must be held accountable by the latter's direct participation in the formulation of his instructions and in the judgement of his performance. Delegate democracy lays great stress on the acceptance of majority decisions, on the mandating of representatives and in their reporting back to those who confer the mandate upon them. It may be regarded as a form of Labour movement politics transposed into local govern- ment....If the voters return a Labour council to power on the basis of a specific manifesto then the local Labour party becomes the guardian of the voters' mandate and on behalf of the voters the party must ensure that councillors keep faith with their election pledges.
>
> (Cmnd 9801 1986: 129)

The epitome (and, in the view of its critics, the nadir) of this model was perhaps the Liverpool City Council dominated by the Militant Tendency in the mid-1980s (see Taafe and Mulhearn 1988). Nonetheless, it is a view of representation which still resonates in many Labour Councils in the 1990s, despite the countervailing tendencies of individual citizens to seek 'representation' through issue-specific groups rarely associated with the major political parties (see Pratchett and Wilson 1996: 232–3).

Local governance, associationalism and problems of representative democracy

> Policy-making for local government has generated a policy mess because of the failure to appreciate that disaggregation, differentia- tion, interdependence and policy networks are central characteristics of the British polity. In one short phrase,...local government [has been replaced] with local governance.
>
> (Rhodes 1997: 133–4)

The concept of 'local governance' has at its core the same features as those noted in the wider debate on governance (see Chapter 6; Stoker 1998: 17–28). At its starkest it is a model of complexity which acknowledges that 'nearly 5000 bodies, not directly elected...are involved nowadays in the governance of our local communities, and spending well over half the total money spent by elected local government' (Wilson and Game 1998: 316). For present purposes the most significance aspect of the concept is that it provides a fundamental challenge to the traditional model of representative local government.

The way to mitigate this challenge has been seen variously to 'empower' groups through the development of notions of 'community government' (Stewart 1995; Cochrane 1996: 205; Burns *et al.* 1994: 265–6); to 'democratise' local decision making through active citizen involvement – including direct participation; or to develop an 'associative form' of local democracy (Hirst 1994: 33–43). All of these proposals recognise the failings of representative government as presently constituted at the local level, and all raise the fundamental issue of how such schemes of reform fit 'in relation to the decisional competence of elected councillors, whose representative credentials are more secure, and who are also publicly accountable for their decisions' (Beetham 1996: 44). All, with the exception of direct citizen participation through referenda, do not envisage, however, the replacement of representative democracy. The various schemes of 'democratisation' are not conceived, therefore, as alternatives to the process of territorial representation. Instead, they are additional forms of representation and consultation. As Phillips notes, other associations and groups might be able 'to claim some level of legitimacy from their networks or their organisational base...but they cannot claim the same kind of legitimacy that comes from a popular vote' (1996a: 36). If this is the case, then:

> electing representatives to act on the citizens' behalf has to remain the major component – and not only from pragmatic reasons, but also from egalitarian concerns. The great advantage of representative democracy is that elections put the voters on a potentially equal footing, for they make no excessive demands on the citizens' energy or time.
>
> (Phillips 1996a: 28)

Thus suffusing the discussion of 'local governance' is an appreciation of the general legitimation afforded by electoral modes of representation (see Beetham 1996; Phillips 1996a: 36). Part of this appreciation entails an acknowledgement of the paradoxes entailed in 'enhancing democracy' alongside the established representative process. In this vein Cochrane (1996: 207) criticises Hirst's scheme of associationalism for painting 'too rosy a picture of pluralism to be entirely convincing'. In particular, it is unclear how differences in power between associations will be dealt with, how consensus will be built, or how unorganised interests are to be reflected in the decision making process. Hence, the electoral process and territorial representation within localities will remain central, for precisely the reasons adumbrated in Chapter 6 (see also Cochrane 1996: 207). This point is recognised implicitly in Burns *et al.*'s (1994: 280) attempt to combine an associative model with the representative democracy of 'community government'. In their scheme priority is afforded to representative government as an active and important means of correcting the divisions and inequalities of power endemic in any associational system. 'Because local government…derive[s] legitimacy from [its] role as the focal point for representative politics in the locality, [it] would have the power to orchestrate the networks of internally devolved service units and non-statutory service providing organisations' (Burns *et al.* 1994: 280). Even so the tensions stemming from the differing claims to 'legitimacy' on behalf of associations and elected local politicians – stemming from their differing organisational and representational bases – would remain endemic to this scheme. Phillips rightly concludes, therefore, that 'each extension of democracy leads to new problems as well as solutions' (1996a: 36). The problems are both normative and practical and are centred on the meaning of representation and the form that representation takes. In other words, they are the problems identified at the national level in preceding chapters.

The European level

The European Union provides a third level of representation. In a book dealing with the theory and practice of representation in Britain, the inclusion of the 'European' level is both necessary and problematic. It is necessary because elections to the European Parliament provide yet another set of representatives chosen directly by the British electorate, and raise specific questions about the nature of these representatives, as well as more general questions about the bases of legitimation of EU policies and the nature of European 'governance'. Obviously, these questions raise far broader issues than can be dealt with adequately here, so the problem is how to deal with the major political and constitutional dimension of 'Europe' while still keeping a clear focus on our main concern of representation in Britain. The answer is: first, to restrict the following discussion exclusively to the analytical concerns pursued throughout the preceding chapters; and, second, to assume a basic knowledge of the institutional structure of the EU (for background see Nugent 1994; Dinan 1994; Richardson 1996, Wallace and Wallace 1996).

Elections and British representatives in the European Parliament

Four elections to the European Parliament have taken place since the first direct election was held in 1979. Unlike Westminster, each parliament has a fixed term of five years. In 1994, 87 UK representatives were returned to the Strasbourg parliament, 84 from mainland Britain and 3 from Northern Ireland. The representatives from Northern Ireland were elected for a single three-member constituency on the basis of the single transferable voting system, while those from Britain were returned for single member constituencies on the basis of the first-past-the-post system. The territorial basis of British representation was unique amongst EU states. All other states employed some proportional voting system: either based on single national lists or on regional lists. However, the decision to hold the 1999 EP elections on the basis of a regional list system will bring Britain into line with other EU states. In 1999, England will be divided into nine electoral regions, each electing between six and eleven MEPs. Scotland, Wales and Northern Ireland will each constitute single regions and elect, respectively, eight, five and three MEPs. Voting will be on the basis of 'closed' party lists, whereby electors can only vote for a party and not for individual candidates.

Of the 87 UK MEPs elected in 1994, 16 (18.4 per cent) were women – a higher proportion of women than at Westminster at the time. Of the total of 567 MEPs elected in 1994, 146 (25.9 per cent) were women. After the accession of Austria, Sweden, and Finland in 1995 the total number of MEPs increased to 626, of whom 173 were women (28 per cent). There were considerable national variations, with 44 per cent female representation among Danish MEPs, but with only 8 per cent among Portugal's representatives. Even though there is a higher proportion of female representatives in the EP than in national parliaments, the debate about the representational merits of a more microcosmic parliament is as intense, and for the same reasons, as that outlined in Chapter 2.

Party representation

British representatives at Strasbourg are no exception to the general rule that MEPs owe their selection and election almost exclusively to national parties. Alone of all representatives from member states in 1994, British MEPs were chosen by local parties rather than regional or national electoral committees (Hix and Lord 1997: 60). Local constituency parties were grouped for the purpose of choosing candidates for EP elections, often encompassing some seven or eight Westminster constituencies. These large, aggregate groupings had the dual effect of making it difficult for individual constituency parties to track the activities of 'their' MEP, while simultaneously reducing the direct capacity of national party leaders to influence their party representatives in Strasbourg (Hix and Lord 1997: 86). This was particularly significant for the Labour party, given that 62 of the 84 British MEPs were members of the Labour Group in the EP. Indeed, in anticipation of the introduction of a regional list system for the 1999 European elections, the Labour party's NEC proposed a new selection procedure for its MEPs in January 1998. Prospective candidates would, as a first stage, have to win a One Member One Vote ballot in an existing Euro-constituency. In these ballots each voter would vote for one man and one woman. The second stage would involve a joint panel of NEC members and regional representatives, which would determine the rank-order of candidates on the list. Critics of the new system believed that it was designed to tighten central party control by ensuring that: 'effectively the leadership will determine who gets in' (Ken Livingstone MP quoted in the *Guardian*, 28 January 1998). Similar fears were also expressed within the Conservative party about the role of the party leadership in the new selection procedure for MEPs.

Characteristically, national party leaderships in Britain have afforded a low priority to the EP and its elections. This relative lack of concern has found reflection both in the nature of the Euro-election campaigns and in the constrained development of transnational party groups within the EP itself. As we will examine in more detail below, European elections have largely revolved around national campaigns conducted by national parties and with political debate focused upon national issues rather than wider European concerns. In 1994 for example, despite the existence of transnational party federations (Party of European Socialists, European People's Party, European Liberal and Democratic Reform and the European Federation of Green Parties) which produced agreed Euro-manifestos, there was little sense of the elections being 'European' (see Smith 1995: 53). In part, this reflected the bland and uncontentious nature of the manifestos produced by the transnational parties. No detailed commitments and no substantive proposals for a five-year legislative programme were included. In addition, each national party made the final decision on exactly how much use was made of the transnational manifesto and what weighting was to be placed on the 'European' dimension in the campaign (see Smith 1996: 279–80; Hix and Lord 1997: 91–2). The significance of this for our purposes is that the national focus of elections and the absence of a 'European electoral programme' offered to the electorate undermines the theory of 'party representation' at the EU level. This is not to deny that 'party' is of major importance for British MEPs, but simply to note that 'party' does not provide an unambiguous focus of representation. At best it provides a bifurcated vision – of national party concerns and transnational party issues – with no single 'mandate' for the individual MEP to act upon.

Manifestly, the parliamentary activities of MEPs are organised within the frame provided by national party groups and transnational party groupings at Strasbourg (see Corbett *et al.* 1995: 87–95; Westlake 1994: 184–209). However, because party groups within the EP 'are less directly linked than national parties to mass electoral politics, or to the executive functions of government' (Hix and Lord 1997: 138), it means that the prerequisites of the theory of 'party representation' – a common manifesto, an electoral mandate, and responsibility for effecting a legislative programme – do not pertain at the EU level. In this sense the potential 'independence' of MEPs from party is far greater than at Westminster. While there is considerable party cohesion in the EP, with the two main party groups displaying levels of cohesion at around 90 per cent in recorded votes (Hix and Lord 1997: 142–3; see also Bardi 1994: 364–9), it is difficult to ascribe such unity to notions of 'party representation'. Generally, MEPs are less beholden to party direction than MPs and find it relatively easy to conform with Rule 2 of the EP's standing orders which states: 'Members of the European Parliament shall exercise their mandate independently. They shall not be bound by any instructions and shall not receive a binding mandate' (European Parliament 1996). Overall, therefore, as Hix and Lord conclude: 'European level parties fall far short of the role of parties in a party democracy', in particular 'they are weakest of all...on the most vital criteria of all: the question of electoral legitimacy' (1997: 213). We will examine the general question of 'legitimacy' below, but, first, we need to examine the issue of constituency representation.

Euro-constituency representation

The web page of the UK Office of the European Parliament states unequivocally that the role of British MEPs 'is to represent their constituency in the European Parliament' (http: //www.cec.org.uk/directry/meps/). The average size of a British constituency for the 1994 elections for the European Parliament was just over 506,000; some seven times the size of a Westminster constituency. Not surprisingly, the very size of European constituencies impacts on the performance of representative roles by British MEPs.

Overall, throughout the EU, it has been found that MEPs from district/constituency based systems engage in behaviour which 'is more readily geographically targeted' (Bowler and Farrell 1993: 56). A 1996

survey of MEPs confirmed this in its conclusion that: 'The more dispro-
portional – or the more majoritarian – an electoral system, the more MEPs
tend to focus on their constituency rather than on the party voters or the
people of their nation' (Wessels 1997: 19). In practice this means that UK
MEPs (along with those from Ireland) are more likely to emphasise the
constituency dimension in their focus of representation than MEPs elected
under a national list or regional list electoral system. In terms of links with
the constituency this means that British (and Irish) MEPs are more likely to
have permanent offices in their constituency (some 94 per cent) than MEPs
elected from national lists (55 per cent) (Bowler and Farrell 1993: 56). The
exact degree of contact between British constituents and MEPs, however,
is far lower than that between Westminster MPs and their constituents. A
recent survey of British MEPs estimated that they received an average of
30 to 40 letters each week from individual constituents (Shephard 1997:
444) – far fewer than received by MPs. Indeed, Shephard estimates that
only 1 in 240 electors contact their MEP in a year, compared to 1 in 25
who contact their MP in the same period. Typically, contact entails
requests to: assist in securing grants or other EU funds; deal with problems
relating to administrative agencies in national or local government; or
address some policy related matter (often dealing with environmental, agricultural, or VAT issues). Many communications between constituents and
MEPs take the form of requests for information rather than the redress of
individual grievances (Bowler and Farrell 1993: 52). MEPs may also be
called upon to take up 'cross-border' issues – such as matters dealing with
restrictions on trade or movement – by individuals, groups, or local or
national representatives within their Euro-constituency. These cross-border
cases often entail interactions between elected representatives at the local,
national and European levels.

Problems of legitimacy

As we saw in Chapter 1 the concept of representation has traditionally
been linked with issues of legitimation. Traditionally, decision makers have
invoked the process of representation to establish their credentials to act
on behalf of those not actually present at the point of decision, and to
assert their responsibility and accountability for the decisions taken.
Historically, therefore, the representative assembly in Western liberal
democratic states has been an intrinsic part of the decision making
process, serving to legitimate outputs of that process and to secure consent
within the wider polity. The defining characteristics of modern representative systems of government have thus been most apparent in states that
have had a territorially defined 'polity' and an inclusive idea of 'demos'. A

singular conception of legitimacy – derived from a process of representation based upon free, competitive elections – has tended to prevail in these states.

However, when the decision making process in the European Union is examined, such traditional models of representative government and democracy are difficult to apply. The reason is obvious:

> The European Parliament is the first, and so far the only experiment in trans-national democracy. No other institution in the world brings together under one roof representatives from different states, who have been directly elected to that institution and who have been given a range of legally entrenched powers. Nowhere is there an equivalent body.
>
> (Corbett *et al.* 1995: xxi)

Indeed, some commentators have argued variously that there is no European polity, no European 'demos', and hence no source of legitimation upon which such a transnational experiment could prosper (for an overview of these arguments see Weiler *et al.* 1996: 4–39; Weiler 1997: 254–84). In contrast, others have argued that the EU can be conceived as a polity (Caporaso and Keeler 1995; Wessels 1996: 68–70; Cram 1996: 53–5) and that a European 'demos' might yet emerge out of the formal proclamation of European citizenship in Article 8 of the Maastricht Treaty (Council of the European Communities 1992) and the informal realisation of 'democratic citizenship' in the EU (see Meehan 1993: 155–6; Newman 1996: 138–58). But this very contestation points to the fact that no simple, single source of legitimation can be identified within the EU.

At best a dual process of legitimation can be discerned – drawing upon processes of representation at both the national and the European levels. Thus, although there is a tendency to analyse the national and supranational processes independently, it is important to note that they have been closely linked. From the outset under the Treaty of Paris in 1951, the creation of a Common Assembly, as part of the institutional structure of the European Coal and Steel Community (ECSC), intertwined supranational and national modes of representation in an uneasy synergetic relationship. The Common Assembly, composed of seventy-eight Members nominated from national parliaments, was firmly rooted in national processes of representation; yet, simultaneously, it was the 'first international assembly in Europe with legally guaranteed powers' (Westlake 1994: 11). The Assembly's role was limited initially to debating the policies drafted by the High Authority of the ECSC (later the Commission of the EC). It was to be the High Authority – acting as a supranational technocratic institution offering leadership in Europe – which was expected to drive the integrationist project. The problem was, and is, that the Commission 'is a *sui generis* organization established without any direct, public means of legitimation' and as such is 'denied the kind of parliamentary legitimacy normally possessed by national cabinets' (Featherstone 1994: 163). In which case, practical legitimation of ECSC, and later EC, policies had to be sought from the indirect democratic sources of national parliaments and national ministerial representatives in the Council of Ministers. In this respect national parliaments proved effective in providing the legitimating frame within which further European integration could take place (Judge 1996: 94–6). Hence, as Neunreither notes, one variant of legitimacy is based on:

> the democratic institutions of member states and the fact that national parliaments have agreed by ratification of the EC Treaty and its amendments to the partial transfer of powers to the European Union and the exercise of power by the Community institutions according to those treaties. It is obvious that all Community institutions…rely on this first basis of legitimacy.
>
> (1994: 312)

Certainly in Britain this mediated form of legitimation was seen as something both to defend (in the case of the Conservative party metaphorically to die for as an electoral force in the mid-1990s) and to be sceptical of at the same time. It was worth defending because it challenged the democratic credentials of a directly elected European Parliament. This defence was most actively articulated by Conservative Euro-sceptics. Yet, simultaneously, some scepticism was in order because, if the 'United Kingdom Parliament exercised no control over Community legislation other than through the voice and vote of United Kingdom Ministers in the Council of Ministers' (HL 149 1986: 7), then 'strong party government' placed inherent limitations upon the capacity of MPs to control executive actions in Brussels. Key elements of the scrutiny system at Westminster have been found to be 'wholly inadequate' (HC 51-xxvii 1996: xxiv) – the conclusion reached by some commentators is that 'there is a full British input into European decisions, but it is not from…Parliament' (Riddell 1998: 45).

The second source of legitimation within the EU stems from direct elections to the European Parliament. And it is precisely these electoral credentials that Euro-sceptics in Britain, and elsewhere, are prone to challenge. One example will suffice. In the period immediately before the 1996 Inter-Governmental Conference and the signing of the Treaty of Amsterdam in 1997, Norman Lamont, ex-Chancellor of the Exchequer and Euro-sceptic convert, asked the question: 'Do we need a European Parliament?' Not surprisingly, perhaps, his answer was 'no'. His reasons were that: 'The European Parliament is not a proper parliament'; 'elections for the European Parliament are simply a series of opinion polls about political popularity in different countries'; and that 'at the last European elections the turn-out was only 36 per cent. Some MEPs were elected by only 15 or 16 per cent of the electorate, but went straight off to the European Parliament proclaiming their democratic mandate to build Europe' (Lamont 1995: 78; see also Spicer 1992: 47–51). This partisan assessment did reflect, however, more considered academic concerns about the democratic credentials of the EP.

The first is the extent to which elections for the European Parliament are 'first order' elections or 'second order national elections'. In making this analytical distinction Reif (1985; Reif and Schmitt 1980) defined the former in terms of national elections – concerned primarily with power distribution and government formation – which are characterised by high profile campaigns and a high level of electoral participation. 'Second order elections', in contrast, tend to engender less public interest, lower levels of campaigning and electoral turn-out, and do not involve national power distribution or government formation. In a major cross-national study, van der Eijk and Franklin (1996) concluded that Reif's notion of second-order national elections provided an accurate characterisation of the 1989 and 1994 European elections. These elections were 'treated as opportunities to discuss national political differences and to register support for, or opposition to, political parties on the basis of these differences' (Franklin *et al.* 1996: 367). Given the national foci of elections, Franklin *et al.* could not find the expression of a single electoral verdict and, so, reached the conclusion that, 'the European Parliaments elected in 1989 and 1994 had no mandate whatsoever in terms of the European arena' (1996: 368). In contrast, Westlake takes to task those who criticise the 'non-Europeanness' of EP elections for basing their argument on a false premise. What should also be considered in his view is that 'the 'Europeanness' of the elections relates not only to the substance of political debate but also to their simultaneity and the common institution involved' (Westlake 1994: 100).

Nonetheless, those concerned with electoral 'crisis' point further to the low turnout at EP elections. Franklin notes that 'many commentators have suggested that low turnout should be considered to indicate a lack of legitimacy of the EC/EU since citizens appear by their failure to vote to be withholding their support for European institutions' (1996: 191). However, empirical evidence does not support such a charge. In the first instance, there is considerable variation in turnout, in 1994 ranging from 96 per cent to 36 per cent. Second, the variations in turnout can be largely explained by divergent national contexts in which European elections take place. Third, there is evidence that 'European voters already constitute a single electorate' (Franklin *et al.* 1996: 331). Overall, therefore, 'there is no evidence that low turnout corresponds to lack of support for the European project' (Franklin 1996: 193).

Democratic deficits

Closely linked to the debate about the deficiencies of EU elections is a concern with the deficiencies of the institutional structure of the EU. The notion of 'democratic deficit' has become a preoccupation of politicians and academics alike, and it is now widely argued that there is, at least, a dual democratic deficit. At the EU level there is an imbalance between the directly elected element, the EP, and the unelected Commission, and the indirectly accountable Council of Ministers and European Council. The implicit assumptions are that the representatives of the 'European people' make only a marginal contribution to EU decision making, and that there is a basic lack of direct accountability of EU executive institutions to those representatives. At this level 'the preoccupation with the "democratic deficit" rests partly on the assumption that these European institutions should be subject to tests of accountability similar to those applied to the individual member states' (Wallace and Wallace 1996: 26). Whether these assumptions are valid – in what is, by any definition, an 'unusual pattern of institutions' (Wallace and Wallace 1996: 25), or 'a mixed polity', or even a 'new polity' (Wessels 1996: 59–69) – remains an open question. Nonetheless, most of the proposals to redress this perceived deficit have conceived of the relationship between the EP and the Council and the Commission *as if* it conformed to established modes of legislative–executive relations (see Corbett *et al.* 1995: 245–98; Lodge 1996: 194–6; Newman 1996: 174–88; Dankert 1997: 215–25).

At the national level, the 'democratic deficit' is held to be compounded by the 'failure' of national parliaments either to influence or to scrutinise effectively the actions of national ministers in the Council of Ministers. The House of Commons' Select Committee on European Legislation identified the problem clearly:

> None of the Institutions of the European Union – not the Commission, the European Parliament, the European Court of Justice, the European Court of Auditors, nor, collectively, the Councils of Ministers – is answerable to any individual National Parliament. It follows that National Parliaments can exert their powers and influence *directly* only upon their own Ministers as national representatives

(rather than delegates) in the Council of Ministers. Making this process effective must be the main aim of a scrutiny system.

(HC 51-xxvii 1996: ix)

Indeed, making scrutiny processes more effective has become of increasing concern for national parliaments since Maastricht (see HC 239 1995; Judge 1996; Norton 1996; HC 51-xxvii 1996; HC 51-xxviii 1996). All national parliaments have re-examined their scrutiny procedures. In addition, closer cooperation between national parliaments and the European Parliament has been sought through the Conference of European Affairs Committees (COSAC) and enhanced through the Protocol on the Role of National Parliaments appended to the Amsterdam Treaty (see Council of the European Union 1997). Yet, in spite of this activity, there is still a strong belief that the EU is plagued by 'a continuing democratic deficit' (HC 36-xiii 1997: xx).

Crisis of legitimacy?

Combining the issues identified above – the 'participation deficit' of European elections, and the 'democratic deficit' apparent in the limited contributions of national parliaments and the EP to the EU policy process – leads back to a consideration of legitimation within the EU. Influential commentators are convinced that there is a 'democratic legitimacy crisis' (Lodge 1996: 207); and that 'the crisis of legitimacy...[is] endemic to the current structure of political representation within the European Community' (Franklin and van der Eijk 1996: 7).

Yet such commentators also acknowledge, at the same time, that the EP is 'the vehicle through which democratic legitimacy is conferred on EU laws drafted by authorities who are seen to exercise power in a lawful way' (Lodge 1996: 210). Manifestly, the opportunity to vote at a 'European level' is, in itself, of fundamental importance in conferring such legitimacy (whether that opportunity is fully exercised or not). The very opportunity to vote (given 'their simultaneity and the common institution involved' to echo Westlake's phrase) provides a symbolic and normative illustration of the conferring of consent at the European level. Not surprisingly the EP in its official publications subscribes to this view: 'election by direct universal suffrage gives the European Parliament its legitimacy' (European Parliament 1995: 26). By this view the European electoral process, in itself, is sufficient for the EP to claim that it has 'legitimacy'.

A more complex defence against the charge of a 'legitimacy crisis' within the EU is to argue that traditional conceptions of representative government in liberal democratic states – and notions of the conferring of

legitimacy derived therefrom – are inappropriate for conceptualising legitimation within the unique institutional structure of the EU. The full
complexity of the details of this argument need not detain us here, what is
important is the general claim that a 'new polity' is emerging in the EU. If
this is the case, then, as part of a 'unique phenomenon', the processes of
legitimation will not resemble those found in existing liberal democratic
states (whether unitary or federal). As Wessels (1996: 69) states: 'democratic
legitimacy is not to be found in familiar terms. But this does not mean that
it does not exist at all'. Instead, there is a 'fusion process' whereby
'Europeanisation' comes to imply a 'new exercise in indirect democracy
and is, in this sense, a "saut qualitatif" in democracy: a new kind of
democracy for a larger area – not perfect but a major step forward'
(Wessels 1996: 64). The 'Europeanisation' process leads, therefore, to an
acknowledgement that the EP and national parliaments are not competi-
tors in the process of legitimation, and that this process is not a zero-sum
game – where the legitimacy of the EP necessarily detracts from legitimacy
derived from national or sub-national representative processes. There are
multiple sources of legitimation – both direct and indirect – within the EU
stemming from different levels of territorial representation. Some have
argued that the 'line of delimitation…between the legitimising rationales'
of these levels of representation has not been clearly drawn and the result
is likely to be a 'confusion of processes that would make them opaque and
inaccessible to outsiders' (Obradovic 1996: 206). Certainly proponents of
the 'crisis of legitimacy' would subscribe to this view.

An alternative response, however, would be to dismiss the need for 'a
line of demarcation' and to accept a multi-level, complex process of representation. The notion of a 'prismatic political system' captures this
complexity. In such a system 'rays of activity and authority are scattered or
focused more or less effectively through institutions and social forces'
(Laffan 1997: 6). From the perspective of an individual citizen looking
through this 'prism', the range of institutions and social forces which
attract his or her attention will vary across policy areas and time, as will the
sources of legitimation. For the individual citizen a detailed understanding
of how the prism 'works' is not required, nor is active participation.
Instead, a 'permissive consensus' – one which accepts that policies are
legitimate because of the variegated contribution of different representatives in different institutional contexts – is perhaps sufficient. But the
proponents of a 'new polity' or a 'prismatic political system' would take
the argument one stage further and maintain that the density and
complexity of institutional linkages reflects a multitude of different sources
of direct and indirect, legal, democratic and *functional* legitimacy.
Legitimation stems not only from elected representatives at various

territorial levels but also from the inclusion of functional representatives in the decision processes. As Wessels observes: 'From the highest political authorities in the European Council to the sectoral interest groups the actors within the EC/EU system bring their respective legitimacy into the new polity' (1996: 63). Indeed, Wessels and Diedrich believe that in this new polity 'the principle of representation is increasingly defined in new terms, shifting away from territorial/parliamentary to functional self-representation' (1997: 9). Whether this constitutes a 'new definition' of representation is questionable (see Chapter 6 and below). What Wessels and Diedrich do acknowledge, however, is that 'the sources and dimensions of legitimacy are progressively getting merged' in a multi-level system of governance (1997: 9).

European governance

This is not the place to engage in a detailed analysis of 'European governance' given the many interpretations of the concept itself. One variant is provided by Marks *et al.* who present a model of 'multi level governance' (1996: 347). This model acknowledges that states are an integral and powerful part of the EU, but also recognises that member states do not monopolise control over many activities that take place in their respective territories. Their conclusion, therefore, is that a 'multi-level Euro-polity' has developed since the 1980s. But this conception of 'governance' is largely distinct from the theories of 'governance' examined elsewhere in this book. In criticising Marks' approach, Rhodes (1997: 140) argues that the concept of 'multi-level governance' may describe the changing structure of EU policy making but it does not explain why the structure varies or why it has changed over time. Instead, Rhodes (1997: 159) believes that a 'theory impregnated' concept of policy networks has greater utility in analysing the EU. This view is shared by a host of commentators (admittedly each with a slightly different starting premise, see Peterson 1995a: 76–80; Peterson 1995b: 389–407; Richardson 1996: 6–11; Börzel 1997; Laffan 1997: 6). The result is that 'scholars of the European Union now almost accept it as given that the EU policy process is best characterised as a multi-level, multi-arena, multi-venue game' (Richardson 1997: 23–4). In other words, if complexity, differentiation, blurred boundaries between public and private policy actors, multiplicity of actors in each policy area, interdependence, and asymmetries of power are now the hallmarks of policy making at local and national levels in the UK then these characteristics are even more pronounced in the EU decision making process.

For our purposes these characteristics refocus attention back onto the process of territorial representation and the position of elected representatives in this complex process of decision making. In contrast, however, many commentators (see for example Rhodes 1997; Andersen and Burns 1996) maintain that parliaments – at both national and European levels – are residualised analytically, and challenged normatively, in these models. In this context, the terms 'democratic deficit', 'legitimacy crisis' and 'post-parliamentary governance' are treated as accurate descriptions rather than as analytical concepts. Without repeating the discussion outlined in Chapter 6, the importance – indeed the prior importance of parliamentary representation – to the processes of legitimation in the EU still needs to be borne in mind. In the analysis of European governance the continuing importance of territorial representation can be acknowledged alongside the development of networks, communities and other forms of interest inter-mediation. Indeed, one fruitful line of research is the extent to which, in certain policy areas, MEPs are integrated into networks. Kohler-Koch, for one, is in no doubt that: 'There are…issue areas where Members of the Parliament are considered the natural ally of an advocacy coalition and become members of a policy community' (1997: 7).

More generally, other analysts are willing to accept that in a multi-level system of governance the EP has an important say as 'part of a European legitimacy complementary to the national and functional [elements]' (Wessels and Diedrich 1996: 9). Even Andersen and Burns (1996: 237), while identifying a 'representational complex' which differs 'substantially from territorial, parliamentary representation', have to concede that formal responsibility for policy making still 'resides in the system of representative democracy' (1996: 238), and that the institutions of representative democracy 'at least in public mythology' are still of importance. Indeed, they maintain that 'parliamentary democracy…still remains the major basis for legitimising political authority' (1996: 228), but believe that it will be increasingly difficult to maintain the 'public myth in the face of growing democratic deficits' (1996: 244). We will return to this issue in Chapter 8, but, in the meantime, it is sufficient to note that territorial representation continues to feature in theories of 'organic governance' (often as a paradox, or as a problem for those theories). Ultimately, however, the crucial point is that 'specialised organic forms are not particularly effective at legitimising the system of modern governance. Typically, the formal democratic arrangements, in particular parliament, still remain essential in this respect' (Andersen and Burns 1996: 246).

8 Representation in the twenty-first century

One thing that history teaches us is that the future rarely turns out the way that we expect. It is perhaps unwise, therefore, to speculate about the future of representation in Britain in the twenty-first century. However, sufficient analytical threads have been identified in preceding chapters to alert us to the major issues worthy of consideration. Even if we are not in a position to know the exact answers, we have a good idea, at least, of what the questions are.

In fact, the basic questions are those that have confronted theorists of representation throughout history: who or what is to be represented; how; and for what purpose? The answers to these questions entail, in turn, detailed consideration of the issues that have recurred throughout this book: the distinction to be drawn between representative democracy and representative government; the associated ideas of legitimacy, consent, authorisation; the paradoxes of representation, and; notions of the 'crisis of representation'.

The 'crisis of representation' has manifested itself in various guises in successive chapters of this book. Notions of crisis are evident at all levels – local, sub-national, national and European – and are posited in both normative and practical terms. When couched in terms of a 'legitimation crisis' these notions point both to the centrality of processes of territorial representation and to the modern challenge posed by representation rooted in 'function' or 'presence'. The claims to legitimacy derived from the former are counterposed by the claims to legitimacy by the latter. Differing conceptions of representation are held to be in conflict with each other – and hence a paradox arises. This paradox may be resolved, however, simply by asserting that the language of legitimacy in Britain is grounded in an understanding of the accepted constitutional rules of the game. These rules specify that elected representatives from geographically defined areas authorise and consent to policies on behalf of their constituents. In this process, policies are transposed into *public* or 'general' policies (generally accepted as legitimate if not generally applicable to every citizen). It is this general acceptance, or general legitimation, which distinguishes the claims of territorial representation from other modes of representation and their attendant claims to legitimacy (see Chapter 6). In this sense, at least, there is no 'crisis of legitimacy' – as the claims of territorial representation, of representative democracy, are still accepted as normatively superior by most citizens (see Norris 1997b). The *principle* of representative democracy, especially after the collapse of an alternative model (of state socialist democracy in the former Soviet Union), is unchallenged.

What is challenged, however, is the *practice* of representation in Britain. The vagaries of the first-past-the-post electoral system and its ramifications for the 'strength' and 'responsiveness' of representative government, and the limited opportunities for public participation in decision making and hence the limited form of representative democracy itself, have been sufficient to prompt concern about a growing de-legitimation of representative processes in Britain. Such concern has merely been heightened by empirical descriptive studies of 'governance' (see Chapters 6 and 7). A further paradox supplants the initial paradox. While the ideals of representation and the constitutional rules of the game derived from the electoral principle remain paramount, the practical application of those rules – and their biased interpretation in favour of leadership and considerations of government over citizen participation and considerations of democracy – have generated, in the eyes of reformist groups at least, a 'crisis of representation' in Britain.

It is this 'crisis' that the Labour government elected in May 1997 sought to redress. And it did so by reasserting the values of representative *democracy* over those of representative *government*. That there were manifest contradictions in its strategy – that the grip of notions of strong and responsible government was harder to shake off in Westminster than in Edinburgh, Cardiff, or the localities in Britain – needs simply to be noted. What needs to be examined here is the trajectory of reform and the attempts at rejuvenating the democratic elements of representative democracy.

Representation and democratisation

Our aim is no less than to set British political life on a new course for the future...Labour is committed to the democratic renewal of our country.

(Labour Party 1997c: 1–4)

One key dimension of this manifesto pledge for the Labour government after 1 May 1997 was an extension of representative processes in Britain. In essence there was to be 'more' representation – through the creation of new levels of representation, and the extension of representative principles to new institutions and organisations at existing levels – particularly at the local level.

New levels of representation: Scotland and Wales

The Labour party's manifesto gave a clear commitment that: 'A sovereign Westminster Parliament will devolve power to Scotland and Wales' (Labour Party 1997c: 33). The express intention was the extension of democratic control over the responsibilities exercised by the Scottish and Welsh Offices respectively. Legislation to enact the devolution commitments was promised within the first year of the new parliament after referendums had been held on Labour's proposals. In July 1997 two White Papers, *Scotland's Parliament* (Cm 3658 1997) and *A Voice for Wales* (Cm 3718 1997), were published. On 11 September 1997 referendums were held in Scotland and Wales. The questions asked in Scotland were that 'there should be a Scottish Parliament' and that 'a Scottish Parliament should have tax-varying powers'; to which 74.3 per cent and 63.5 per cent of Scottish voters respectively answered 'yes'. In Wales, only one question was asked, that 'there should be a Welsh Assembly', and the answer was far less decisive with only 50.3 per cent of voters answering 'yes'.

In turn, the referendums were followed, in November 1997, by the introduction of the Wales Bill, and, a month later, by the introduction of the Scotland Bill. In December it was also announced that the first elections to the Scottish parliament would be held on 6 May 1999; and, in January 1998, it was decided that the Scottish parliament would be located in a new building at Holyrood in Edinburgh.

One thing is certain, therefore, that in the year 2000 Scotland will have an elected parliament and Wales will have an elected Assembly. The precise powers and responsibilities of these representative institutions need not detain us here, nor need we dwell upon the historical campaigns which culminated in their creation (see Constitution Unit 1996; Mitchell 1996). Moreover, given the comparatively restricted powers of the Welsh national assembly and its primarily deliberative role, we will concentrate upon the more fundamental debate surrounding the creation of a Scottish parliament. More particularly we will focus upon the representational issues which have been at the heart of that debate.

The Scottish Constitutional Convention

Issues of representation underpinned *A Claim of Right for Scotland* (Campaign for a Scottish Assembly 1988), which acknowledged 'the sovereign right of the Scottish people to determine the form of government best suited to their needs' and which pledged that its actions were directed at agreeing a scheme for an assembly or parliament for Scotland; mobilising support for such a scheme; and securing the scheme's implementation.

To pursue the objectives of *A Claim of Right* a Scottish Constitutional Convention was established in March 1989 as a cross-party campaign for constitutional change. It drew upon a wide cross-section of Scottish society and included in its membership Labour and Liberal Democrat MPs, Labour MEPs, local authorities, the Scottish Trade Union Congress, as well as civic groups, businesses and church representatives. Given its membership, it is unsurprising, perhaps, that the Convention's recommendations were not always framed with the precision of constitutional lawyers. Thus, for example, the Convention's views on sovereignty aroused academic criticism (see Levy 1992: 225–7; Mitchell 1992: 102–3). Although pledged to create a representative assembly or parliament, the Convention was convinced that 'sovereignty rests with the Scottish people' (Scottish Constitutional Convention 1990: 6) and that 'a Scottish Parliament securely based on legislative power will give responsive and *direct* government to the Scottish people' (1990: 7, emphasis added). In practice, however, what *Towards Scotland's Parliament* proposed was the exercise of sovereignty by the representatives of the people in a 'directly elected Scottish Parliament within the United Kingdom...working with Westminster and within the guidelines of national policy' (1990: 10–11). The ultimate aim was to 'encourage an open, accessible and democratically accountable government and a participatory democracy which will bring Parliament and people close together in determining what is best for Scotland' (1990: 12).

In 1993, the Convention appointed a Scottish Constitutional Commission to examine in detail how this aim could be achieved. The Commission recognised from the outset that there were problems in reconciling the six principles of representation identified in *Towards Scotland's Parliament*. These were: first, the electoral system for the new parliament should provide a closer correspondence between seats and votes than provided by the first-past-the-post system; second, there should be effective positive action to bring about equal representation of men and women, and fairer representation of ethnic and other minority groups; third, a 'real link' should be preserved between representatives and their constituents;

fourth, the electoral system should be simple to understand; fifth, adequate representation for less populous areas should be secured; and sixth, 'the greatest possible power' should be placed in the hands of the electorate.

In producing its report, *Further Steps Towards a Scheme for Scotland's Parliament*, in October 1994, the Commission endorsed the additional member system (AMS), whereby each voter would cast two votes: one for a constituency Member of the Scottish parliament (MSP) and one for a representative from a party or group of his or her choice. The former were to be drawn from Westminster constituencies on a first-past-the-post basis, the latter were to be allocated from party lists covering Euro-constituencies. The Commission also identified the creation of a Scottish parliament as 'a unique opportunity to start afresh on a fair and equal footing and to open political debate and decision making to a wealth of human experience at present unjustifiably marginalised' (Scottish Constitutional Commission 1994: 12). From this neo-Benthamite premise, the Commission maintained (1994: 12) that it was essential to secure a critical mass of female representatives in the new parliament in order to take full account of 'their distinctive experience and priorities'. However, if agreement upon the aim of equal gender representation was easily reached, the means for achieving this objective divided both the Commission and wider Scottish opinion (see Scottish Constitutional Commission 1994: 15–17; Brown 1998).

In 1995, the Convention produced its final report *Scotland's Parliament, Scotland's Right* (Scottish Constitutional Convention 1995). Under the heading *Making Scotland's Parliament Truly Representative* the report was 'resolute' that 'men and women [would be] fairly represented in numbers broadly proportionate to their shares of the population, and which would actively encourage the participation of all groups, including ethnic minority groups, in its consultative processes' (Scottish Constitutional Convention 1995). The report went on to specify that there would be 129 Members of the new parliament: 73 constituency Members based on the 72 Westminster constituencies (with Orkney and Shetland divided into two constituencies); and an additional 56 Members, seven from each of the eight Euro-constituencies in Scotland, to be drawn from party lists.

In outlining its vision of how the Scottish parliament would work, the report emphasised the participatory advantages to be derived from a new representative institution. In the first instance, its physical location in Scotland would mean that it would 'by definition be physically more accessible to the people of Scotland'. Second, however, this very proximity would be 'reinforced by the introduction of an information strategy designed expressly to encourage understanding of the parliament's workings and participation in its decision-making by all organisations and individuals'. Moreover, the report repeatedly stressed 'the greatest possible involvement by the people of Scotland' and the need to ensure that 'parliament remains responsive to the wishes and values of the Scottish people' (Scottish Constitutional Convention 1995).

The White Paper and the Scotland Bill

As noted above, a White Paper, *Scotland's Parliament* (Cm 3658 1997), was published in July 1997. In terms of the electoral arrangements for the new parliament the White Paper reflected exactly the Convention's proposal for 129 MSPs, 73 Members to be elected for constituencies and 56 additional Members to be drawn from regional party lists. An 'essential foundation' of representation in the new parliament was thus seen to be 'a constituency link' (Cm 3658 1997: 27), with additional Members returned to ensure greater proportionality between votes cast and seats won. The White Paper also went some considerable way in endorsing the microcosmic aspirations of the Convention in its statement:

> The Government are keen to see people with standing in their communities and who represent the widest possible range of interests in Scotland putting themselves forward for election to the Scottish Parliament. In particular the Government attach great importance to equal opportunities for all – including women, members of ethnic minorities and disabled people. The Government urge all political parties offering candidates for election to the Scottish Parliament to have this in mind in their internal candidate selection processes.
>
> (Cm 3658 1997: 27–8)

Further reflection of the Convention's democratic conviction came in the pledges to create a participatory and accessible parliament. While the Labour government stated that it did not wish to infringe the Scottish parliament's capacity to determine its own mode of working, it 'expected', nonetheless, that the parliament in Edinburgh would 'adopt modern methods', be 'accessible, open and responsive to the needs of the public' and that 'participation will be encouraged' (Cm 3658 1997: 30). The White Paper also stipulated that the new parliament should 'harness the best of modern technology'.

Naturally when the White Paper was published, and later when the Scotland Bill was announced and considered in the House of Commons, most public, media and parliamentary attention was focused upon the exact powers to be devolved to the Edinburgh parliament. In essence these were to make laws in relation to matters long devolved administratively to the Scottish Office and other Scottish departments. Most of the devolved matters affect directly the daily lives of the citizens of Scotland and include: health, education, local government, housing, economic development, transport, legal affairs, environmental protection, agriculture, sport and the arts. Ultimately, the legislation establishing the Scottish parliament sought to list matters reserved to the UK parliament rather than to specify exactly which matters were to be devolved. Thus Westminster was to retain control over: constitutional matters; foreign policy; defence and national security; fiscal, monetary and macroeconomic policies; employment; social security policy and administration; transport safety and regulation, and other specified matters (see Cm 3658 1997: 10–11). For our purposes, however, the importance of the Scotland Bill is that it created another level of representation in Britain and another 129 elected representatives.

Indeed, in introducing the devolution legislation, Donald Dewar the Secretary of State for Scotland, proclaimed it as 'a catalyst for change. We want literally to create a new politics in Scotland, bringing back popular legitimacy' (HC Debates 12 January 1998, vol. 304: col. 22). Hence, a new parliament would have to be 'fit for the purpose, equipped for the future, modern, efficient and accessible' (HC Debates 12 January 1998, vol. 304: col. 27). The ultimate objective was to provide 'a more pluralist, outward-looking democracy that is in tune with the modern world. We want to build a system of government that people can access easily, feel part of, and take part in' (HC Debates 12 January 1998, vol. 304: col. 34).

REPRESENTATIVE GOVERNMENT VERSUS REPRESENTATIVE DEMOCRACY

At the heart of the devolution proposals was thus a conception of a revitalised system of representation in Scotland which would secure 'popular legitimacy' for government from Edinburgh. For several participants in the parliamentary debate the issue was not one of securing localised representative government but rather of establishing a new variant of 'representative *democracy*'. Indeed, some MPs seemed to demand more than indirect democracy. In this vein, Malcolm Bruce for the Liberal Democrats maintained that the 'days of the Westminster Parliament are, thankfully, numbered and that sovereignty will be returned to where it came from – to the people, *not to the arrogation of people elected in a representative Parliament*. Ultimately, the people should decide' (HC Debates 13 January 1998, vol. 304: col. 172). Denis Canavan, Labour MP and signatory of the Constitutional Convention's *Claim of Right*, shared the belief that 'the sovereignty of the people of Scotland is surely at the heart of the matter' and that the Bill offered 'the first democratic parliament in Scotland's history'. In his view Scotland would have, for the first time, 'a modern, democratic Parliament for the people of Scotland, elected by the people of Scotland and accountable to the people of Scotland' (HC Debates 13 January 1998, vol. 304: col. 183).

Considerations of executive government and control within parliament did not feature in these assessments. Instead, consensus was to be the new style of politics with a 'balanced partnership between the executive and legislative branches of the state in Scotland' based upon 'more give and take; more listening; more cooperation' (Dewar, HC Debates 12 January 1998, vol. 304: col. 30). Some MPs were, however, a little more sanguine about the long-term prospects of consensus in the new parliament (see for example Dr Liam Fox, HC Debates 13 January 1998, vol. 304: col. 167; Sir Teddy Taylor, HC Debates 13 January 1998, vol. 304: col. 179). Nonetheless, the clear intention was to move away from the adversarial politics of Westminster and to inculcate 'grown-up, civilised' behaviour in Edinburgh (Anne Begg, HC Debates 13 January 1998, vol. 304: col. 177). The intention was to develop 'representative democracy' in Scotland and to refocus the political debate away from traditional concerns of 'representative government' at Westminster.

CONSTITUENCY VERSUS LIST MEMBERS

The government's twin desire of retaining 'a constituency link as the essential foundation of the new Scottish Parliament' (Cm 3658 1997: 27), while simultaneously seeking greater proportionality through adding Members from regional lists, came under close scrutiny in the debate on the Scotland Bill. Donald Dewar saw 'the decision to move to a more proportional system as an unusual example of principle triumphing over narrow political interests' (HC Debates 12 January 1998, vol. 304: col. 27). Dewar's statement frankly acknowledged that the long-term electoral dominance of the Labour party in Scotland had rested upon the weighted results of the simple plurality voting system. Even some of those Labour MPs who were initially 'not very enthusiastic about the abandonment of first-past-the-post' acknowledged the need to 'carry all of the people of Scotland with us'. This entailed a further recognition that this could be achieved 'only if there is a Parliament in which everyone feels that there is a place for them' (Martin O'Neill, HC Debates 12 January 1998, vol. 304: col. 57).

However, other Labour Members remained unconvinced of the merits of the proposed voting system. Ian Davidson, for example, believed that it would provide for first-class and second-class MSPs. He argued that: 'First-class [constituency] Members will be accountable for their selection and election to real people, whereas there is some doubt about exactly to whom second-class [list] Members will be accountable' (HC Debates 12 January

1998, vol. 304: col. 74). Conservative MP Dr Liam Fox had no doubt, however, as to whom the latter would be accountable: 'I have served in the Government Whips Office. I know the power of patronage and the techniques that Whips may use to twist arms. However, there is no power remotely as great as that of dropping people from a party list if they do not back the party line' (HC Debates 13 January 1998, vol. 304: col. 162). Sir Teddy Taylor subscribed to the same view: 'Those members without constituency responsibilities will simply be a party of hacks, people who have been presented by their parties and put on a list' (HC Debates 13 January 1998, vol. 304: col. 162).

A second issue raised by the addition of MSPs from regional lists was what would their relationship be to territorial representation? If constituency was the 'essential foundation' of representation, how would added members operate in the new parliament? For some MPs the experience of other European countries with additional member systems suggested that: 'List Members often end up with more work than constituency Members because electors who do not agree with their elected constituency Members turn to list Members' (Roseanna Cunningham, HC Debates 13 January 1998, vol. 304: col. 180). For others the reverse possibility – of list Members doing less work – seemed more likely. Thus, Ian Davidson speculated: 'Second-class Members will have no identifiable constituents…and will have the opportunity to freeload on the back of constituency work done by individual constituency members' (HC Debates 12 January 1998, vol. 304: col. 73). What he found even more worrying was the potential for list MSPs to 'intervene mischievously' in the work of constituency MSPs:

> We can imagine what will happen over a matter such as a school closure, for example, when a local Member is wrestling with the potential difficulties. An outside Member with no real responsibility in the area could be as mischievous and partisan as he or she liked and then walk away; the constituency Member would be left to pick up the pieces.
>
> (HC Debates 12 January 1998, vol. 304: col. 73)

Examination of the practical experience of AMS in Germany, for example, does little to resolve this argument. In large part this is because the role of grievance chaser is not pre-eminent in the role expectations of MPs in the Bundestag (see Bogdanor 1997: 71). While German MPs engage in 'territorial advocacy' and other promotional activities (including self-promotional activities to enhance their electoral support), any differences in constituency work between 'constituency' and 'list' is attributable more to party factors than how the MP was elected. MPs from small parties, elected primarily on the basis of regional lists, 'find themselves in a local political environment dominated by rival parties in which there are fewer (and qualitatively different) opportunities for constituency work' (Patzelt 1997: 76).

However, comparative empirical evidence held little resonance for those MPs convinced that the adoption of AMS in Scotland would result in an 'horrendous nightmare' (Sir Teddy Taylor, HC Debates 13 January 1998, vol. 304: col. 181).

EQUALITY OF REPRESENTATION: WEST LOTHIAN AND BEYOND

If the relationship between representatives in the Edinburgh parliament gave rise to 'nightmares' for some MPs, then an even greater nightmare was envisaged in the future relationship between MSPs in Edinburgh and MPs at Westminster. Richard Shepherd saw 'only conflict' in this relationship:

> Scottish Members of the [Westminster] Parliament will have no competence for matters such as social security and education, the bread and butter of our daily lives. In Edinburgh, for the same constituencies, there will be Members of the Scottish Parliament who will be competent for those matters. I see only divisiveness there. Even if, as is likely on the basis of current constituencies, both Members come from the same party, where will it lead? The aspiration and ambition of constituency Members…is to cry out for the alleviation of problems in their constituencies.
>
> (HC Debates 13 January 1998, vol. 304: col. 203)

This was not, however, seen to be a problem on the Labour benches. Maria Fyfe predicted on the basis of her present experience where she 'frequently ha[d] housing cases, although that is really a matter for the local authority', that 'I am sure that when we have a Scottish Parliament, people will still come to my surgery and to the surgery of the Member of the Scottish Parliament' (HC Debates 13 January 1998, vol. 304: col. 226).

Of more concern was the representational relationship between MPs within Westminster. The 'welfare officer' role and 'service delivery' on behalf of the constituency, as noted in Chapter 7, has become an increasingly important part of the Westminster MP's job. One result of the creation of a Scottish parliament identified by its critics would be that Scottish MPs in Westminster would have to 'abandon their responsibilities for the education, health, housing and local problems of their constituents and to become, effectively, part-time Members of Parliament' (Michael Ancram, HC Debates 12 January 1998, vol. 304: col. 39). In which event, there would be 'no parity of responsibility or quality of constituency representation. Scottish Members of Parliament at Westminster will have considerably less to do than their English counterparts' (Michael Ancram, HC Debates 12 January 1998, vol. 304: col. 42).

However, Ancram's assessment conflates two separate issues. The first is about 'parity of responsibility', and raises fundamental issues about the performance of representational roles. The second concerns workload and work patterns of MPs. The standard response to the second charge is to assert, generally, that 'there is still a very important job for Scottish MPs to do in Westminster' (Malcolm Bruce, HC Debates 13 January 1998, vol. 304: col. 173); or, more specifically, to list matters still to be decided in London after devolution: 'There will still be immigration and nationality and social security issues – the Child Support Agency alone could keep me going – as well as foreign affairs and international development' (Maria Fyfe, HC Debates 13 January 1998, vol. 304: col. 226). The issue here was not that there would be little for Scottish MPs to do, but that they would have to change their established patterns of substantive policy interest and engagement at Westminster (see Judge and Finlayson 1975 for an examination of this issue during the 1970s' devolution debate).

The more fundamental issue concerned the equality of representatives in Westminster. For James Paice, the Scotland Bill would produce the result of some MPs exerting 'different levels of power over the activities and public services provided in the areas that they represent' (HC Debates 13 January 1998, vol. 304: col. 156). For Richard Shepherd, this constituted 'the most distressing aspect of the construction of the Bill'. It did so because there was no recognition of the 'question of our equality as citizens within the government of this island'. Shepherd believed that the 'magnificence of this Parliament lies in its being the representative institution of us, the people' and as such it asserts 'the essential quality of us as citizens and *us as elected representatives*, holding within our core all the powers of the state to ensure equality across the land' (HC Debates 13 January 1998, vol. 304: col. 201, emphasis added). After the year 2000 there would no longer be such equality of representatives in Westminster.

There are two dimensions to this inequality. One is that Scottish MPs would be unable to deal with many important issues of direct concern to their constituents. The other is that, in contradistinction, 'Scottish Members of Parliament...will have a competence in areas that are denied to English Members of Parliament in relation to Scotland' (Shepherd, HC Debates 12 January 1998, vol. 304: col. 94). The latter inequality is at the heart of what has become known as the 'West Lothian question'. The West

Lothian question is named after Tam Dalyell, the Member for the then constituency of West Lothian. Throughout the debates on the earlier devolution Bills in 1977 and 1978, Dalyell remorselessly pointed to the fact that after devolution Scottish MPs at Westminster would no longer be able to vote on Scottish domestic policies, such as education, housing and health, but would still be able to vote on English domestic policies. In addition, it would be possible for a future Labour government, dependent for its majority on MPs returned for Scottish seats, to legislate successfully on English domestic matters on the strength of support from MPs from Scotland; unfortunately, this would be the very same government which could not, and MPs who could not, legislate for corresponding matters in Scotland. The dilemma was vividly restated by Tam Dalyell in the debate on the Scotland Bill in 1998:

> To put it in practical terms, I suppose that it is really the Two Feathers in Hebden Bridge question so beloved of Bernard Ingram. I will spare the House the expletives, but the Two Feathers question is this, 'What are those *** jocks doing coming *** telling us what to do when they've got a *** Parliament of their own? That is the question that will be asked.
>
> (HC Debates 4 March 1998, vol. 307: col. 1081)

The answers to this question have been many and varied. They have ranged from, at one extreme that there is no need to provide an answer, to the other extreme that there is no answer within the context of the UK as a unitary state. In between there are multiple answers. The most common are: first, the complete exclusion of Scottish MPs from Westminster; second, an 'in and out' solution where Scottish MPs would vote only on matters not transferred to the Scottish parliament; third, a reduction in the number of Scottish MPs at Westminster; fourth, allow Scottish MSPs to serve concurrently as MPs; fifth, some variant of an 'English solution' through the creation of English regional assemblies, or an English Grand Committee within Westminster; sixth, a UK-wide system of federal government; or, seventh, independence for Scotland (for details on aspects of these schemes see Judge and Finlayson 1975: 287–92; Dalyell 1977: 245–54; Bogdanor 1979: 161–2; McLean 1995: 267–8; Constitution Unit 1996: 108–11; Bogdanor 1997: 35–40).

An examination of the constitutional intricacies of each of these answers would take us far beyond the immediate concern of this book. Instead what needs to be remembered is simply that at the centre of the devolution debate in the UK has been the issue of representation (and has been so for over a century – see Bogdanor 1979: 10–24; Judge 1993:

163–79; Mitchell 1996: 68–107). In seeking to enhance representation in Scotland – through the election of more representatives in an Edinburgh-based parliament – the prevailing logic of representation at other levels within the UK is brought under scrutiny. The West Lothian question prompts the response that there is no logical solution to the representational dilemma within a unitary/union UK state. Equally, however, the response could be that representation is a matter of practice as much as *a priori* reasoning (see Mount 1992: 254–5; Bogdanor 1997: 39–40). Indeed, history teaches us that theories of representation have often reflected and justified representative practice of the time. The future of Scottish representation might yet confirm this pattern.

EQUALITY OF REPRESENTATION: MICROCOSMIC CONSIDERATIONS

As noted above, the White Paper, *Scotland's Parliament*, attached great importance to equal opportunities for the representation of women, members of ethnic minorities and disabled people. In particular it urged 'all political parties offering candidates for election to the Scottish Parliament to have this in mind in their internal candidate selection processes' (Cm 3658 1997: 28). Both the Labour party and the Liberal Democratic party had had this consideration 'in mind' throughout their negotiations in the Scottish Constitutional Convention. The problem was that they were not of 'one mind' as to how to secure parity of gender representation and fairer representation of other social groups.

The Scottish Labour party advocated 'active intervention' whereby there would be a statutory imposition on political parties to select a man and a woman for each constituency. This would have required each voter to have cast votes in three separate ballots: one for a male representative, one for a female, and one for a party or group on the regional list. When the Scottish Constitutional Commission examined this proposal it concluded that there were several ideological and practical objections to this scheme. 'Profound reservations' were expressed about the limitation of direct competition between men and women for constituency seats; as each would be separated on discrete lists. Some members of the Commission found the proposal, at best unnecessary, given 'the progress towards equal representation now being made inside political parties'. Others found it, at worst, 'patronising towards women' (Scottish Constitutional Commission 1994: 16). On a practical level, it was pointed out that a double ballot on gender lines would effectively double the number of constituency MSPs, and if a corresponding adjustment was made to the number of additional Members the result would be a parliament of over 224 Members. Redrawing existing Westminster boundaries to produce a smaller number of larger constituencies, effectively 36 'double constituencies', prompted the objections that not only would boundary redistribution slow down the implementation of devolution legislation, but it would also result in 'more remote constituency units' (Scottish Constitutional Commission 1994: 16).

The Scottish Constitutional Commission, while acknowledging that a 'double ballot' system was 'the most straightforward way of ensuring equal representation of men and women in the Scottish Parliament' (1994: 15), eventually reported that it could not recommend the introduction of such a system. Instead, it proposed a voluntary scheme in which parties should seek to attain a target of at least 40 per cent female representation in the new parliament. This conclusion was greeted with dismay by women activists in Scotland, but it prompted further efforts to find an agreed alternative proposal (for details see Brown 1996: 36–7; Brown 1998). The alternative eventually arrived at, in November 1995, and considered by the executives and conferences of the Labour and Liberal Democratic parties, took the form of an 'Electoral Contract'. The Contract committed the two parties to the principle that there should be an equal number of men and women candidates at the first Scottish parliamentary elections. (Securing equal representation at the parliament's inception was deemed to be particularly important, as it would become more difficult to institute parity should gender imbalance became institutionalised through default in the first Edinburgh parliament.) The mechanisms for ensuring gender equality – in the selection of candidates in winnable seats, and their distribution between constituency and additional members – was to be left to the discretion of each party.

The Labour party embarked upon a campaign to ensure that as many women as men were returned to the Scottish parliament. The principle of 'twinning' was approved by the party's NEC and endorsed at conference in October 1997. Under this proposal, winnable constituencies would be twinned, with Labour party members in paired constituencies choosing two candidates, one drawn from a list of women and one from a list of men. At the October 1997 conference, Joan Ruddock, the minister responsible for women's issues, proclaimed: 'There are no no-go areas for women. Women want fairness. 50–50, that is our party's principled position' (quoted in the *Scotsman*, 1 October 1997). The problem confronting the Labour party, however, was that its 'principled position' had earlier been undermined by the 'legal position' specified in equal opportunities legislation. Without a change in the Sex Discrimination Act the twinning strategy ran the risk of a legal challenge.

The experience of quotas and women-only shortlists in the Labour party (after the 1993 conference had agreed to such shortlists in 50 per cent of all vacant seats held by Labour and in 50 per cent of 'winnable' marginals) demonstrated the legal problems of 'active intervention'. In addition to male resistance in some, especially northern, constituency parties (for details see Perrigo 1995: 414–5; Perrigo 1996: 128–9; Squires 1996: 71–6; Criddle 1997: 190–1), and a cooling of support by the party leader after July 1995; the ruling of an industrial tribunal in January 1996 that all-women shortlists were illegal meant the termination of the programme of positive discrimination well before the May 1997 general election. The ruling was brought about by the cases of two disgruntled male Labour candidates, Peter Jepson and Roger Dyas Elliot, who had sought selection in constituencies with women-only shortlists. They claimed that the shortlists were in breach of the 1975 Sex Discrimination Act and a 1976 European Community Directive on equal treatment.

The Jepson ruling weighed heavily in the legal advice offered to the Scottish Secretary when he proposed that the Sex Discrimination Act should be amended to allow political parties to pursue discriminatory processes in favour of the selection of women for the first Scottish parliamentary elections. In a leaked cabinet committee minute (*Guardian*, 3 March 1998) the Lord Chancellor, Lord Irvine, was reported to have advised the Scottish Secretary that selection processes which discriminated in favour of women would, in the opinion of the government's law officers, be liable to challenge – both along the lines of the Jepson case, and also under the European Equal Treatment Directive. In which case, the Scottish Secretary's proposal for securing equal gender representation was considered to be 'a high risk course', and could not be supported by the Labour government. Nonetheless, the minute did recognise that 'the Government did have a responsibility to consider whether legally acceptable ways, which might command consensus, of addressing the problem of increasing the representation of women across the range of democratic bodies could be found'.

The Lord Chancellor's assessment of the legal difficulties was not shared, however, by several Labour contributors to the deliberations on the Scotland Bill. Malcolm Chisholm, in asking his government colleagues to consider introducing a temporary special measure to exclude the first Scottish parliamentary elections from the Sex Discrimination Act, pointed out that:

> A statutory quota is in place in Belgium…under a law of 24 May 1994, whereby 33.3 per cent of candidates must be female. That is less than we want, but the principle is established. Under the Danish equality of treatment legislation, sexual discrimination is not allowed but exemption from the Act may be granted…[if] equality of treat-

ment is promoted for both sexes in a transitional period by giving one sex preferential treatment to redress actual inequality.

(HC Debates 12 January 1998, vol. 304: col. 95)

The principle of introducing some form of immunity for political parties from possible challenge under the Sex Discrimination Act was also supported by James Wallace, Leader of the Scottish Liberal Democrats (HC Debates 12 January 1998, vol. 304: cols 52–3). Wallace's support was met with evident irritation on the part of Labour backbenchers, who noted that the Liberal Democrats in the Constitutional Convention had opposed the creation of a legislative framework to secure equality of representation. Nonetheless, Wallace maintained that: 'there has been no change in our position. The state should not legislate on how political parties select their candidates. We are saying that political parties should not be open to challenge in the courts because they have tried to achieve some gender balance' (HC Debates 12 January 1998, vol. 304: col. 53). In practice, however, the likelihood of a challenge within the Liberal Democratic party was more remote than in the Labour party. The Liberal Democrat's strategy of achieving gender balance rested upon the process of 'zipping' – of using the regional lists to select female members – to compensate for any imbalance within the (comparatively small) number of constituency seats expected to be won by the party. (On electoral projections from the 1997 general election, the Liberal Democrats could expect to win a greater proportion of list seats than constituency seats.)

An attempt by Maria Fyfe to introduce a new clause into the Scotland Bill, to exempt political parties in Scotland from the provisions of the Sex Discrimination Act of 1975, was defeated heavily (HC Debates 31 March 1998, vol. 309: cols 1,135–48). The advancement of gender equality was left, therefore, to the discretion of individual political parties. In the event, the selection processes in the Labour and Liberal Democratic parties had, by the end of July 1998, secured respectively 69 and 21 female candidates. A new dawn in Scottish politics was awaited:

It has been shown that when women are fairly represented alongside men in the decision making process, there is a difference in the way things are done and in policy priorities. Not only can the Scottish Parliament be a shining example of new politics, it can begin to promote new politics.

(Sandra Osborne, HC Debates 13 January 1998, vol. 304: col. 192)

Modernising local government: 'new democratic legitimacy'

Just as the Scottish parliament was expected to bring about a 'new politics', so too did the Labour government expect reform of local government to 'bring government back to the people' (DETR 1998: 3). John Prescott, Deputy Prime Minister and Secretary of State for the Environment, Transport and the Regions, in his preface to the consultative document *Modernising Local Government*, made it clear that: 'Our agenda is the renewal of local democratic government, leading local communities and serving local people. We want councils to gain a new democratic legitimacy' (DETR 1998: 3). The starting assumption was that the legitimacy of local government was presently undermined by low levels of electoral turnout, a culture of apathy, the unrepresentative nature of councillors in microcosmic terms and a mixed record of achievement in service delivery. The need for change was apparent in the belief that: 'Unless they engage their local people...councils cannot have the democratic legitimacy they need if they are to lead their local communities, and fulfil their responsibilities for local services' (DETR 1998: 11).

The election of representatives was identified as the 'prime way in which the political will of a community is expressed on the policies and services' (DETR 1998: 15). Participation in elections was crucial, as 'the more people vote, the greater the democratic legitimacy of the actions taken by those elected' (DETR 1998: 15). Moreover, the tradition of close links between constituents and representatives drawn from identifiable constituencies was seen to be 'vital to ensuring councils engage effectively with their local communities' (DETR 1998: 21). What the government sought, therefore, was the *enhancement* of the representative process, by enabling more people to vote, and to vote more often through annual elections. In addition, it also expected local authorities to develop clear strategies on involving local people in between elections. Consultation and participation were to be the keystones of local decision making processes in the future. To achieve these objectives, five broad types of democratic initiative were identified under the headings: seeking the views of the citizen; increasing community involvement in direct decision making; influencing policy on specific issues; scrutinising council activities; and opening up local authorities.

Under the first heading, citizens' juries, focus groups, conferences and deliberative opinion polls were listed as possible mechanisms for eliciting the views of citizens. Greater direct involvement in decision making could be secured through standing citizens' panels, community forums and area-based neighbourhood committees, or user group forums. On specific issues or decisions, referendums would provide the electorate with direct influence. An enhancement of the scrutiny role could possibly be effected through panels of inquiry or public scrutiny committees drawn from the public. Finally, public question times at council meetings, or even the co-option of members of the public onto council committees, would serve to 'open up' local authorities (for details see DETR 1998: 24–7).

Many of the consultation processes listed in *Modernising Local Government* had already been tried in a variety of local authorities. Indeed, some authorities had launched 'democracy plans' aimed at comprehensive and coordinated attempts at local democratic renewal (see for example Bristol City Council 1998). Clearly visible in these local democratic experiments was an acceptance that enhanced citizen participation and influence would still 'respect the authority of citizens' democratically elected representatives' (Bristol City Council 1998: 24). Yet, throughout the Department of the Environment, Transport and the Regions' (DETR) consultative document, there was a concern to ensure that the various consultative forums, committees, juries and panels were representative in themselves of either the community at large or of specific sections of the community. More representative institutions were thus proposed, and clashes of 'legitimacy' between directly elected, territorially-based councillors and other 'community representatives' were stipulated away in the statement that the latter were to act in a 'consultative' or 'advisory' capacity (with the exception of direct participation through referendums).

However, the practical experience of neighbourhood forums and 'local town halls' in the 1980s and 1990s in the London boroughs of Islington and Tower Hamlets pointed to a less positive proposition. As Desmond King observes on the experience of neighbourhoods in Tower Hamlets: 'Because [they] were based on geographical area, rigidly demarcated, consultation processes were quickly exploited by groups *unrepresentative* of the local community at the expense of other groups' (1996: 220, emphasis added). Similarly, the use of surveys and juries has within them a potential for the expression of biased and irresponsible opinion in the absence of the 'long shadow' cast by the electoral process (see Cochrane 1996: 209).

More fundamentally, perhaps, the proposals for democratisation of local government leave unresolved the 'legitimacy' dilemma. On the one hand, the question of a 'legitimacy deficit' stemming from low electoral turn-out is addressed, and redressed, through proposals for increased participation in elections (and more elections). These proposals are believed to be sufficient to reassert the legitimacy of elected representatives in the decision making process. However, in themselves they do not confront the alternative claims to legitimacy – stemming, for example, from 'expertise' in bureaucracies and policy networks, or from shared 'experiences' in user groups. As noted in Chapter 6, these alternative sources have traditionally posed both normative and practical challenges to territorial representation. This challenge is unlikely to diminish in the future as 'local governance' prevails over 'local government'; and as participatory institutions, such as user groups and forums, seek delegated authority for service provision. In the latter instances, participants may claim a legitimacy derived from personal experience of the service provided (see Stoker 1996: 199) or indeed from being elected from within a neighbourhood. Ultimately, however, and in-line with the discussion in Chapter 7, the superior claim of elected councillors is that 'they are the elected representatives of all the city's residents, and have the power and responsibility to make decisions on their behalf in the common interest' (Bristol City Council 1998: Appendix: 1). The challenge of the future is to sustain that claim.

Local political leadership: disentangling representative government from representative democracy?

In Chapter 1 a distinction was made between 'representative democracy' and 'representative government'. The former was conceived in terms of the overall structure of the political system itself – as a *political process* entailing indirect citizen participation in decision making. The basic claim to be 'democratic' is dependent upon the process itself. This allows for the possibility of further 'democratisation', through increasing the number of representative institutional forms and opportunities to elect more representatives. Essentially this is the logic underpinning many of the reforms sketched in *Modernising Local Government*. 'Representative government' on the other hand is concerned more with institutions of decision or political leadership – and the claim to be 'representative' distils into a claim to be 'responsible'.

Modernising Local Government reveals an awareness of this basic distinction and notes that 'there is strong argument for separating the executive and representational functions of councillors' (DETR 1998: 30). The traditional organisational structure of most councils, centred around committees, provides one of the strongest arguments in itself; being widely perceived to be too burdensome, too inefficient and too ineffective. In particular, it blurred responsibility, allowing councillors to disclaim responsibility for corporate decisions and preventing open scrutiny of executive decisions. As the consultative document noted: 'political leadership can be performed most effectively and openly where it is clear who has the power to take the decisions'. It argued that the benefits of clear leadership would be 'the greater, the more the representative role and the executive role are separated' (DETR 1998: 31). In which case, the government was 'very attracted to the model of a strong executive directly elected mayor'. The comparative advantages and disadvantages of this model have been well rehearsed and need not detain us here (see Hodge *et al.* 1997; Stoker and 6 1997). Instead, our concern is with the model's emphasis upon scrutiny and enhanced executive responsibility to local citizens and their representatives. One consequence of the separation of roles would, in the DETR's view, be an enhancement of the individual councillor's representative role, enabling them to 'become, in a much clearer way, the advocate of the local people, channelling their grievances and demands' (DETR 1998: 31). In envisaging a future less time-consuming, but more high profile, more effective and more rewarding role for individual councillors, the expressed hope was that 'high calibre people from all walks of life...including from those groups which are under-represented at the moment (e.g. those in employment, women, the young, ethnic minorities)' would be encouraged to serve as councillors.

In proposing a distinction between representational roles and leadership roles, the government acknowledged the fundamental distinction between representative *government* and representative *democracy*. In making this distinction it sought the simultaneous enhancement of both. This objective was apparent in the referendum of 7 May 1998 on the creation of an elected Mayor and an Assembly in a new Greater London Authority. Of those who voted, 72 per cent – around one million Londoners – voted in favour of the new Authority. However, the turnout was only 34 per cent of eligible voters. Confronted by even lower turnouts elsewhere in local elections in England on the same day, Tony Blair took this as an indication that: 'we are right to press on with the modernisation of local government' (*Guardian*, 9 May 1998) and confirmed the government's commitment to the revitalisation of local democracy and an extension of the London experiment to other parts of Britain. Other members of the Labour Party were less sanguine, however, about the voters' desire for enhanced 'participation'. Alan Chedzoy, Labour Leader of Dorset County Council, noted in a letter to the *Guardian* (11 May 1998) that his experience of canvassing for the local elections provided 'no evidence that voters wanted more elections, more referenda and more consultations, which are the sort of things suggested by believers in "participatory" democracy. My judgement is that our people favour representative democracy every time'. Nonetheless, the government promised to introduce a White Paper on the revitalisation of local democracy including proposals for annual elections, slimmed down authorities and elected mayors. While it is beyond our remit to speculate upon the likely success of this strategy, it does provide a good example of how theory guides political practice. At the very least, elected executive

mayors will bring yet another layer of representation and electoral responsibility to the British political system. One thing is certain, therefore, the
future holds the prospect of more elections and 'more' representation.

The beginning and the end: electoral systems and the consequences for representation

Throughout this book it has been taken for granted that elections are at
the heart of modern representative processes in Britain. Elections are the
vital link between representatives and the represented. They provide both
a mechanism for choosing representatives and for controlling them. Where
the emphasis is placed – whether upon choosing or on controlling – helps
to condition views upon the efficacy of the electoral system itself. In turn,
these relative weightings become entwined with assessments about whether
representative government – and political leadership – is the primary
objective of representation; or representative democracy – and the incorporation of the political values of equality, freedom and participation into
general rules of the political game – is the central feature. Naturally these
concerns are pivotal to the study of electoral systems and to the debate
about electoral reform. Equally naturally, the closing paragraphs of this
book are not the place to embark upon a detailed analysis of the relative
merits of different electoral systems (for such analyses see Dummett 1997;
Farrell 1996; Bogdanor 1997). Instead we simply need to note that by the
year 2000 there will be a variety of electoral systems in use in the UK.

Elections for the Scottish parliament and the Welsh national assembly
will be based on the additional member system, MEPs will be elected on
closed regional lists, Northern Ireland will continue to use the single transferable vote system for local and Euro-elections, an elected London Mayor
will be elected by a supplementary vote and some variant of proportional
representation might be introduced for local government elections. One
further possibility is an elected and reformed House of Lords in the
twenty-first century, which would add yet another tier of representation to
those examined in Chapter 7.

Despite these innovations, the first Westminster election of the new
millennium, to be held no later than May 2002, is still likely to be
contested on the basis of the first-past-the-post system. In December 1997
the Labour government established an Independent Commission on
Voting Systems, chaired by Lord Jenkins, to examine 'broadly proportional' alternatives to the simple plurality system. This fulfilled the first part
of Labour's manifesto commitment on electoral reform; the other part, a
referendum on the voting system for Westminster elections, was to follow
the report of the Commission. While the government signalled its inten-

tion of scheduling a referendum before the next election (*Guardian*, 10 March 1998), it also indicated that any change to the electoral system was unlikely to be initiated before 2002.

It is hardly surprising that at the end of the twentieth century elections for the House of Commons should provide a last bastion against encroaching proportionality in Britain. Throughout the century, with only a temporary and limited exception in the period 1916–18, official discourse has afforded priority to arguments about representative *government* over representative *democracy*. Even in 1998 the grip of history was still clearly apparent in William Hague's (speech to the Centre for Policy Studies) observation that 'I would argue [the] overriding feature of our Britishness is our long history of accountable government'. He proceeded to argue:

> Practical political power in our country resides primarily with the national government, not with individual Members of Parliament....That power is derived from the national government commanding a working majority in the House of Commons. That working majority is bestowed on political parties by the British people at the ballot box. There is a clear line of accountability. We know who to praise when things go well, and, more importantly, we know who to blame when they do not. And when things do not go well, our voting system allows us to do something about it and kick the Government out.
>
> (Hague 1998)

The twin virtues of strong and responsive government are paramount in this defence of the 'Westminster model'. It should be remembered that these virtues pre-date the extension of the franchise and the adoption of the term 'representative democracy'. Indeed, part of the continuing attachment to such notions of representative government in Britain stems from the very persistence of the model itself. As Norris (1995: 68) notes, plurality elections have been a well-established part of the British constitution since 1264.

In the Westminster model, strong government means single-party government and is associated with party notions of manifestos and mandates (considered in Chapter 4). It makes a virtue of the exaggerative bias in the electoral system which 'manufactures' parliamentary majorities. In reverse, the system removes the need for post-election bargaining between coalition partners in government, and ensures that, as long as a government maintains the support of its own backbenchers, it can legislate pretty much when and how it likes. In this model the voter knows what the government promises and knows what to do if it fails to deliver on its promises. Equally, the government is aware that, in a competitive two party system, a relatively small swing in the vote at the next election can overturn its parliamentary majority. Hence, the actions of single-party governments are authorised through the electoral process; and, equally importantly, governments are also held responsible for their actions through that process. Proponents of the first-past-the-post system have traditionally maintained, therefore, that 'power is shackled with account-ability' (Norris 1995: 66).

Opponents of the simple plurality system, while questioning the basic premises of the Westminster model – both its strength and its responsibility – ultimately base their own advocacy of a more proportional voting system upon a radically different conception of representation. The emphasis is now placed upon choosing representatives and the aggregate representa-tiveness of parliament. Obviously what representatives 'do', and the nature of legislative outputs, remains a concern, but the assumption is that outputs will be directly influenced by the 'inputs' made by elected repre-sentatives. Supporters of electoral reform thus have in common a belief that 'the purpose of an election is to choose a representative parliament' (Bogdanor 1997: 54). They maintain that the present electoral system is inherently 'unfair': it discriminates against small parties whose vote is geographically dispersed; against voters (often the majority) who did not vote for the successful candidate in a constituency, or who did not vote for the successful national party (always the majority of voters in the post-war period), and; against women and against ethnic minorities. From this perspective the first-past-the-post system 'stands condemned as inequitable, inefficient and socially divisive' (Bogdanor 1997: 64). The question then becomes: 'what are the most relevant respects in which MPs should represent their constituents, and Parliament be representative of the electorate as a whole' (Beetham 1992b: 467). The answer, for McLean at least, is: 'If you think it is important to ask "Are there the same propor-tion of Liberals [Scottish Nationalists, women, Afro-Caribbeans, etc.]" in Parliament as in the country?...you are drawn to PR [proportional repre-sentation]' (1991: 174). Moreover, if the present electoral system is judged deficient in meeting the criteria of fairness and equality of representation a corollary is that the very legitimacy of the system of government is undermined. If the system is not fair and equal, but government *is* strong and responsive, then a case can be made that government outputs are at least authorised and accepted as legitimate because of the 'long shadow' cast by the electoral process. However, should the shadow become hazy, should governments be held to be neither strong nor responsive, then the theory of 'representative government' is insufficient in itself to sustain a lasting claim to legitimacy. It was precisely these circumstances which led reformers to identify a 'crisis of legitimacy' at the heart of British parliamentary government in the 1980s and 1990s (see for example Hirst 1990; Harden 1991; Blackburn 1992; Barnett *et al.* 1993; Bogdanor 1997; Barnett 1997). The paradox was that the very characteristics upon which the legitimacy of the representative process in Britain had rested traditionally – strong and responsive *government* – were now seen to be the source of the de-legitimisation of British government. The virtues of representative *democracy*, and of a legitimacy derived from participatory processes, were now deployed by reformers *against* elite legitimation derived from notions of representative government. In this process, different theories of representation were used to defend or criticise existing representative practices and to outline possible alternatives for the future.

Towards the future: echoes of the past

By 2002, and the last possible date for the termination of the parliament elected in 1997, British constitutional topography will have been subjected to several seismic upheavals. The familiar landscape featuring the smooth contours of 'representative and responsible' government, sketched so clearly by Birch in 1964, will have been replaced with more dramatic representative scenery. Underpinning the Labour government's claim to be democratising British government there will be more elections, at more levels, contested on a greater diversity of electoral rules. Simply stated, there will be more representatives drawn from more socially diverse backgrounds.

The British constitutional landscape will also have been transformed by Labour's, pragmatic as much as principled, use of referenda. By 2002, referendums will have been held, scheduled, or proposed for: a Scottish parliament and Welsh national assembly, an elected mayor and strategic local authority for London; possible devolution for English regions; electoral reform, and; at some future date in the next parliament, entry to the European Economic and Monetary Union. In addition, other direct modes of political participation by means of citizens' juries, focus groups and even citizen's initiatives, will have been thoroughly discussed under the DETR's 'democratic renewal' project. All of these participatory initiatives will be reinforced by developments in information technologies and the government's commitment to use these technologies to expand the interface between the represented and their representatives (see Cm 3658 1997: 30–1; Parliamentary Office of Science and Technology 1998).

The degree to which these developments will enlarge the scope of direct citizen participation in practice remains uncertain. What does remain certain, however, is that 'indirect participation' through representative processes will continue to define and delimit the democratic credentials of the British political system in the twenty-first century. Intrinsic to that definition will be those elements identified in Chapter 1 – the inclusion–exclusion paradox, the 'principle of distinction', the mechanisms of choice and control of representatives, the focus and style of representation and the very meaning of legitimacy and the sources of legitimation.

Without doubt, theories of representation will remain central to any normative conception of legitimation in Britain. Equally, the practice of representation will continue to be shaped by, and, simultaneously, also serve to shape those theories. If representation is 'an irreducible necessity' of modern liberal democratic politics (Beetham 1992a: 53), then an understanding of the concept and its practice will remain an 'irreducible necessity' for any student of British politics in the twenty-first century.

References

Adonis, A. (1993) *Parliament Today*, Manchester University Press, Manchester.

Alderman, G. (1984) *Pressure Groups and Government in Great Britain*, Longman, London.

Allaun, F., Mikardo, I. and Sillars, J. (1972) *Labour: Party or Puppet?*, Tribune Group, London.

Andersen, S.S. and Burns, T. (1996) 'The European Union and the Erosion of Parliamentary Democracy: A Study of Post-Parliamentary Governance', in S.S. Andersen and K.A. Eliassen (eds) *The European Union: How Democratic Is It?*, Sage, London.

Arblaster, A. (1984) *The Rise and Decline of Western Liberalism*, Basil Blackwell, Oxford.

Arblaster, A. (1987) *Democracy*, Open University Press, Milton Keynes.

Aristotle [c.335–322 BC] (1962) *The Politics*, Penguin, Harmondsworth.

Baker, D., Gamble, A. and Ludlam, S. (1993) 'Whips or Scorpions? Conservative MPs and the Maastricht Paving Motion Vote', *Parliamentary Affairs*, 46, 2: 151–66.

Baker, D., Gamble, A. and Ludlam, S. (1994) 'The Parliamentary Siege of Maastricht 1993', *Parliamentary Affairs*, 47, 1: 61–72.

Ball, T. (1992) *James Mill: Political Writings*, Cambridge University Press, Cambridge.

Banks, O. (1993) *The Politics of British Feminism, 1918–1970*, Edward Elgar, Aldershot.

Bardi, L. (1994) 'Transnational Federations, European Parliamentary Groups, and the Building of Europarties', in R.S. Katz and P. Mair (eds) *How Parties Organise*, Sage, London.

Barnett, A. (1997) *This Time: Our Constitutional Revolution*, Vintage, London.

Barnett, A., Ellis, C. and Hirst, P. (1993) *Debating the Constitution*, Polity, Cambridge.

Bealey, F. (1988) *Democracy in the Contemporary State*, Clarendon Press, Oxford.

Beer, S.H. (1969) *Modern British Politics* (2nd edn), Faber & Faber, London.

Beetham, D. (1992a) 'Liberal Democracy and the Limits of Democratization', *Political Studies*, 40, 5: 40–53.

Beetham, D. (1992b) 'The Plant Report and the Theory of Political Representation', *Political Quarterly*, 63, 4: 460–7.

Beetham, D. (1996) 'Theorising Democracy and Local Government', in D. King and G. Stoker (eds) *Rethinking Local Democracy*, Macmillan, Houndmills.

Benn, T. (1982)*Arguments for Democracy*, Penguin, Harmondsworth.

Bentham, J. [1789] (1843) *Essay on Political Tactics*, in *Works*, vol. 2, ed. J. Bowring, William Tait, Edinburgh.

Bentham, J. [1817] (1843) *Plan of Parliamentary Reform*, in *Works*, vol. 3, ed. J. Bowring, William Tait, Edinburgh.

Bentham, J. [1830] (1843) *The Constitutional Code*, in *Works*, vol. 9, ed. J. Bowring, William Tait, Edinburgh.

Berrington, H. (1995) 'Political Ethics: The Nolan Report', *Government and Opposition*, 30: 431–51.

Berry, S. (1993) 'Lobbying: A Need to Regulate', *Politics Review*, February: 23–6.

Birch, A.H. (1964) *Representative and Responsible Government*, Unwin, London.

Birch, A.H. (1971) *Representation*, Macmillan, London.

Birch, A.H. (1975) 'The Theory of Representation and British Practice' in S.E. Finer (ed.) *Adversary Politics and Electoral Reform*, Anthony Wigram, London.

Birch, A.H. (1993) *The Concepts and Theories of Modern Democracy*, Routledge, London.

Black, J. (1993) *The Politics of Britain: 1688–1800*, Manchester University Press, Manchester.

Blackburn, R. (1992) 'The Ruins of Westminster', *New Left Review*, 191: 5–35.

Bogdanor, V. (1979) *Devolution*, Oxford University Press, Oxford.

Bogdanor, V. (1984) *What is Proportional Representation?* Martin Robertson, Oxford.

Bogdanor, V. (1997) *Power and the People: A Guide to Constitutional Reform*, Gollancz, London.

Börzel, T.A. (1997) 'What's So Special About Policy Networks: An Exploration of the Concept and its Usefulness in Studying European Governance', *European Integration Online Papers* No. 16, http: //eiop.or.at/eiop/texte/ 1997—016a.htm

Bowler, S. and Farrell, D. (1993) 'Legislator Shirking and Voter Monitoring: Impacts of European Parliament Electoral Systems upon Legislator-Voter Relationships', *Journal of Common Market Studies*, 31, 1: 45–70.

Bracher, K. D. (1967) 'Problems of Parliamentary Democracy in Europe', in S.R. Gaubard (ed.) *A New Europe?*, Beacon Press, Boston.

Brazier, R. (1991) *Constitutional Reform*, Clarendon Press, Oxford.

Bressers, H., O'Toole, L.J. and Richardson, J.J. (1994) 'Networks as Models of Analysis: Water Policy in Comparative Perspective', *Environmental Politics*, 3: 1–23.

Bristol City Council (1998) *Bristol Democracy Plan*, Bristol City Council, Bristol.

Brown, A. (1996) 'Women and Politics in Scotland', *Parliamentary Affairs*, 49, 1: 26–40.

Brown, A. (1998) 'Deepening Democracy: Women and The Scottish Parliament', *Regional and Federal Studies*, 8, 1: 103–19.

Budge, I. (1996) *The New Challenge of Direct Democracy*, Polity, Cambridge.

Burke, E. [1774] (1801) 'Speech to the Electors of Bristol', in *Works*, vol. 3, Rivington, London.

Burke, E. [1780a] (1801) 'Speech at Bristol Previous to the Election', in *Works*, vol. 4, Rivington, London.

Burke, E. [1780b] (1801) 'Speech at Bristol at the Conclusion of the Poll', in *Works*, vol. 4, Rivington, London.

Burke, E. [1780c] (1812) 'Speech on a Bill for Shortening the Duration of Parliament', in *Works*, vol. 10, Rivington, London.

Burke, E. [1780d] (1801) 'Speech on a Plan for the Better Scrutiny of the Independence of Parliament and the Economic Reformation of the Civil and Other Establishments', in *Works*, vol. 3, Rivington, London.

Burke, E. [1790] (1967) 'Letter 26 February 1790', in A. Cobban and R.A Smith, *The Correspondence of Edmund Burke*, vol. 6, Cambridge University Press, Cambridge.

Burke, E. [1792] (1801) 'Letter to Sir Hercules Langrishe', in *Works*, vol. 6, Rivington, London.

Burke, E. [1796] (1801) 'First Letter on a Regicide Peace', in *Works*, vol. 8, Rivington, London.

Burnell, J. B. (1980) *Democracy and Accountability in the Labour Party*, Spokesman, Nottingham.

Burnheim, J. (1985) *Is Democracy Possible? The Alternative to Electoral Politics*, Polity, Cambridge.

Burns, D., Hambleton, R. and Hoggett, P. (1994) *The Politics of Decentralisation: Revitalising Local Democracy*, Macmillan, Houndmills.

Butt, R. (1969) *The Power of Parliament*, Constable, London.

Butt, R. (1989) *A History of Parliament: The Middle Ages*, Constable, London.

Bystydzienski, J.M. (1992) 'Influence of Women's Culture on Public Politics in Norway', in J.M. Bystydzienski, *Women Transforming Politics*, Indiana University Press, Indianopolis.

Cain, B.E., Ferejohn, J.A. and Fiorina, M.P. (1979) 'The House is Not a Home: British MPs in Their Constituencies', *Legislative Studies Quarterly*, 4: 501–23.

Cain, B.E., Ferejohn, J.A. and Fiorina, M.P. (1984) 'The Constituency Service Basis of the Personal Vote for U.S. Representatives and British Members of Parliament', *American Political Science Review*, 78: 110–25.

Cain, B.E., Ferejohn, J.A. and Fiorina, M.P. (1987) *The Personal Vote: Constituency Service and Electoral Independence*, Harvard University Press, Cambridge MA.

Callaghan, J. (1990) *Socialism in Britain*, Blackwell, Oxford.

Camerilleri, J.A. and Falk, J. (1992) *The End of Sovereignty*, Edward Elgar, Aldershot.

Campaign for a Scottish Assembly (1988) *A Claim of Right for Scotland*, Campaign for a Scottish Assembly, Edinburgh.

Canavan, F.P. (1960) *The Political Reason of Edmund Burke*, Duke University Press, Durham NC.

Caporaso, J. and Keeler, J. (1995) 'The European Union and Regional Integration Theory' in S. Mazey and C. Rhodes (eds) *The State of the European Union* (vol. 3), Lynne Reiner/Longman, Boulder.

Carpenter, L.P. (1976) 'Corporatism in Britain 1930–45', *Journal of Contemporary History*, 11: 3–25.

Cashmore, E. (1991) 'Black Politics: Chasing Five Figure Fantasies', *New Statesman and Society*, 27 September: 32–3.

Cawson, A. (1982) *Corporatism and Welfare*, Heinemann, London.

Cawson, A. (1989) 'Is There a Corporatist Theory of the State', in G. Duncan (ed.) *Democracy and the Capitalist State*, Cambridge University Press, Cambridge.

Churchill, W. (1930) *Parliamentary Government and the Economic Problem*, Oxford University Press, Oxford.

Cm 2850-I (1995) *Standards in Public Life*, Volume 1: Report, First Report of the Committee on Standards in Public Life, HMSO, London.

Cm 2850-II (1995) *Standards in Public Life*, Volume 2: Transcripts of Oral Evidence, First Report of the Committee on Standards in Public Life, HMSO, London.

Cm 3330-II (1996) *Review of Parliamentary Pay and Allowances*, Review Body on Senior Salaries, HMSO, London.

Cm 3658 (1997) *Scotland's Parliament*, Stationery Office, London.

Cm 3718 (1997) *A Voice for Wales*, Stationery Office, London.

Cmnd 9797-I (1986) *The Conduct of Local Authority Business*, Report of the Committee of Inquiry into the Conduct of Local Authority Business, HMSO, London.

Cmnd 9801 (1986) *The Conduct of Local Authority Business*, Research Volume IV, Report of the Committee of Inquiry into the Conduct of Local Authority Business, HMSO, London.

Coates, D. (1975) *The Labour Party and the Struggle for Socialism*, Cambridge University Press, Cambridge.

Cochrane, A. (1996) 'From Theories to Practices: Looking for Local Democracy in Britain', in D. King and G. Stoker (eds) *Rethinking Local Democracy*, Macmillan, Houndmills.

Cohen, J. and Rodgers, J. (1995) 'Secondary Associations and Democratic Governance', in E.O. Wright (ed.) *Associations and Democracy*, Verso, London.

Cole, G.D.H. (1917) *Self Government in Industry*, Hutchinson, London.

Cole, G.D.H. (1920a) *Social Theory*, Methuen, London.

Cole, G.D.H. (1920b) *Guild Socialism Restated*, Leonard Parsons, London.

Conservative Party (1970) *A Better Tomorrow*, Conservative Central Office, London.

Conservative Party (1983) *Manifesto*, Conservative Central Office, London.

Conservative Party (1997a) The 114th Conservative Party Conference: Speeches, http://www.tory.org.uk/

Conservative Party (1997b) *You Can Only Be Sure With the Conservatives*, Conservative Central Office, London.

Conservative Party (1998) *The Fresh Future*, http://www.tory.org.uk/

Constitution Unit (1996) *Scotland's Parliament: Fundamentals For a New Scotland Act*, The Constitution Unit, London.

Coole, D. (1993) *Women in Political Theory* (2nd edn), Harvester Wheatsheaf, London.

Corbett, R., Jacobs, F. and Shackleton, M. (1995) *The European Parliament* (3rd edn), Cartermill, London.

Council of the European Union (1992) *Treaty on European Union*, Office for Official Publications of the European Communities, Luxembourg.

Council of the European Union (1997) *Treaty of Amsterdam Amending the Treaty on European Union, the Treaties Establishing the European Communities and Certain Related Acts*, Office for Official Publications of the European Communities, Luxembourg.

Cowley, P. (1998) 'Unbridled Passions? Free Votes, Issues of Conscience, and the Accountability of Members of Parliament', *Journal of Legislative Studies*, 4, 2: 70–88.

Cowley, P. and Stuart, M. (1997), 'Sodomy, Slaughter, Sunday Shopping and Seatbelts', *Party Politics*, 3, 1: 19–30.

Cox, A. (1988a) 'Neo-Corporatism versus the Corporate State', in A. Cox and N. O'Sullivan (eds) *The Corporate State*, Edward Elgar, Aldershot.

Cox, A. (1988b) 'The Failure of Corporatist State Forms and Policies in Postwar Britain', in A. Cox and N. O'Sullivan (eds) *The Corporate State*, Edward Elgar, Aldershot.

Craig, F.W.S. (1989) *British Election Facts 1832–1987*, Dartmouth, Aldershot.

Cram, L. (1996) 'Integration Theory and the Study of the European Policy Process', in J.J. Richardson (ed.) *European Union: Power and Policy-Making*, Routledge, London.

Crewe, I. (1993) 'Voting and the Electorate', in P. Dunleavy, A. Gamble, I. Holliday and G. Peele (eds) *Developments in British Politics 5*, Macmillan, London.

Crick, B. (1964) *In Defence of Politics*, Penguin, Harmondsworth.

Criddle, B. (1997) 'MPs and Candidates', in D. Butler and D. Kavanagh (eds) *The British General Election of 1997*, Macmillan, London.

Crouch, C. (1977) *Class Conflict and the Industrial Relations Crisis*, Heinemann, London.

Crouch, C. (1982) 'The Peculiar Relationship: The Party and the Unions', in D. Kavanagh (ed.) *The Politics of the Labour Party*, Allen & Unwin, London.

Curtice, J. and Jowell, R. (1997) 'Trust in the Political System', in R. Jowell, J. Curtice, A. Park, L. Brook, K. Thomson and C. Bryson, *British Social Attitudes: the 14th Report*, Ashgate, Aldershot.

Dahl, R.A. (1956) *A Preface To Democratic Theory*, University of Chicago Press, Chicago.

Dahl, R.A. (1961) *Who Governs?*, Yale University Press, New Haven.

Dahl, R.A. (1989) *Democracy and Its Critics*, Yale University Press, New Haven.

Dalyell, T. (1977) *Devolution: The End of Britain?*, Jonathan Cape, London.

Dankert, P. (1997) 'Pressure From the European Parliament', in G. Edwards and A. Pijpers (eds) *The Politics of European Treaty Reform: The 1996 Intergovernmental Conference and Beyond*, Pinter, London.

Darcy, R., Welch, S. and Clark, J. (1994) *Women, Elections and Representation* (2nd edn), University of Nebraska Press, Nebraska.

Daugbjerg, C. and Marsh, D. (1998) 'Explaining Policy Outcomes: Integrating the Policy Network Approach with Macro-Level and Micro-Level Analysis', in D. Marsh (ed.) *Comparing Policy Networks*, Open University Press, Buckingham.

Denver, D. (1997) 'The Government That Could Do No Right' in A. King (ed.) *New Labour Triumphs: Britain at the Polls*, Chatham House, London.

DETR (1998) *Modernising Local Government: Local Democracy and Community Leadership*, Department of the Environment, Transport and the Regions, London.

Dicey [1885] (1959) *An Introduction to the Study of the Law of the Constitution* (10th edn), Macmillan, London.

Dinan, D. (1994) *Ever Closer Union?*, Macmillan, Houndmills.

Dinwiddy, J. (1989) *Bentham*, Oxford University Press, Oxford.

Doig, A. and Wilson, J. (1995) 'Untangling the Threads of Sleaze: the Slide into Nolan', *Parliamentary Affairs*, 48: 562–78.

Dummett, M. (1997) *Principles of Electoral Reform*, Oxford University Press, Oxford.

Dunleavy, P., Weir, S. and Subrahmanyam, G. (1995) 'Sleaze in Britain: Media Influences, Public Response and Constitutional Significance', *Parliamentary Affairs*, 48: 602–16.

Dunn, J. (1979) *Western Political Theory in the Face of the Future*, Cambridge University Press, Cambridge.

Easton, D. (1966) *A Systems Analysis of Political Life*, Wiley, New York.

Eccleshall, R. (1986) *British Liberalism: Liberal Thought from the 1640s to 1980s*, Longman, London.

Ellis, J. and Johnson, R.W. (1974) *Members from the Unions*, Fabian Society, London.

Erskine May (1989), *Treatise on the Law, Privileges, Proceedings and Usage of Parliament* (21st edn), Butterworths, London.

European Parliament (1995) *The European Parliament*, Office for Official Publications of the European Communities, Luxembourg.

European Parliament (1996) *Rules of Procedure* (11th edn), European Parliament, Luxembourg.

Evans, E.J. (1996) *The Forging of the Modern State: Early Industrial Britain 1783–1870* (2nd edn), Longman, London.

Farrell, D.M. (1996) *Comparing Electoral Systems*, Prentice Hall, London.

Featherstone, K. (1994) 'Jean Monnet and the 'Democratic Deficit' in the European Union', *Journal of Common Market Studies*, 32: 149–70.

Femia, J. (1993), *Marxism and Democracy*, Oxford University Press, Oxford.

Fenn, R.A. (1987) *James Mill's Political Thought*, Garland, New York.

Fenno, R.E. (1978) *Home Style: House Members in Their Districts*, Little Brown, Boston.

Finer, H. (1923) *Representative Government and a Parliament of Industry*, Fabian Society/Allen & Unwin, London.

Finer, H. (1949) *Theory and Practice of Modern Government*, Holt and Company, New York.

Finer, S.E. [1958] (1966) *Anonymous Empire: A Study of the Lobby in Great Britain*, (2nd edn), Pall Mall Press, London.

Foote, G. (1985) *The Labour Party's Political Thought*, Croom Helm, London.

Franklin, M. (1996) 'European Elections and the European Voter', in J.J. Richardson (ed.) *European Union: Power and Policy-Making*, Routledge, London.

Franklin, M. and van der Eijk, C. (1996) 'The Problem: Representation and Democracy in the European Union', in C. van der Eijk and M. Franklin (eds) *Choosing Europe? The European Electorate and National Politics in the Face of Union*, Michigan University Press, Ann Arbor.

Franklin, M., van der Eijk, C. and Marsh, M. (1996) 'Conclusions: The Electoral Connection and the Democratic Deficit', in C. van der Eijk and M. Franklin (eds) *Choosing Europe? The European Electorate and National Politics in the Face of Union*, Michigan University Press, Ann Arbor.

Fraser, E. (1996) 'The Value of Locality', in D. King and G. Stoker (eds) *Rethinking Local Democracy*, Macmillan, Houndmills.

Game, C. and Leach, S. (1996) 'Political Parties and Local Democracy', in L. Pratchett and D. Wilson (eds) *Local Democracy and Local Government*, Macmillan, Houndmills.

Geddes, A. (1995) 'The 'Logic' of Positive Action?', *Party Politics*, 1, 2: 275–85.

Gerth, H.H. and Mills, C.W. (1970) *From Max Weber: Essays in Sociology*, Routledge, London.

Goulbourne, H. (1990) *Black Politics in Britain*, Avebury, Aldershot.

Grant, W. (1995) *Pressure Groups, Politics and Democracy in Britain* (2nd edn), Harvester Wheatsheaf, London.

Greenleaf, W.H. (1983) *The British Political Tradition: The Ideological Heritage* (vol. 2), Methuen, London.

Hague, W. (1998) 'Change and Tradition: Thinking Creatively About the Constitution', Speech to the Centre for Policy Studies, 24 February, Conservative Central Office, London.

Hanf, K. and O'Toole. L.J. (1992) 'Revisiting Old Friends: Networks, Implementation Structures and the Management of Inter-Organizational Relations', *European Journal of Political Research*, 21: 163–80.

Harden, I. (1988) 'Corporatism Without Labour: The British Version', in C. Graham and T. Prosser (eds) *Waiving The Rules*, Open University Press, Milton Keynes.

Harden, I. (1991) 'Review Article: The Constitution and Its Discontents', *British Journal of Political Science*, 21: 489–510.

Harrop, M. and Miller, W.L. (1987), *Elections and Voters: A Comparative Introduction*, Macmillan, Houndsmill.

Hayek, F. A. (1982) *Law, Legislation and Liberty, Volume 3. The Political Order of a Free People*, Routledge & Kegan Paul, London.

Hayter, D. (1982), 'Democracy at Stake', *New Socialist*, March/April: 13–14.

HC 161 (1931) *Procedure on Public Business*, Special Report from the Select Committee on Procedure, Session 1930–3, HMSO, London.

HC 118 (1947) *Report from the Committee of Privileges*, Session 1946–47, HMSO, London.

HC 57 (1969) *Report from the Select Committee on Members' Interests (Declaration)*, HMSO, London.

HC 634 (1975) *Complaint Concerning a Resolution of the Yorkshire Area Council of the National Union of Mineworkers*, Second Report from the Committee of Privileges, Session 1974–75, HMSO, London.

HC 108 (1991) *The Interests of Chairmen and Members of Select Committees*, First Report from the Select Committee on Members' Interests, Session 1990–91, HMSO, London.

HC 420 (1991) *Complaint Concerning a Resolution of the Yorkshire Area Council of the National Union of Mineworkers*, Report from the Committee of Privileges, Session 1990–91, HMSO, London.

HC 326 (1992) *Registration and Declaration of Members Financial Interests*, First Report from Select Committee on Members' Interests, Session 1991–92, HMSO, London.

HC 186 (1995) *Register of Members' Interests as at 31st January 1995*, Session 1994–95, HMSO, London.

HC 239 (1995) *The Inter-Governmental Conference: The Agenda, Democracy and Efficiency, The Role of National Parliaments*, Select Committee on European Legislation, 24th Report, Session 1994–5, HMSO, London.

HC 51-xxvii (1996) *The Scrutiny of European Business*, Select Committee on European Legislation, 27th Report, Session 1995–96, HMSO, London.

HC 51-xxviii (1996) *The Role of National Parliaments in the European Union*, Select Committee on European Legislation, 28th Report, Session 1995–96, HMSO, London.

HC 345 (1996) *Register of Members' Interests as at 31st March 1996*, Session 1995–96, HMSO, London.

HC 688 (1996) *The Code of Conduct together with the Guide to the Rules Relating to the Conduct of Members*, Session 1996–97, HMSO, London.

HC 36-xiii (1997) *The Draft Protocol on the Role of National Parliaments*, Select Committee on European Legislation, 13th Report, Session 1996–97, HMSO, London.

HC 181 (1997) *The Register of Members' Interests, Category Four, Sponsorship*, Fourth Report, Standards and Privileges Select Committee, Session 1997–98, HMSO, London.

HC 259 (1997) *Register of Members' Interests as at 31st January 1997*, Session 1996–97, HMSO, London.

HC 291 (1997) *Register of Members' Interests as at 31 October 1997*, Session 1997–98, HMSO, London.

HC 600 (1998) *Modernisation of the House of Commons*, Select Committee on Modernisation of the House of Commons, 4th Report, Session 1997–8, HMSO, London.

Heath, A., Jowell R. and Curtice, J. (1985) *How Britain Votes*, Pergamon Press, Oxford.

Heath, A., Jowell, R., Curtice, J., Evans, G., Field, J. and Witherspoon, S. (1991) *Understanding Political Change: The British Voter 1964–1987*, Pergamon Press, Oxford.

Held, D. (1987) *Models of Democracy*, Polity, Cambridge.

Held, D. (1993) 'Democracy: From City-States to a Cosmopolitan Order? in D. Held (ed.) *Prospects for Democracy*, Polity, Cambridge.

Hibbing, J.R. and Patterson, S.C. (1986) 'Representing a Territory: Constituency Boundaries for the British House of Commons of the 1980s', *Journal of Politics*, 48: 992–1005.

Hill, C. (1986) *The Collected Essays of Christopher Hill, vol. 3: People and Ideas in 17th Century England*, Harvester, Brighton.

Hill, D. (1974) *Democratic Theory and Local Government*, Allen & Unwin, London.

Hirst, P. (1990) *Representative Democracy and Its Limits*, Polity, Cambridge.

Hirst, P. (1993) 'Associational Democracy', in D. Held (ed.) *Prospects for Democracy*, Polity, Cambridge.

Hirst, P. (1994) *Associative Democracy: New Forms of Economic and Social Governance*, Polity, Cambridge.

Hirst, P. (1997) *From Statism to Pluralism*, UCL Press, London.

Hix, S. and Lord, C. (1997) *Political Parties in the European Union*, Macmillan, Houndmills.

HL 149 (1986) *Single European Act and Parliamentary Scrutiny*, Select Committee on the European Communities, 12th Report, Session 1985–6, HMSO, London.

Hodge, M., Leach, S. and Stoker, G. (1997) 'More than the Flower Show: Elected Mayors and Democracy', *Discussion Paper 32*, Fabian Society, London.

Holden, B. (1974), *The Nature of Democracy*, Nelson, London.

Hollingsworth, M. (1991) *MPs for Hire*, Bloomsbury, London.

Immergut, E.M. (1995) 'An Institutional Critique of Associative Democracy', in E.O. Wright (ed.) *Associations and Democracy*, Verso, London.

Ingle, S. (1989) *The British Party System* (2nd edn), Blackwell, Oxford.

Ingle, S. (1997) 'British Political Parties in the Last Fifty Years', in L. Robins and B. Jones (eds) *Half a Century of British Politics*, Manchester University Press, Manchester.

Jessop, B. (1978) 'Capitalism and Democracy: The Best Possible Political Shell?, in G. Littlejohn, B. Smart, J. Wakeford and N. Yuval-Davis (eds) *Power and the State*, Croom Helm, London.

Jessop, B. (1979) 'Corporatism, Parliamentarism and Social Democracy', in P.C. Schmitter and G. Lehmbruch (eds) *Trends Towards Corporatist Intermediation*, Sage, London.

Jessop, B. (1980) 'The Transformation of the State in Post-war Britain', in R. Scase (ed.) *The State in Western Europe*, Croom Helm, London.

Jewell, M.E. (1983) 'Legislator-Constituency Relations and the Representative Process', *Legislative Studies Quarterly*, 8: 303–37.

John, P. (1997) 'Local Governance', in P. Dunleavy, A. Gamble, I. Holliday and G. Peele (eds) *Developments in British Politics 5*, Macmillan, London.

Jordan, A.G. (1990a) 'Policy Community Realism versus 'New' Institutionalist Ambiguity', *Political Studies*, 38, 3: 470–85.

Jordan, A.G. (1990b) 'The Pluralism of Pluralism: An Anti-theory', *Political Studies*, 38, 2: 286–301.

Jordan, A.G. and Richardson, J.J. (1982) 'The British Policy Style or The Logic of Negotiation?' in J.J. Richardson (ed.) *Policy Styles in Western Europe*, Allen & Unwin, London.

Jordan, A.G. and Richardson, J.J. (1987a) *British Politics and the Policy Process*, Allen & Unwin, London.

Jordan, A.G. and Richardson J.J. (1987b) *Government and Pressure Groups in Britain*, Clarendon Press, Oxford.

Judge, D. (1981) *Backbench Specialisation in the House of Commons*, Heinemann Educational Books, London.

Judge, D. (1983a) 'Introduction', in D. Judge (ed.) *The Politics of Parliamentary Reform*, Heinemann Educational Books, London.

Judge, D. (1983b) 'Why Reform? Parliamentary Reform Since 1832', in D. Judge (ed.) *The Politics of Parliamentary Reform*, Heinemann Educational Books, London.

Judge, D. (1990a) *Parliament and Industry*, Dartmouth, Aldershot.

Judge, D. (1990b) 'Parliament and Interest Representation', in M. Rush (ed.) *Parliament and Pressure Politics*, Clarendon Press, Oxford.

Judge, D. (1993) *The Parliamentary State*, Sage, London.

Judge, D. (1995) 'Pluralism', in D. Judge, G. Stoker and H. Wolman (eds) *Theories of Urban Politics*, Sage, London.

Judge, D. (1996) 'The Failure of National Parliaments', in J. Hayward (ed.) *The Crisis of Representation in Europe*, Frank Cass, London.

Judge, D. and Dickson, T. (1987) 'The British State, Governments and Manufacturing Decline', in T. Dickson and D. Judge (eds) *The Politics of Industrial Closure*, Macmillan, London.

Judge, D. and Finlayson, D. (1975) 'Scottish Members of Parliament: Problems of Devolution', *Parliamentary Affairs*, 28, 3: 278–92.

Kateb, G. (1981) 'The Moral Distinctiveness of Representative Democracy', *Ethics*, 91, 3: 357–74.

Keane, J. (1984) *Democracy and Civil Society*, Verso, London.

Kellner, P. (1997) 'Why the Tories Were Trounced', *Parliamentary Affairs*, 50, 4: 616–30.

Kelly, R.N. (1989) *Conservative Party Conferences*, Manchester University Press, Manchester.

King, A. (1997) *New Labour Triumphs: Britain at the Polls*, (ed.) Chatham House, London.

King, D. (1996) 'Conclusion', in D. King and G. Stoker (eds) *Rethinking Local Democracy*, Macmillan, Houndmills.

King, D. and Stoker, G. (1996) *Rethinking Local Democracy*, (eds) Macmillan, Houndmills.

Klingemann, H. D., Hofferbert, R. I. and Budge, I. (1994) *Parties, Policies and Democracy*, Westview Press, Boulder.

Kogan, D. and Kogan, M. (1982) *The Battle for the Labour Party*, Fontana, Glasgow.

Kohler-Koch, B. (1997) 'Organised Interests in the EC and the European Parliament', *European Integration Online Papers* No 9, http: //eiop.or.at/eiop/texte/1997—009a.htm

Kornberg, A. and Clarke, H. D. (1992), *Citizens and Community: Political Support in a Representative Democracy*, Cambridge University Press, Cambridge.

Kruthoffer, A. (1992) 'Voters, Quotas, and Women in the House', in G. Smyth (ed.) *Refreshing the Parts*, Lawrence & Wishart, London.

Labour Party (1907a) *Annual Conference Report*, Labour Party, London.

Labour Party (1907b) *NEC Report and Balance Sheet*, Labour Party, London.

Labour Party (1918) *Annual Conference Report*, Labour Party, London.

Labour Party (1935) *Annual Conference Report*, Labour Party, London.

Labour Party (1970) *Annual Conference Report*, Labour Party, London.

Labour Party (1997a) *Labour Into Power: A Framework for Partnership*, Labour Party, London.

Labour Party (1997b) *Partnership in Power*, Labour Party, London.

Labour Party (1997c) *New Labour: Because Britain Deserves Better*, Labour Party, London.

Laffan, B. (1997) 'The European Union: A Distinctive Model of Internationalisation?', *European Integration Online Papers* No. 18, http: //eiop.or.at/eiop/texte/ 1997—018a.htm

Lamont, N. (1995) *Sovereign Britain*, Duckworth, London.

Layton-Henry, Z. (1992) *The Politics of Immigration*, Blackwell, Oxford.

Lehmbruch, G. (1979) 'Liberal Corporatism', in P.C. Schmitter and G. Lehmbruch (eds) *Trends Towards Corporatist Intermediation*, Sage, London.

Leigh, D. and Vulliamy, E. (1997) *Sleaze: The Corruption of Parliament*, Fourth Estate, London.

Leoni, B. (1961) *Freedom and Law*, Van Nostrand, Princeton.

Levy, R. (1992) 'The Scottish Constitutional Convention, Nationalism and the Union', *Government and Opposition*, 27: 222–34.

Leys, C. (1989) *Politics in Britain* (2nd edn), Verso, London.

Lijphart, A. (1984) *Democracies: Patterns of Majoritarian and Consensus Governments in Twenty One Countries*, Yale University Press, New Haven.

Loades, D. (1997) *Tudor Government: Structures of Authority in the Sixteenth Century*, Blackwell, Oxford.

Lodge, J. (1996) 'The European Parliament', in S.S. Andersen and K.A. Eliassen (eds) *The European Union: How Democratic Is It ?*, Sage, London.

Loughlin, M. (1996) 'The Constitutional Status of Local Government, in L. Pratchett and D. Wilson (eds) *Local Democracy and Local Government*, Macmillan, Houndmills.

Lovenduski, J. (1993), 'Introduction: The Dynamics of Gender and Party', in J. Lovenduski and P. Norris (eds) *Gender and Party Politics*, Sage, London.

Lovenduski, J. and Norris, P. (1989) 'Selecting Women Candidates: Obstacles to the Feminisation of the House of Commons', *European Journal of Political Research*, 17, 4: 533–62.

Lovenduski, J. and Randall, V. (1993) *Contemporary Feminist Politics*, Oxford University Press, Oxford.

Ludlam, S. (1996) 'The Spectre Haunting Conservatism: Europe and Backbench Rebellion', in S. Ludlam and M.J. Smith (eds) *Contemporary British Conservatism*, Macmillan, Basingstoke.

McCrone, D.J. and Stone, W.J. (1986) 'The Structure of Constituency Representation: On Theory and Method', *Journal of Politics*, 48: 956–75.

MacInnes, J. (1987) *Thatcherism at Work*, Open University Press, Milton Keynes.

McKenzie, R.T. (1963) *British Political Parties*, Mercury Books, London.

McLean, I. (1989) *Democracy and the New Technology*, Polity, Cambridge.

McLean, I. (1991) 'Forms of Representation and Systems of Voting', in D. Held (ed.) *Political Theory Today*, Polity, Cambridge.

McLean, I. (1995) 'Are Scotland and Wales Over-Represented in the House of Commons?', *Political Quarterly*, 66, 4: 250–68.

Macmillan, H. (1933) *Reconstruction: A Plea for National Unity*, Macmillan, London.

Macpherson, C.B. (1977) *The Life and Times of Liberal Democracy*, Oxford University Press, Oxford.

Madison, J., Hamilton, A. and Jay. J. [1788] (1987) *The Federalist Papers*, Penguin, Harmondsworth.

Mair, P. (1994) 'Party Organizations: From Civil Society to the State', in R.S. Katz and P. Mair (eds) *How Parties Organize*, Sage, London.

Maitland, F. W. (1908), *The Constitutional History of England*, Cambridge University Press, Cambridge.

Maloney, W. and Richardson, J.J. (1994) 'Water Policy-Making in England and Wales: Policy Communities Under Pressure?', *Environmental Politics*, 3: 110–38.

Maloney, W., Jordan, G. and McLaughlin, A.M. (1994) 'Interest Groups and Public Policy: The Insider/Outsider Model Revisited', *Journal of Public Policy*, 14: 17–38.

Mancuso, M. (1995) *The Ethical World of British MPs*, McGill-Queens University Press, Montreal.

Manin, B. (1997), *The Principles of Representative Government*, Cambridge University Press, Cambridge.

Marks, G., Hooghe, L. and Blank, K. (1996) 'European Integration from the 1980s', *Journal of Common Market Studies*, 34: 341–78.

Marquand, D. (1988) *The Unprincipled Society*, Fontana, London.

Marsh, D. and Rhodes, R.A.W. (1992a) *Policy Networks in British Government*, (eds) Clarendon Press, Oxford.

Marsh, D. and Rhodes, R.A.W. (1992b) *Implementing Thatcherism*, Open University, Milton Keynes.

Mayo, H.B. (1960) *An Introduction to Democratic Theory*, Oxford University Press, Oxford.

Meehan, E. (1993) *Citizenship and the European Community*, Sage, London.

Mellors C. (1978) *The British MP*, Saxon House, Farnborough.

Middlemas, K. (1979) *Politics in Industrial Society*, André Deutsch, London.

Miliband, R. (1972) *Parliamentary Socialism* (2nd edn), Merlin, London.

Miliband, R. (1977) *Marxism and Politics*, Oxford University Press, Oxford.

Miliband, R. (1982) *Capitalist Democracy in Britain*, Oxford University Press, Oxford.

Mill, J. [1820] (1992) 'An Essay on Government', in T. Ball (ed.) *James Mill: Political Writings*, Cambridge University Press, Cambridge.

Mill, J.S. [1859] (1910) *On Liberty*, Dent, London.

Mill, J.S. [1861] (1910) *Considerations on Representative Government*, Dent, London.

Minkin, L. (1980) *The Labour Party Conference*, Manchester University Press, Manchester.

Minkin, L. (1992) *The Contentious Alliance*, Edinburgh University Press, Edinburgh.

Mitchell, J. (1992) 'Shibboleths and Slogans: Sovereignty, Subsidiarity and Constitutional Debate', *Scottish Government Yearbook 1992*, Unit for the Study of Scottish Government, Edinburgh.

Mitchell, J. (1996) *Strategies for Self-Government: The Campaigns for a Scottish Parliament*, Polygon, Edinburgh.

Mount, F. (1992) *The British Constitution Now*, Heinemann, London.

Muller, W. D. (1977) *The 'Kept Men': The First Century of Trade Union Representation in the British House of Commons 1874–1975*, Harvester, Sussex.

Murphy, W.F. (1993) 'Constitutions, Constitutionalism and Democracy', in D. Greenberg, S.N. Katz, M. Oliviero and S.C. Wheatley (eds) *Constitutionalism and Democracy: Transitions in the Contemporary World*, Oxford University Press, Oxford.

Neunreither, K. (1994) 'The Democratic Deficit of the European Union: Towards Closer Cooperation Between the European Parliament and the National Parliaments', *Government and Opposition*, 29: 299–314.

Newman, M. (1996) *Democracy, Sovereignty and the European Union*, Hurst, London.

Newton, K. (1976) *Second City Politics: Democratic Processes and Decision-Making in Birmingham*, Clarendon Press, Oxford.

Norderval, I. (1985) 'Party and Legislative Participation among Scandanavian Women', in S. Basevkin (ed.) *Women and Politics in Western Europe*, Frank Cass, London.

Norris, P. (1995) 'The Politics of Electoral Reform in Britain', *International Political Science Review*, 16, 1: 65–78.

Norris, P. (1996) 'Woman Politicians: Transforming Westminster?', *Parliamentary Affairs*, 49, 1: 89–102.

Norris, P. (1997a) 'The Puzzle of Constituency Service, *Journal of Legislative Studies*, 3: 29–49.

Norris, P. (1997b) 'Designing Democracies: Institutional Arrangements and System Support', Paper for Workshop on Confidence in Democratic Institutions, August, Washington DC.

Norris, P. and Lovenduski, J. (1989) 'Women Candidates for Parliament: Transforming the Agenda', *British Journal of Political Science*, 19, 1: 106–15.

Norris, P. and Lovenduski, J. (1993a) 'If Only More Candidates Came Forward: Supply Side Explanations of Candidate Selection in Britain', *British Journal of Political Science*, 23, 4: 373–408.

Norris, P. and Lovenduski, J. (1993b) 'Gender and Party Politics in Britain' in J. Lovenduski and P. Norris (eds) *Gender and Party Politics*, Sage, London.

Norris, P. and Lovenduski, J. (1995) *Political Representation: Gender, Race and Class in the British Parliament*, Cambridge University Press, Cambridge.

Norton, P. and Mitchell, A. (1997) 'Meet the New Breed' *The House Magazine*, 13 October: 10–13.

Norton, P (1981) *The Commons in Perspective*, Martin Robertson, Oxford.

Norton, P. (1993) *Does Parliament Matter?*, Harvester Wheatsheaf, London.

Norton, P. (1994) 'Factions and Tendencies Within the Conservative Party', in H. Margetts and G. Smith (eds) *Turning Japanese?*, Lawrence and Wishart, London.

Norton, P. (1997) 'The United Kingdom: Restoring Confidence?', *Parliamentary Affairs*, 50: 357–72.

Norton, P. and Wood, D.M. (1993) *Back From Westminster: British Members of Parliament and Their Constituents*, University Press of Kentucky, Lexington.

Nugent, N. (1994) *The Government and Politics of the European Union* (3rd edn), Macmillan, Houndmills.

Obradovic, D. (1996) 'Policy Legitimacy and the European Union', *Journal of Common Market Studies*, 34: 191–222.

O'Gorman, F. (1973) *Edmund Burke: His Political Philosophy*, Allen & Unwin, London.

Oliver, D. (1991) 'The Parties and Parliament: Representative or Intra-party Democracy?', in J. Jowell and D. Oliver (eds) *The Changing Constitution* (2nd edn), Oxford University Press, Oxford.

Oliver, D. (1997) 'Regulating the Conduct of MPs. The British Experience of Combating Corruption', *Political Studies*, 45: 539–58.

Olsen, J.P., Roness, P. and Saetren, H. (1982) 'Norway: Still Peaceful Coexistence and Revolution in Slow Motion?' in J. J. Richardson (ed.) *Policy Styles in Western Europe*, Allen & Unwin, London.

Pahl, R. and Winkler, J. (1974) 'The Coming Corporatism', *New Society*, October 10.

Paine, T. [1792] (1984) *The Rights of Man*, Penguin, Harmondsworth.

Panitch, L. (1979) 'The Development of Corporatism in Liberal Democracies' in P.C. Schmitter and G. Lehmbruch (eds) *Trends Towards Corporatist Intermediation*, Sage, London.

Panitch, L. (1980) 'Recent Theorisations of Corporatism: Reflections on a Growth Industry', *British Journal of Sociology*, 31: 159–87.

Panitch, L. and Leys, C. (1997)*The End of Parliamentary Socialism*, Verso, London.

Parliamentary Office of Science and Technology (1998) *Electronic Government: Information Technologies and the Citizen*, Parliamentary Office of Science and Technology, Stationery Office, London.

Parry, G. and Moran, M. (1993) *Democracy and Democratization*, Routledge, London.

Pateman, C. (1970) *Participation and Democratic Theory*, Cambridge University Press, Cambridge.

Pattie, C.J., Johnston, R.J. and Stuart, M. (1998) 'Voting Without Party?' in P. Cowley (ed.) *The Conscience of Parliament*, Frank Cass, London.

Patzelt, W.J. (1997) 'German MPs and Their Roles', *Journal of Legislative Studies*, 3, 1: 55–78.

Percy, E, (1931) *Democracy on Trial: A Preface to an Industrial Policy*, Eyre, London.

Perrigo, S. (1995) 'Gender Struggles in the British Labour Party from 1979–1995', *Party Politics*, 1, 3: 407–17.

Perrigo, S. (1996) 'Women and Change in the Labour Party', *Parliamentary Affairs*, 49, 1: 116–129.

Peterson, J. (1995a) 'Decision-making in the European Union: Towards a Framework for Analysis', *Journal of European Public Policy*, 2: 69–94.

Peterson, J. (1995b) 'Policy Networks and European Union Policy Making: A Reply to Kassim', *West European Politics*, 18: 389–407.

Phillips, G. (1992) *The Rise of the Labour Party 1893–1931*, Routledge, London.

Phillips Griffiths, A. (1960) 'How Can One Person Represent Another', *Proceedings of the Aristotelian Society*, 34.

Phillips, A. (1991) *Engendering Democracy*, Polity, Cambridge.

Phillips, A. (1993) *Democracy and Difference*, Polity, Cambridge.

Phillips, A. (1995) *The Politics of Presence*, Clarendon Press, Oxford.

Phillips, A. (1996a) 'Why Does Local Government Matter?', in L. Pratchett and D. Wilson (eds) *Local Democracy and Local Government*, Macmillan, Houndmills.

Phillips, A. (1996b) 'Feminism and Attractions of the Local', in D. King and G. Stoker (eds) *Rethinking Local Democracy*, Macmillan, Houndmills.

Pitkin, H. (1967) *The Concept of Representation*, University of California Press, Berkeley.

Pollard, A.F. (1926) *The Evolution of Parliament* (2nd edn), Longmans, London.

Potter, A. (1961) *Organised Groups in British National Politics*, Faber & Faber, London.

Power, G. (1997) *Reinventing Westminster: The MP's Role and Reform of the House of Commons*, Charter 88, London.

Pratchett, L. and Wilson, D. (1996) 'What Future for Local Democracy?', in L. Pratchett and D. Wilson (eds) *Local Democracy and Local Government*, Macmillan, Houndmills.

Pross, A.P. (1986) *Group Politics and Public Policy*, Oxford University Press, Toronto.

Pugh, M. (1992) *Women and the Women's Movement in Britain 1914–1959*, Macmillan, London.

Radice, L., Vallence, E. and Willis, V. (1990) *Member of Parliament: The Job of a Back-bencher* (2nd edn), Macmillan, Houndmills.

Rawlings, R. (1990) 'The MP's Complaints Service', *Modern Law Review*, 53: 22–42.

Reeve, A. and Ware, A. (1992) *Electoral Systems: A Comparative and Theoretical Introduction*, Routledge, London.

Reif, K. (1985) 'Ten Second-Order Elections', in K. Reif (ed.) *Ten European Elections: Campaigns and Results of the 1979 First Direct Elections to the European Parliament*, Gower, Aldershot.

Reif, K. and Schmitt, H. (1980) 'Nine Second-Order Elections: A Conceptual Framework for the Analysis of European Election Results', *European Journal of Political Research*, 8: 3–444.

Rhodes, R.A.W. (1985) 'Power Dependence, Policy Communities and Inter-Governmental Networks', *Public Administration Bulletin*, 49: 4–29.

Rhodes, R.A.W. (1988) *Beyond Westminster and Whitehall*, Unwin Hyman, London.

Rhodes, R.A.W. (1990) 'Policy Networks: A British Perspective', *Journal of Theoretical Politics*, 2: 292–316.

Rhodes, R.A.W. (1997) *Understanding Governance: Policy Networks, Governance, Reflexivity and Accountability*, Open University Press, Buckingham.

Rhodes, R.A.W. and Marsh, D. (1992a) 'New Directions in the Study of Policy Networks', *European Journal of Political Research*, 21: 181–205.

Rhodes, R.A.W. and Marsh, D. (1992b) 'Policy Networks in British Politics', in D. Marsh and R.A.W. Rhodes (eds) *Policy Networks in British Government*, Clarendon Press, Oxford.

Richardson, J.J. (1993) 'Interest Group Behaviour in Britain: Continuity and Change', in J.J. Richardson (ed.) *Pressure Groups*, Oxford University Press, Oxford.

Richardson, J.J. (1996) *European Union: Power and Policy-Making*, Routledge, London.

Richardson, J.J. (1997) 'Interest Groups, Multi-Arena Politics and Policy Change', Paper presented at the American Political Science Association Annual Meeting, Washington DC.

Richardson, J.J. and Jordan. A.G. (1979) *Governing Under Pressure*, Martin Robertson, Oxford.

Riddell, P. (1998) *Parliament Under Pressure*, Gollancz, London.

Riker, W. (1982) *Liberalism Against Populism*, Freeman and Company, San Francisco.

Roper, J. (1989) *Democracy and Its Critics*, Unwin Hyman, London.

Rose, R. (1982) *Understanding the United Kingdom: The Territorial Dimension in Government*, Longman, London.

Rose, R. (1984) *Do Parties Make a Difference?* (2nd edn), Macmillan, London.

Ross J.F.S. (1944) *Parliamentary Representation*, Yale University Press, New Haven.

Ross, J.F.S. (1948) *Parliamentary Representation*, Eyre and Spottiswoode, London.

Rousseau, J.J. [1762] (1973) *The Social Contract and Discourses*, Everyman, London.

Rush, M. (1988) 'The Members of Parliament', in M. Ryle and P.G. Richards (eds) *The Commons Under Scrutiny*, Routledge, London.

Rustin, M. (1985) *For A Pluralist Socialism*, Verso, London.

Saggar, S. (1992) *Race and Politics in Britain*, Harvester Wheatsheaf, London.

Saint-Germain, M.A. (1989) 'Does Their Difference Make a Difference?', *Social Science Quarterly*, 70, 4: 956–68.

Sanders, D. (1997) 'Voting and the Electorate', in P. Dunleavy, A. Gamble, I. Holliday and G. Peele (eds) *Developments in British Politics 5*, Macmillan, London.

Sartori, G. (1987) *The Theory of Democracy Revisited*, Chatham House, Chatham, NJ.

Schmitter, P.C. (1979) 'Modes of Interest Mediation and Models of Societal Change in Western Europe', in P.C. Schmitter and G. Lehmbruch (eds) *Trends Towards Corporatist Intermediation*, Sage, London.

Schmitter, P.C. (1982) 'Reflections on Where the Theory of Neo-Corporatism Has Gone and Where the Praxis of Neo-Corporatism May Be Going', in P.C. Schmitter and G. Lehmbruch (eds) *Patterns of Corporatist Policy-Making*, Sage, London.

Schumpeter, J.A. [1943] (1976) *Capitalism, Socialism and Democracy* (5th edn), Allen & Unwin, London.

Scottish Constitutional Commission (1994) *Further Steps Towards a Scheme for Scotland's Parliament*, Scottish Constitutional Commission, Edinburgh.

Scottish Constitutional Convention (1990) *Towards Scotland's Parliament*, Scottish Constitutional Convention, Edinburgh.

Scottish Constitutional Convention (1995) *Scotland's Parliament: Scotland's Right*, Scottish Constitutional Convention, Edinburgh.

Searing, D.R. (1985) 'The Role of the Good Constituency Member and the Practice of Representation in Great Britain', *Journal of Politics*, 47: 348–81.

Searing, D. R. (1994) *Westminster's World: Understanding Political Roles*, Harvard University Press, Cambridge MA.

Seyd, P. (1987) *The Rise and Fall of the Labour Left*, Macmillan, Houndmills.

Sharpe, L.J. (1970) 'Theories and Values of Local Government', *Political Studies*,18, 2: 153–74.

Shaw, E. (1994) *The Labour Party Since 1979*, Routledge, London.

Shephard, M. (1997) 'The European Parliament: Laying the Foundations for Awareness and Support', *Parliamentary Affairs*, 50: 438–52.

Skard, T. and Haavio-Mannila, E. (1985) 'Women in Parliament', in E. Haavio-Mannila *et al.* (eds) *Unfinished Democracy: Women in Nordic Politics*, Pergamon, Oxford.

Smith, J. (1995) *The Voice of the People: The European Parliament in the 1990s*, RIPA, London.

Smith, J. (1996) 'How European are European Elections', in J. Gaffney (ed.) *Political Parties and the European Union*, Routledge, London.

Smith, M.J. (1991) 'From Policy Communities to Issue Network: Salmonella in Eggs and the New Politics of Food', *Public Administration*, 69, 2: 235–55.

Smith, T. (1979) *The Politics of the Corporate Economy*, Martin Robertson, Oxford.

Solomos, J. and Back, L. (1993) 'Migration and the Politics of Race', in P. Dunleavy, A. Gamble, I. Holliday and G. Peele, (eds) *Developments in British Politics 4*, Macmillan, London.

Sophal, R. and Muir, C. (1996) 'Survey of Councillors', in *Facing the Challenge: Report of the First National All-Party Convention of Black, Asian and Ethnic Minority Councillors*, LGIU, London.

Spicer, M. (1992) *A Treaty Too Far: A New Policy For Europe*, Fourth Estate, London.

Squires, J. (1996) 'Quotas for Women: Fair Representation', *Parliamentary Affairs*, 49, 1: 71–88.

Stewart, J. (1995) 'A Future for Local Authorities as Community Government' in J. Stewart and G. Stoker (eds) *Local Government in the 1990s*, Macmillan, Houndmills.

Stewart, J.D. (1958) *British Pressure Groups*, Oxford University Press, Oxford.

Stoker, G. (1996) 'Redefining Local Democracy', in L. Pratchett and D. Wilson (eds) *Local Democracy and Local Government*, Macmillan, Houndmills.

Stoker, G. and 6, Perri (1997) *Bringing It All Together: A New Model For London Governance*, Association of London Government, London.

Stoker, G. (1998) 'Governance as Theory: Five Propositions', *International Social Science Journal*, 155: 17–28.

Strinati, D. (1979) 'Capitalism, the State and Industrial Relations', in C. Crouch (ed.)*The State and Economy in Contemporary Capitalism*, Croom Helm, London.

Strinati, D. (1982) *Capitalism, the State and Industrial Relations*, Croom Helm, London.

Studlar, D.T. (1986) 'Non-white Policy Preferences, Political Participation and the Political Agenda in Britain', in Z. Layton-Henry and P.B. Rich (eds) *Race, Government and Politics in Britain*, Macmillan, London.

Studlar, D. T. and McAlistair, I. (1996) 'Constituency Activity and Representational Roles Among Australian Legislators', *Journal of Politics*, 58: 69–90.

Taafe, P. and Mulhearn, T. (1988) *Liverpool: A City That Dared to Fight*, Fortress Books, London.

Tether, P. (1996) 'The Party in the Country II', in P. Norton (ed.) *The Conservative Party*, Prentice Hall, London.

Thomas, J.A. (1939) *The House of Commons 1832–1901*, University of Wales Press, Cardiff.

Thomas, S. (1991) 'The Impact of Women on State Legislative Policies', *The Journal of Politics*, 53, 4: 958–76.

Thomas, S. (1994) *How Women Legislate*, Oxford University Press, Oxford.

Thomas, S. and Welch, S. (1991) 'The Impact of Gender on the Activities and Priorities of State Legislatures', *Western Political Quarterly*, 44, 2: 445–56.

Thompson, D. F. (1976) *John Stuart Mill and Representative Government*, Princeton University Press, Princeton, NJ.

Tocqueville, A. [1862] (1968) *Democracy in America*, Fontana, London.

Topf, R. (1994) 'Party Manifestos' in A. Heath, R. Jowell and J. Curtice (eds) *Labour's Last Chance*, Dartmouth, Aldershot.

Truman, D. (1951) *The Governmental Process*, A.A. Knopf, New York.

Vallance, E. (1979) *Women in the House*, Athlone Press, London.

van der Eijk, C. and Franklin, M. (1996) *Choosing Europe? The European Electorate and National Politics in the Face of Union*, (eds) Michigan University Press, Ann Arbor.

Wahlke, J.C., Eulau, H., Buchanan, W. and Ferguson, L.C. (1962) *The Legislative System*, Wiley, New York.

Walkland, S.A. (1968) *The Legislative Process in Great Britain*, Allen & Unwin, London.

Wallace, H. and Wallace, W. (1996) *Policy-Making in the European Union*, Oxford University Press, Oxford.

Webb, P.D. (1994) 'Party Organizational Change in Britain: The Iron Law of Centralization', in R.S. Katz and P. Mair (eds) *How Parties Organize*, Sage, London.

Weiler, J.H.H. (1997) 'Legitimacy and Democracy of Union Governance', in G. Edwards and A. Pijpers (eds) *The Politics of European Treaty Reform: The 1996 Inter-governmental Conference and Beyond*, Pinter, London.

Weiler, J.H.H., Haltern, U.R. and Mayer, F.C. (1996) 'European Democracy and its Critique', in J. Hayward (ed.) *The Crisis of Representation in Europe*, Frank Cass, London.

Welch, S. (1985) 'Are Women More Liberal than Men in the US Congress?', *Legislative Studies Quarterly*, 10, 1: 125–34.

Wessels, B. (1997) *Members of the European Parliament: Motivations, Role Orientations and Attitudes Towards Enlargement of the European Union*, Budapest Papers on Democratic Transition, no. 213, Hungarian Centre for Democracy Studies, Budapest.

Wessels, W. (1996) 'The Modern West European State and the European Union: Democratic Erosion or a New Kind of Polity', in S.S. Andersen and K.A. Eliassen (eds) *The European Union: How Democratic Is It?*, Sage, London.

Wessels, W. and Diedrich, U. (1997) 'A New Kind of Legitimacy for a New Kind of Parliament: the Evolution of the European Parliament', *European Integration Online Papers* No. 6, http://eiop.or.at/eiop/texte/ 1997—006a.htm

Westlake, M. (1994) *A Modern Guide to the European Parliament*, Pinter, London.

Whiteley, P., Seyd, P. and Richardson, J.J. (1994) *True Blues*, Oxford University Press, Oxford.

Williams, S. (1985) *Conflict of Interest: The Ethical Dilemma in Politics*, Gower, London.

Wilson, D. and Game, C. (1998) *Local Government in the United Kingdom* (2nd edn), Macmillan, Houndmills.

Winkler, J.T. (1976) 'Corporatism', *European Journal of Sociology*, 18: 100–36.

Winkler, J.T. (1977) 'The Corporatist Economy: Theory and Administration' in R. Scase (ed.) *Industrial Society: Class, Cleavage and Control*, Allen & Unwin, London.

Witt, L., Paget, K.M. and Matthews, G. (1994) *Running as a Woman: Gender and Power in American Politics*, Free Press, New York.

Wood, D.M. (1987) 'The Conservative Member of Parliament as Lobbyist for Constituency Economic Interests', *Political Studies*, 35: 393–409.

Wood, D.M. and Young, G. (1997) 'Comparing Constituency Activity by Junior Legislators in Great Britain and Ireland', *Legislative Studies Quarterly*, 22: 217–32.

Wright, T. (1994) *Citizens and Subjects: An Essay on British Politics*, Routledge, London.

Wright. A.W. (1979) *G.D.H. Cole and Guild Socialism*, Clarendon Press, Oxford.

Young, A. (1983) *The Reselection of MPs*, Heinemann, London.

Index

bureaucratic accommodation 138
Burke, E. 120; on collective relationship
of representatives 52–4; on
constituency-representative
relationship 49–52; on interest
representation 100–1; on territorial
and functional representation 47–9;
on trustee theory 47–54, 56–9, 62,
65–9
Burnell, J.B. 65
Burnheim, J. 3
Burns, D. 164, 165
Burns, T. 121, 139, 140, 141, 177
Burt, Alistair 94
Butt, R. 48, 99, 127, 128, 150
Butterfill, John 109
Bystydzienski, J.M. 41

Cain, B.E. 152, 153, 154, 156
Callaghan, J. 75, 76
Camerilleri, J.A. 18
Cameron, Doreen 43
Canavan, Dennis 184
Canavan, F.P. 50
capital punishment 61–4
Caporaso, J. 170
Carpenter, L.P. 128
Carttiss, Michael 94
'cash for questions' scandal 117
Cashmore, E. 43
Cawson, A. 132
Central Office (Conservative Party) 90
Chedzoy, Alan 197
Chisholm, Malcolm 192
Churchill, Winston 127–8
citizenship 4
civic virtue 4
civil service: expertise of 122; and
pressure groups 131
Clarke, H.D. 12, 141
Clwyd, Ann 153
Coaker, Vernon 109
Coates, D. 76, 79, 80–1
Cochrane, A. 164, 165, 195
Cohen, J. 147
Cole, G.D.H. 123–5, 124, 126, 143
Colvin, Michael 109
community government 164

conference sovereignty, Labour Party
77–80; reduction of 85
conscience issues and trustee theory
60–4
Conservative Party: democracy in 89;
and Europe 67–8; legal identity, lack
of 89–90; and mandate 74, 93–5;
party delegates of 64–5; party
theory 88–95; reform of 91–2;
review of 91
constituencies of MPs 152
constituency matters, MPs' time on 154
constituency representation 151–7
constituency-representative
relationship: Burke on 49–52; and
interest representation 101–2
constituency service 153–5; local
promotion in 155–6; welfare in
156–7
Constitutional Settlement (1689) 16, 48
Coole, D. 28
Corbett, R. 168, 170, 173
corporatism in post-parliamentary
governance 132–6
Cowley, P. 60–1, 69
Cox, A. 132, 135
Craig, F.W.S. 36
Cram, L. 170
Crewe, I. 73
Crick, B. 2
Criddle, B. 33, 108, 192
Critchley, Julian 66
Crouch, C. 79, 132
Cryer, Ann 40
Cryer, Bob 109
Cunningham, Roseanna 186
Curtice, J. 115, 156

Dahl, R.A. 3, 10, 128, 131, 142
Dalyell, Tam 189
Dankert, P. 173
Darcy, R. 36, 37, 38, 40
Daugbjerg, C. 140, 141–2
Davidson, Ian 185, 186
democracy 2–13; direct *see* direct
democracy; indirect *see* indirect
democracy; as tyranny, Burke on
524

Riddick, Graham 117
Riker, W. 11, 12
Robathan, Andrew 63–4
Rodgers, J. 147
Rodgers, William 65
Roper, J. 17–18
Rose, R. 73, 155
Ross J.F.S. 30–2, 45, 108
Rousseau, J.J. 8, 11
Ruddock, Joan 191
Rumbold, Dame Angela 108
Rush, M. 32
Rustin, M. 82

Saggar, S. 42, 43
Sainsbury, Lord 107
Saint-Germain, M.A. 39
Saklatvala, Shapurji 42
Sanders, D. 73
Sartori, G. 5, 6, 9, 10, 11
Sarwar, Mohammed 42
Schmitt, H. 172
Schmitter, P.C. 135–6
Schumpeter, J.A. 7
Scotland, representation in 180–93;
    constituency vs. list members 185–7;
    elections 198; equality of
    representation in 187–90;
    representative government and
    representation democracy in 184–5
Scotland Bill 183–93
Scottish Constitutional Commission
    181, 190, 191
Scottish Constitutional Convention
    181–3
Scottish Parliament 180
Searing, D.R. 150, 152, 153, 154, 155
sectorisation in post-parliamentary
    governance 137–8
self-exclusion in representative
    democracy 9
Sex Discrimination Act 191–3
Seyd, P. 82
Sharpe, L.J. 158
Shaw, E. 83
Shephard, M. 169
Shepherd, Richard 187, 188
Shore, Peter 107, 119
Singh, Marsha 42

sinister interests (Mill) 102–4
Skard, T. 39
Skinner, Dennis 110
Smith, J. 167
Smith, John 84, 112
Smith, M.J. 140
Smith, T. 128
Social Democratic Federation 75
Social Democratic Party: Labour Party
    defection to 66, 83
Solomos, J. 41
Sophal, R. 161
Spicer, M. 172
Squires, J. 192
Stanbrook, Ivor 66
Stewart, J. 164
Stewart, J.D. 129–30
Stoker, G. 158, 159, 163, 196, 197
Stone, W.J. 151
Straw, Jack 63–4
Strinati, D. 132, 133
Stuart, M. 61
Studlar, D.T. 42, 151
Sweden: women in politics 41

Taafe, P. 163
Taylor, Ann 112
Taylor, Sir Teddy 185, 186, 187
technology and direct democracy 6
territorial advocacy 155–6
territorial representation 149–77; Burke
    on 47–9; and Europe *see* European
    Parliament; European Union; and
    functional representation 139–40;
    and local government *see* local
    government
Tether, P. 90
Thatcher, Margaret 66, 93, 136
Thomas, J.A. 98
Thomas, S. 39, 40
Thompson, D.F. 55, 103
Tocqueville, A. 10
Topf, R. 71, 73, 93
trade unions: corporatism with
    government 132–3; dominance of
    78–9; interest representation of
    113–14; and Labour Party 75–6;
    sponsoring MPs 110–12, 113–14
Trades Union Congress 75